Studies in Jewish Civilization,
Volume 14:
Women and Judaism

Proceedings
of the Fourteenth Annual Symposium
of the Klutznick Chair in Jewish Civilization-
Harris Center for Judaic Studies
October 28-29, 2001

D1715013

Studies in Jewish Civilization,
Volume 14:
Women and Judaism

Editors

Leonard J. Greenspoon
Ronald A. Simkins
Jean Axelrad Cahan

The Klutznick Chair in Jewish Civilization
The Harris Center for Judaic Studies
The Center for the Study of Religion and Society

Creighton
UNIVERSITY
PRESS

Distributed by the University of Nebraska Press

Library of Congress Cataloguing-in-Publication Data

Studies in Jewish Civilization, Volume 14: Women and Judaism/
    Leonard J. Greenspoon, Ronald A. Simkins, and Jean Axelrad
       Cahan, editors.
    p. c.m—(Studies in Jewish civilization, ISSN 1070-8510; 14)
    "Proceedings of the fourteenth annual Symposium of the Klutznick Chair
    in Jewish Civilization-Harris Center for Judaic Studies, October 28-29,
    2001"
    Half t.p.
    ISBN 1-881871-43-6 (paper)
    1. Women's Studies, Jewish—History, criticism, theology, interpretation,
    etc.
    Congresses. I. Greenspoon, Leonard J. (Leonard Jay), Simkins, Ronald
    A., Cahan, Jean Axelrad.
    II. Klutznick Chair in Jewish Civilization-Harris Center for Judaic Stud-
    ies (14th : 2001: Creighton University)
    III. Series

EDITORIAL   MARKETING & DISTRIBUTION
Creighton University Press   University of Nebraska Press
2500 California Plaza   233 North 8th Street
Omaha, NE 68178   Lincoln, NE 68588-0255

Printed in the United States of America

Dedicated to

Roz Friedman

Table of Contents

Acknowledgments

The Fourteenth Annual Klutznick-Harris Symposium, "Women and Judaism," was held on Sunday, October 28, and Monday, October 29, 2001. The second symposium to be jointly sponsored by Creighton University's Klutznick Chair in Jewish Civilization and the Harris Center for Judaic Studies at the University of Nebraska-Lincoln, it marked the first time Sunday sessions were held on the Lincoln campus. In honor of this event, the Harris Center sponsored a luncheon keynote at which Brenda Brasher delivered the paper, "Gender and Religious Aggression in the Middle East: Case Study of the Western Wall." Special thanks go to Jean Axelrad Cahan and Doreen Wagenaar of the Harris Center, and Joy Ritchie, director of the UNL Women's Studies Program, for their hard work in making the Lincoln events possible.

According to tradition, Sunday evening events, including dinner, keynote, and reception, were held at the Omaha Jewish Community Center. We thank Kathy McGauvran and Carolyn Novicoff for their able assistance with set-up and arrangements there. Also following tradition, Monday events were held at the Creighton Skutt Student Center. We thank Susan and David Davies, owners of Soul Desires book store, for providing book displays at all locations.

An additional event was held on Saturday evening at the Omaha Sheraton Hotel, coordinated and hosted by Adrian Koesters, Senior Editorial Specialist and Program Coordinator for the Klutznick Chair. This soiree featured music by Willis Ann Ross, storytelling by Ozzie Nogg, and a poetry reading by Symposium participant Esther Fuchs. We are grateful to Adrian Koesters for the smooth operation of all activities and events connected with the Symposium; she has also overseen and was a key participant in the editorial process by which initial abstracts have been turned into the chapters that now comprise this volume. Jean Cahan served as an editor for the first time; as ever, deep thanks are due Ronald Simkins, director of the Creighton Center for the Study of Religion and Society, for agreeing to edit this volume, his fourth contribution as series' editor.

Ten of the papers included here were presented at the Symposium. Unfortunately, Marjorie Lehman, Keren R. McGinity, and Reina Rutlinger-

Reiner were not able to attend. We are pleased to include their contributions here, as well as papers by Morris M. Faierstein and Ori Z. Soltes.

This Symposium was held only weeks after the events of September 11. Amid the uncertainty of that time, it was a comfort to know that we could continue to rely on the generosity of our benefactors. They include:

The Ike and Roz Friedman Foundation
Dorothy and Henry Riekes
The Eve and Louis Wintroub Endowment
Jewish Educational and Library Services (JELS)
The Henry Monsky Lodge of B'nai B'rith
The Creighton College of Arts and Sciences
The Creighton University Committee on Lectures, Films, and Concerts
The University of Nebraska-Lincoln Women's Studies Program
Mdwest Express Airlines

The long-standing support of the Ike and Roz Friedman Foundation has been a mainstay of the Symposia. Mrs. Friedman has graciously and unobtrusively insured that we are in a position to offer this event annually. In gratitude, we dedicate this volume to her.

Leonard J. Greenspoon
The Klutznick Chair in Jewish Civilization
Creighton University
Omaha, Nebraska
July, 2003
ljgrn@creighton.edu

Editors' Introduction

In traditional Jewish homes every Shabbat evening (Friday night) the husband recites a portion of Psalm 31 in honor of his wife. Known as "eshet chayil," after its first words, this biblical passage encompasses vv 10-31 and comprises a poetical catalogue of attributes associated with an ideal female. In American homes this phrase has been variously translated as "a virtuous woman" (Isaac Leeser and Alexander Harkavy), "an accomplished woman" (ArtScroll), and "a capable wife" (JPS TANAKH). But almost certainly the most popular English rendering, and the one that most accurately captures its meaning, is "a woman of valor," coined by the JPS translators of the 1917 version and adopted by the Living Nach.

No matter how the expression "eshet chayil" is understood and no matter how we assess its application to women in antiquity or in contemporary Jewish society, "Women and Judaism" is a topic both timely and timeless. The fifteen essays included in this volume demonstrate the enormous range of subject matter and approaches or perspectives that are relevant to the study of the theme of the Fourteenth Annual Klutznick-Harris Symposium. As in previous Symposia and their volumes, we place great value on the individual contributions contained herein and on the light they collectively shed on a topic of singular importance. We do not claim, nor should we, that we have covered the field exhaustively.

We have organized the volume's fifteen chapters into three categories. As always, such divisions are approximations, indicating what are in our opinion some of the useful connections and contexts in which to situate these articles. We anticipate that users of this volume will draw additional links among these articles and between them and other ongoing research. The three divisions are text, arts and literature, and history. The first includes papers that, for the most part, provide in-depth analysis or close reading of texts that have been central to Judaism. The second division presents contributions covering literature, sculpture, painting, print-making, photography, and theater, among others. Chapters that emphasize the historical, social, and religious contexts in which particular women lived make up the third division.

In Judaism, almost all study involves text and its interpretation. Even works of art characteristically represent interaction with text, whether or not words actually appear on the canvas or the photograph. Thus, as a brief summary of each chapter, we include a text that represents its theme.

Part 1: Text

1. Susan A. Brayford, "The Domestication of Sarah: From Jewish Matriarch to Hellenistic Matron"

> "And Sarah laughed to herself, saying, 'Now that I am withered, am I to have enjoyment—with my husband so old?' Then the LORD said to Abraham, 'Why did Sarah laugh, saying, "Shall I in truth bear a child, old as I am?" Is anything too wondrous for the LORD? I will return to you at the same season next year, and Sarah shall have a son.'" (Genesis 18:12-14 [JPS TANAKH])

2. Charles David Isbell, "Nice Jewish Girls: Liquor, Sex, and Power in Antiquity"

> "'Come, let us make our father [Lot] drink wine, and let us lie with him, that we may maintain life through our father.' That night they made their father drink wine, and the older one went in and lay with her father; he did not know when she lay down or when she rose." (Genesis 19:32-33 [JPS TANAKH])

3. Sidnie White Crawford, "Traditions about Miriam in the Qumran Scrolls"

> "Then Miriam the prophetess, Aaron's sister, took a timbrel in her hand, and all the women went out after her in dance with timbrels. And Miriam chanted for them: Sing to the LORD, for He has triumphed gloriously; Horse and driver He has hurled into the sea." (Exodus 15:20-21 [JPS TANAKH])

4. Marjorie Lehman, "Women and Passover Observance: Reconsidering Gender in the Study of Rabbinic Texts"

> "And affirmative precepts limited to time, women are exempt. Whence do we know it?—It is learned from phylacteries: just as women are exempt from phylacteries, so are they exempt from all affirmative precepts limited to time." (*b. Kiddush.* 34a [Soncino edition])

5. Jayne K. Guberman, "*Weaving Women's Words*: Gendered Oral Histories for the Study of American Jewish Women"

> "I think justice is a very big part of the Jewish ethic, and I feel that justice is fundamental to the whole family planning and reproductive health movement. Justice for women, for poor women, justice for families all over the world." (Laurie Schwab Zabin, reproductive health activist and researcher)

Part 2: Arts and Literature

6. S. Daniel Breslauer, "Stories and Subversion"

> "From the day of Miriam's death, peace be with her, no one had removed this sign of mourning. Raphael pulled aside the end of the sheet, looked into the mirror, and saw his own face, and the east-wall embroidery across the room, and the scroll he had written, with the hollow, outlined letters at its end. At that moment his soul stirred and he returned to the table, took the quill, and filled in the letters in the scroll he had written in memory of his wife's soul." (S. Y. Agnon, "The Tale of the Scribe")

7. Henry Abramson, "A Derivative Hatred: Images of Jewish Women in Modern Anti-Semitic Caricature"

"Thou shalt have no intercourse with the Jew. Avoid all contact and community with the Jew and keep him away from thyself and thy family, especially thy daughter." (Theodor Fritsch, "The Racist's Decalogue" [1883])

8. Dan W. Clanton, Jr., "Judy in Disguise: D. W. Griffith's *Judith of Bethulia*"

"She [Judith] went up to the bedpost near Holofernes' head, and took down his sword that hung there. She came close to his bed, took hold of the hair of his head, and said, 'Give me strength today, O Lord God of Israel!' Then she struck his head twice with all of her might, and cut off his head." (Judith 13:6-8 [NRSV])

9. Reina Rutlinger-Reiner, "Creative Expressions of Resistance: Original Theater of Orthodox Israeli Women"

"I, Orly, daughter of Aviva, am honored to light this torch in honor of all the women here who reinforce the spirit of the Jewish woman— in honor of my mother, yours, theirs; it is only thanks to their righteousness that we are present today." (from the script, "In Honor of the State of Israel")

10. Ori Z. Soltes, "Fixing It and Fitting In: Contemporary Jewish American Women Artists"

"Somehow, it seems to take forty years for survivors to come to terms with their personal Holocaust experiences. It took me just over forty years to return to the places in western Slovakia where I was hidden as a child. Ever since that trip, I have been working out my feelings about this part of my past through images on canvas and paper." (artist Kitty Klaidman)

11. Gail Twersky Reimer, "Women on the Wall"

"I felt the same about suffrage as I felt about the interracial problem. I have never understood why we must talk and talk about it. It seems not a question for people to grow eloquent about. It is so obvious that to treat people equally is the right thing to do." (Gertrude Weil, Goldboro, NC [1964])

Part 3: History and Criticism

12. Esther Fuchs, "Jewish Feminist Scholarship: A Critical Perspective"

"At the heart of feminist scholarship in all fields of study is an awareness of the problem of women's oppression and the ways in which academic inquiry has subtly subsidized it, a sense of the possibilities for liberation, and a commitment to make scholarship work on women's behalf." (feminist scholar Ellen Carol du Bois)

13. Morris M. Faierstein, "Women as Prophets and Visionaries in Medieval and Early Modern Judaism"

"And likewise she told me that there seemed to be another higher place above her head where there was much murmuring, and that she asked the Angel: 'What are those sounds above?' And the Angel said to her: 'Friend of God, those that make sounds up there are those who…are now in glory.'" (eyewitness to Ines of Herrera)

14. Keren R. McGinity, "Immigrant Jewish Women Who Married Out"

"Today I find myself pulled by old forgotten ties, through the violent projection of an immensely magnified Jewish problem. It is one thing to go your separate way, leaving friends and comrades behind.…It is another thing to fail to remember them when the world is casting them out.…The least I can do, in my need to share the sufferings of my people, is declare that I am as one of them." (Mary Antin)

15. Karla Goldman, "Finding Women in the Story of American and Omaha Reform Judaism"

> "Sarah likewise wept and said, 'Master of the Universe! I had no prior inclination, but when you said, "Leave your homeland," I believed your words.'" (*Midrash Tanchuma, Lech Lecha* 5).

Contributors

Henry Abramson

Departments of History and Judaic Studies
Florida Atlantic University
Boca Raton, FL 33431
habramso@fau.edu

Susan A. Brayford

Department of Religious Studies
Centenary College of Louisiana
Shreveport, LA 71134
sbrayfor@centenary.edu

S. Daniel Breslauer

Department of Religious Studies
University of Kansas
Lawrence, KS 66045
barsela@ku.edu

Dan W. Clanton, Jr.

Department of Philosophy
University of Colorado at Colorado Springs
Colorado Springs, CO 80933
dclanton@du.edu

Sidnie White Crawford

Department of Classics & Religious Studies
University of Nebraska-Lincoln
Lincoln, NE 68588
scrawfor@unlserve.unl.edu

Morris M. Faierstein

Meyerhoff Center for Jewish Studies
University of Maryland
College Park, MD 20852
kotsker@yahoo.com

Esther Fuchs

Department of Near Eastern Studies
University of Arizona
Tucson, AZ 85721
fuchs@u.arizona.edu

Karla Goldman   Jewish Women's Archive
                             68 Harvard Street
                             Brookline, MA 02445
                             kgoldman@jwa.edu

Jayne K. Guberman   Jewish Women's Archive
                             68 Harvard Street
                             Brookline, MA 02445
                             jkguberman@jwa.edu

Charles David Isbell   Department of Philosophy and Religious Studies
                             Louisiana State University
                             Baton Rouge, LA 70803
                             cisbell@cox.net

Marjorie Lehman   Department of Talmud and Rabbinics
                             Jewish Theological Seminary
                             New York, NY 10027
                             malehman@jtsa.edu

Keren R. McGinity   Department of History
                             Brown University
                             Providence, RI 02912
                             Keren_McGinity@brown.edu

Reina Rutlinger-Reiner   31 Adam Street
                             Jerusalem 93782
                             Israel
                             reina_j@macam98.ac.il

Gail Twersky Reimer   Jewish Women's Archive
                             68 Harvard Street
                             Brookline, MA 02445
                             greimer@jwa.edu

Ori Z. Soltes   1718 P Street NW, Suite T-9
                             Washington, DC 20036
                             orisoltes@aol.com

The Domestication of Sarah:
From Jewish Matriarch to Hellenistic Matron

Susan A. Brayford

Overhearing a conversation in which one of her husband's mysterious visitors predicts she would have a son, Sarah laughs to herself. Not only has she been barren her whole life, but both she and Abraham are too old to have children. As she reflects on the absurdity of conceiving a child, she also begins to speculate whether she could still have sexual pleasure. Her musings are cut short when the visitors overhear her laughing. YHWH/God,[1] speaking for the group, quickly criticizes her; he presumes that her laughter somehow indicates her lack of faith in his capabilities. However, when Abraham had laughed earlier at the same prediction, he was not criticized by YHWH/God. Why should Sarah's laughter indicate any less faith than that of Abraham? We as readers are not told, but we may speculate. Perhaps Sarah's laughter was not primarily one of doubt, but one of delight. Her laughing thoughts suggest that she was less concerned about the impossibility of progeny than she was about the possibility of pleasure. Thus, it was not Sarah's lack of faith that was the problem; it was her thoughts of experiencing sexual pleasure in her old age and withered state.

YHWH/God was only the first to take exception to Sarah's laughter. Later exegetes of the biblical texts either ignored her laughter or explained it away. The Septuagint[2] translator of the Hebrew Scriptures, however, denied her even more than laughter. Perhaps he also recognized the ambiguity associated with the reason for her laughter, since he omitted it from his otherwise rather literal translation. Refusing to acknowledge that Sarah, the elderly matriarch of Israel, would have thoughts of the pleasures associated with sex, he limits her musings to the possibility of having children. This Alexandrian translator was the first of many who attempted to domesticate Sarah and recast her as a more appropriate first matriarch of Israel for his Hellenistic audience. By the time Sarah appears in the New Testament book of 1 Peter, she is characterized as a submissive wife who obeyed Abraham (1 Pet 3:5-6) and called him "lord." What happened to the Sarah of the Hebrew Bible, who is strong and outspoken? It is she who is the subject of this paper. Before describing her unfortunate transformation, we must first examine her representation in the book of Genesis.

Before the story of Sarah and Abraham officially begins, the biblical narrator sets the stage by introducing the first family of Israel and tracing its roots back to Noah (Gen 11:10-26). At the end of the genealogy, we learn that "Abram and Nahor took wives for themselves; the name of Abram's wife was Sarai and the name of Nahor's wife was Milcah, the daughter of Haran, the father of Milcah and Iscah. Now Sarai was barren, she had no child" (11:29-30).[3] Unlike his brother's wife, for whom family roots are established, Abram's Sarai has neither ancestors nor the possibility of progeny. This becomes even more curious when we later learn that YHWH/God has promised to bless Abraham and make a great nation from him (12:1-3). How will this happen?

By the time Sarah and Abraham have lived in the land of Canaan for many years, YHWH/God reiterates and clarifies the promise of progeny to Abraham. Abraham would himself sire the child that was to be the first heir to YHWH/God's covenantal promise of land and innumerable offspring (15:4-5). However, the narrator once again reminds us: "Sarai, Abram's wife, bore him no children" (16:1). Although Sarah cannot conceive a child, she can and does conceive a plan that involves her Egyptian handmaid Hagar. In the first words that Sarah speaks in the biblical text, she blames YHWH/God for her "closed-up" [עצר] condition. She then tells Abraham to "go into her slave girl," for the implicit purpose of sexual intercourse, a purpose that becomes clear in Sarah's announcement of the potential results [אוּלַי אִבָּנֶה מִמֶּנָּה]. "Perhaps," she says, "I might be 'built up' from her" (16:2).

The wordplay in Sarah's comment implies Hagar's double service. The literal meaning of the Hebrew root בנה [to build] refers to Sarah's improved ("built up") gender status when she is able to provide a child, presumably a son, to Abraham. The presumption of a male child is the basis of the word play between the verb "to build" [בנה] and the noun "son" [בן]. Thus, Sarah hopes that Hagar will be able to build her up by producing a son. As many scholars maintain, Hagar's surrogacy reflects the ancient Near Eastern custom of concubinage or polycoity, whereby a woman of lesser status served as a secondary wife in order to provide an heir for a man whose wife is infertile.[4] Based on comparative anthropological evidence, the status of the child would be different from the status of its mother and could inherit the status and position of its father.[5] However, in the Genesis story it is the status of the two women, Sarah and Hagar, which is highlighted.

At first, it seems as if Sarah's plan worked. "Abraham listened to Sarah's voice" (16:2) and "went into Hagar who conceived" (16:4). However, Hagar does not allow Sarah to achieve her hoped-for gender status improvement. Instead, she exacerbates Sarah's failure by belittling her lack of fertility (16:4). Sarah wants Abraham to restore her status; his refusal (16:5) forces her to banish Hagar (16:6). Now it seems as if Sarah's plan has failed. But YHWH/God intervenes and tells Hagar to go back and suffer abuse if necessary so that Abraham would have his son (16:9). She does and bears Ishmael for Abraham (16:15-16).

Abraham now has the son from his own loins that YHWH/God had promised. Then YHWH/God refines the promise even more. Not only does the son have to be Abraham's, he also has to be Sarah's (17:16)! Of course, Abraham laughs (17:17) when YHWH/God tells him that Sarah would have children, and he pleads that Ishmael may be the son of the promise. YHWH/God, however, has determined that Sarah's son Isaac would be the heir to the promise (17:19). Disguised as an angel, YHWH/God shows up one day, along with two other men (18:1-2). After eating the lavish meal that Abraham has Sarah and his servant boy prepare, YHWH/God announces that he will return the next year and that by then Sarah will have a son. This time Abraham does not laugh at the prediction of his unknown guest, as he had earlier. This time it is Sarah, overhearing the men's conversation, who laughs (18:12).

Before reporting her laughter, however, the narrator once again reminds the reader that Sarah and Abraham were getting old and that Sarah no longer had "the way of women," i.e., menstruation. Not only has she been barren her whole life, but it is now humanly impossible for her to bear children. Knowing this, Sarah perhaps realizes that she will be spared the punishing pains of childbirth, with which YHWH/God had earlier sentenced Eve (3:16) The narrator reports that Sarah laughs to herself, wondering if she could still have sexual pleasure [עֶדְנָה] since she was worn out [בָלֹתִי] and her husband was old (18:12).

The word that Sarah uses to describe herself, בָלֹתִי, based on the root בלה [to become old and worn out], is used most often in the Hebrew Scriptures to describe old sandals and clothes (e.g., Deut 8:4; 29:4; Josh 9:13). This description, put into Sarah's mouth, is hardly a flattering self-image. Yet it does provide a parallel to her comment on Abraham's old age, as well as a stark and realistic basis for her musings about pleasure [עֶדְנָה, *ednah*], a *hapax legomenon*[6] that most academic commentators maintain refers to sexual pleasure. Robert Alter, for example, opines that "the term *ednah* is cognate with Eden and probably suggests sexual pleasure, or perhaps even sexual moistness."[7] Nahum Sarna similarly acknowledges that "Hebrew *ednah* is now known to mean 'abundant moisture' and is an exact antonym of 'withered.'"[8] Lexical relationships aside, the physical aspect of "abundant moisture," from a woman's point of view, implies some degree of sexual stimulation.

Sarah's thoughts, therefore, are of the pleasures of sex. They could also refer to her ability to conceive a child. Female sexual pleasure, according to some ancient scientists, was as much a requirement for reproduction as the pleasure experienced by the male partner. Hypocrites, for example, insisted that a woman will not ejaculate her seed unless she achieves orgasm.[9] Later the prominent first century CE gynecologist Soranus, while denying the woman's seed an active role in conception, nevertheless maintained that a woman's sexual pleasure was necessary for conception.[10] Therefore, Sarah's pondering the possibility of *ednah* could refer to sexual pleasure in and of itself or as a prerequisite to conception. In either case, why not enjoy herself, since Abraham would be sure to do what was necessary to beget his promised son, the son that was to be the covenantal heir?

Sarah's laughing thoughts imply her divinely ordained desire not only for her husband,[11] but also for the pleasure that she might be able to experience. The biggest problem from Sarah's perspective is Abraham's age. YHWH/God, however, interprets the problem differently. Overhearing Sarah's laughter, YHWH/God asks Abraham why she laughed and (mis)reports her laughing thoughts as, "can it really be true that I will bear a child since I am old?" (18:13). His paraphrase shows that YHWH/God mistakenly attributes Sarah's laughter to the impossibility of bearing children. He further misrepresents her concerns as being due not to Abraham's old age, but to her own.[12] YHWH/God refuses to acknowledge Sarah's thoughts of pleasure, refocuses the issue, and redefines the problem. It is Sarah's previous inability to bear children, rather than Abraham's potential inability to provide Sarah pleasure, that becomes central. YHWH/God relieves any performance anxiety on Abraham's part by omitting Sarah's concern about Abraham's age.[13] He likewise relieves what should be Sarah's procreative performance anxiety by announcing that this previously barren woman will conceive within the year. Sarah's concerns, however, were not on her performance, but on Abraham's.

In due time, Sarah does indeed bear the promised child Isaac (21:1-2) and, with YHWH/God's blessing, once again banishes Hagar and Ishmael (21:9-12). Although she herself also disappears from the story, she continues to play a role in other versions of the same stories, the first of which is the Greek translation of the Hebrew Scriptures known as the Septuagint (or LXX).[14] This translation was completed in the mid-third century BCE by Jews living in Alexandria, Egypt, for the benefit of their fellow Jews, who, having adopted the Greek language that was the lingua franca of the Hellenistic world, could no longer read their scripture in its original Hebrew language.

The LXX version of the stories of Sarah and Abraham was both a translation and an interpretation of the Hebrew text. As such, it served as a literary precursor for later attempts by post-biblical authors to idealize the first families of Israel. Like all translations, the LXX was culturally conditioned. A material product of and for its Alexandrian milieu, it both reflected and shaped the identities of the Jews living outside the land and within a thriving Alexandrian community characterized by religious and social diversity. Although the LXX translators followed no explicit guidelines for their translations, they nevertheless produced a relatively literal translation, especially in the book of Genesis. Therefore, the minor differences between the Greek and Hebrew versions of the ancestral stories are significant. According to John Wevers, all differences not caused by linguistic considerations reflect the social background, exegetical understanding, and occasionally the theology of the LXX translators.[15] Likewise, Stafan Oloffson claims that the translators were influenced by their Alexandrian and Hellenistic cultural milieu as well as by the subjective piety of Hellenistic Judaism that was often at odds with the more objective nature of God's revelation in the Hebrew Scriptures.[16]

An even greater incongruity was the Diaspora situation itself. The Jews understood themselves as a people who dwelled apart from their neighbors (Num 23:9). Now that Diaspora Jews no longer lived in geographic isolation, they chose to separate themselves socially and religiously from non-Jews by continuing to adhere to their ancestral customs and traditions.[17] Yet, this understanding of their social and religious differences was often in tension with the temptation on the part of Alexandrian Jews to succumb to the allure of their Hellenistic environment. Some of these Jews did assimilate to various degrees, ranging from the most assimilated wealthy and educated upper classes, which were fully integrated into the political and religious affairs of state, to the least assimilated lower classes, which had little social contact with non-Jews.[18] Most Jewish women, regardless of class, had little or no contact with people outside their family and neighborhood. They were subject to even more restrictions than their sisters back home in Palestine. According to Jewish law, a woman's only guardian was her father until the age of twelve. However, Jewish women in Egypt were subject to guardians their entire life, in accordance with the prevailing custom in Greece.[19]

Thus, many differences and tensions existed within Judaism as well as between Alexandrian Jews and their non-Jewish neighbors. Nonetheless, their religious convictions were a common bond for these Alexandrian Jews and prevented most of them from completely assimilating into the Hellenistic culture. Indeed, as Louis Feldman and others have pointed out, Judaism would not have survived and grown if these Jews had completely abandoned their religious traditions.[20] However, while the central significance of the Torah was not in question, a new interpretation of it was deemed necessary. The LXX translation was the first witness to this new interpretation, which enabled Alexandrian Jews to adapt their religious customs and traditions to their new social environment. Like most products of translation, the LXX destabilized cultural identities and became the means by which a new model of ethnic identity was constructed.[21] Inasmuch as the LXX was also the translation of a foundational religious text within the Jewish community, its re-stabilizing of cultural identities became associated with, and in some cases equivalent to, the Word of God.[22]

Due to their Alexandrian milieu, the Jewish translators of the LXX saw the world through Hellenistic lenses. The feature of this perspective that is most important for Sarah's stories is its view of gender and gender roles. The easiest way to describe the Hellenistic worldview is that it promoted and supported a concept of honor and shame, a concept that still governs the attitudes toward men and women in many parts of the world. In the honor/shame system, honor is more often associated with men and relates to their claimed and recognized social status. Shame, most often linked with women, refers to sensitivity about reputation. A key feature of the version of honor/shame associated with Hellenistic culture was its focus on sexuality and appropriate gender roles, specifically the overt gender-identified behavior displayed in public. According to David Gilmore, social masculinity, namely, the need to polarize "male" and "female," is especially acute in Mediterranean societies. To be "male," one must not only separate from and disparage women and femininity, but also actively demonstrate one's virility. Gilmore characterizes the Mediterranean version of the honor/shame system as "libidinized social reputation"; further, "it is this eroticized aspect of honor—albeit unconscious or implicit—that seems to make the Mediterranean variant distinctive."[23] In order for men to maintain their honor, they must demonstrate virility and vigorously defend the "shame" (modesty or virginity) of their women. LXX Abraham and Sarah well exemplify these socially conditioned gender expectations.

As in the Hebrew text, the first reference to Sarah in LXX includes a comment about her barrenness. However, unlike the Hebrew text that reports she has no children [אֵין לָהּ וָלָד], the Greek comments that she could not bear children (οὐκ ἐτεκνοποίει).[24] This very subtle difference ensures that the couple's lack of offspring is her problem—and thus does not represent a challenge to Abraham's manly honor. Similarly, the Greek version of the story of Sarah's plan emphasizes Abraham's virility and removes all traces of Sarah's expression of hope for an upgrade in her gendered status. The Greek of 16:2 reads: "And Sarah said to Abram, 'Look, the Lord has prevented me from having children. Therefore, go into my servant girl in order that you may have children from her.'"[25] Here Abraham becomes the subject and the beneficiary of Hagar's surrogacy. It is no longer Sarah who is to be "built up" or "sonned," but Abraham (τεκνοποιήσῃς).[26] The intentions of LXX Sarah are focused on the benefits that will accrue to her husband, not to her. Furthermore, LXX's addition of the connective particle οὖν [thus] more directly connects the problem of Sarah's infertility with her proposed solution. The Lord has "hemmed me in so as not to bear, therefore, go into my slave girl." Finally, the Greek translation indicates that the plan will succeed. Gone is the tentativeness of the Hebrew's אוּלַי. Instead LXX Sarah tells her husband to go into her slave girl ἵνα [in order that] he would beget children.

Sarah's domestication is most dramatic in the LXX version of the story of her laughter. This version tells essentially the same story as the Hebrew text about the visitors, YHWH/God's announcement, and Sarah's laughter. However, the differences in the Greek show Abraham's and Sarah's characters to be subtly modified so as to mold them into more ideal ancestors of and for Diaspora Jews. Sarah is more shameful, and Abraham is more honorable. Abraham's social graces are upgraded; he is portrayed as more subservient and an even better host. For example, whereas the Hebrew text reports that Abraham offers his visitors a piece of bread [פַּת־לֶחֶם] and a little water [מְעַט־מַיִם], the LXX omits the adjectives and puts no limit on Abraham's generosity. Therefore, Abraham's level of hospitality, a non-sexual indicator of male honor, is elevated in the LXX.

The LXX also upgrades Sarah's character by removing the implication that she was intentionally eavesdropping on the men's conversation (18:10). The Hebrew text reports that Sarah is listening [שֹׁמַעַת] at the opening of the tent. The following clause, וְהוּא אַחֲרָיו, refers to the tent and the visitor, but the referents of the two masculine pronouns are not clear. Either "he" (i.e., the visitor) was behind "it" (i.e., the tent) or "it" (i.e., the tent) was behind "him" (i.e., the visitor). In either case, the Hebrew text focuses on the location of the visitor vis-à-vis the tent and implies that he was close enough for Sarah, with what John Skinner referred to as "true feminine curiosity,"[27] to be listening to the conversation. The LXX translator, on the other hand, uses the aorist to describe Sarah's activity [ἤκουσεν], i.e., "she heard." This suggests a one time completed action on her part, not the on-going state implied by the Hebrew participle. Furthermore, the reason she heard what the visitor said was her location in relation to him, οὖσα ὁ πισθεν αὐτοῦ, i.e., "she was behind him." Thus, the LXX translation of this clause suggests that Sarah's overhearing was unavoidable, rather than intentional. Like an unobtrusive Hellenistic lady, Sarah knows her place.

Less subtle, however, are the differences in the description of Sarah's laughter. Following YHWH's lead in the Hebrew text, LXX translator either ignores or misunderstands Sarah's musings about sexual pleasure and instead focuses her thoughts more appropriately on childbearing.[28] LXX of Gen 18:12 reads: ἐγέλασεν δὲ Σαρρα ἐν ἑαυτῇ λέγουσα οὔπω μέν μοι γέγονεν ἕως τοῦ νῦν ὁ δὲ κύριός μου πρεσβύτερος. At the beginning and end of verse twelve, the Greek translation is literal, i.e., "so Sarah laughed to herself saying," and "my lord is old." However, the LXX translation for the middle part of the verse is anything but literal. Wevers argues that the translator (mis)read בלתי, not as "my being worn out," but as the negative particle "not, except" and thus translated it as οὔπω, a translation permitted by the consonantal text. This removes Sarah's unflattering self-portrayal as a worn-out old woman. More problematic is עדנה, the word denoting sexual pleasure. Inasmuch as the translator might not have known this *hapax legomenon*, Wevers suggests that he read it as two Hebrew words, הנה and עד, and translated it as ἕως τοῦ νῦν [until now]. Thus, the LXX translation of the middle part of verse twelve might be rendered, "Never yet has it happened to me until now,"[29] with the pronoun "it" occurring in the previous verses and referring to Sarah's ability to have children.[30] Awkward as it is, the translation reflects its immediate literary context.

Although Wevers's explanation of the Greek translation is certainly viable from a philological perspective, it does not, and need not, account for the social implications of the translation. I maintain that the LXX translation, whether intentional or not, represented a modification of the Hebrew text in which Sarah is portrayed as a more fitting first matriarch of Israel for the translator's Hellenistic Alexandrian audience.[31] These differences improve Sarah's physical image and moral character, and substantially censor her thoughts. She is no longer regarded as a worn-out woman, and her thoughts are no longer centered on her own sexual pleasure. Instead, she focuses more appropriately on her spousal duty of producing the required heir for Abraham. Furthermore, by replacing Sarah's thoughts of pleasure with an allusion to her continued barrenness, the LXX places the blame for the couple's lack of progeny on her lips and downplays the significance of Abraham's age. The honor associated with his virility is less threatened, especially since he had earlier sired a son through Hagar. Thus, based in part on notions of honor and shame, both Sarah and Abraham become model ancestors, whose thoughts and deeds are more compatible with the appropriate Hellenized gendered identities that Diaspora Jews desired to adopt. Nevertheless, while the LXX merely upgrades Abraham's character by enhancing his social graces, it redefines Sarah's character by denying her sexuality and refocusing her thoughts toward childbearing.

This apologetic representation of Sarah reflects both the Platonic understanding of the authentic aim of the sexual act and traditional Greek descriptions of a wife's role. As a wife, Sarah is not "kept for the sake of [Abraham's] pleasure." Her duty, to paraphrase Demosthenes, is to "bear legitimate children and be a faithful guardian of her household."[32] LXX Sarah, like her Hellenistic role models, is portrayed as a woman whose value and fate are determined by her reproductive capacities. LXX Sarah, moreover, is not tainted by impure thoughts of sex inappropriate for a Hellenistic lady. She comes close to Perictione, an ideal neo-Pythagorean woman, "who by controlling her desire and passion, becomes devout and harmonious, resulting in her not becoming a prey to impious love affairs."[33] Inasmuch as she no longer thinks about sex, the domesticated Sarah of the LXX also might resemble Semonides' good wife, who is "so chaste that she does not even like to listen to other women who talk about sex."[34] In other words, the process of translation has transformed Sarah into the paradigmatic, "shameful," Hellenistic matron and wife—one who will later provide the model for the obedient wife referenced in 1 Peter.

Later Greek translations of the Hebrew Scriptures, however, showed less concern about Sarah's sexuality. After the Christians adopted the LXX as their scripture and used it to prove that Jesus was the promised messiah, the Jews became suspicious of it. Not only had Christians appropriated their scriptures, they also began to consider their own interpretive glosses as more accurate than the original.[35] Thus, several Palestinian Jews, none of whom had any lexical and/or ideological problems with Sarah's עדנה, undertook a very literal retranslation of the Hebrew text. Aquila restored Sarah's subjectivity in the story of her plan to use Hagar as a surrogate mother. As in the Hebrew text, Sarah's plan will benefit Sarah. She will be "built-up"—thus noticing one aspect of the wordplay in the Hebrew original. He also revised the Greek of Gen 18:12 to read τρυφερία as "softness" or "tenderness." His translation, "after my being worn out, has there been sexual tenderness to me?" restored the physical nature of Sarah's thoughts. [36]

Like Aquila, Symmachus allowed Sarah to benefit from her surrogacy plan. However, he chose to emphasize the other aspect of the Hebrew wordplay by saying that she would be "sonned." In 18:12, he had Sarah pondering her ἀκμή, a translation by which, according to Wevers, Sarah questions her stamina or vigor.[37] However, since ἀκμή also can refer to the highest or culminating point of any condition or act,[38] Sarah could be pondering whether she might reach a climax. Neither of these Palestinian revisers seemed particularly embarrassed about the physical aspects of Sarah's (a)musing thoughts.

The Hebrew Scriptures were also translated into Aramaic during the Second Temple period, when Aramaic became the primary language of the majority of the Jews in Palestine. These translators adopted a much different approach to translating the Hebrew text. Unlike the translators or the revisers of the LXX, Targumim translators followed a process that was explicitly interpretive. The word "Targum," based on the verb תרגם, meaning "translate," "explain," "interpret, " or "read out," refers both to a process that includes translation and interpretation and to the written product of that process, i.e., the Aramaic translation of Hebrew biblical texts.[39] The question, therefore, when examining the texts of the Targumim is not whether, but how much, interpretation is evident. Although each Targum reflects a different interpretive quality and quantity, they all explain and amplify scriptures. The translators considered it necessary not only to translate the text, but also to make it immediately comprehensible and relevant to those hearing or reading it. Gaps, ambiguities, and contradictions in the original were often eliminated. Passages that the translators considered compromising or derogatory to God, Israel, or its ancestors, were revised, explained, or explained away, if not eliminated outright.

Like the translators of the LXX, the Targumim translators were circumspect with regard to Sarah's sexuality. The Palestinian *Pseudo-Jonathan's*, "Shall I become pregnant?" and *Neofiti's*, "Is it possible for me to return to the days of my youth and to have pregnancies?" eliminate the element of Sarah's sexual pleasure. Nevertheless, they retain the biological condition of pregnancy. The Babylonian *Onqelos* removes not only the sexual connotations, but also the physical condition of pregnancy in its translation, "Shall I have youth again?"

The Palestinian revisions of the LXX done by Aquila and Symmachus and the Targumim interpretive translations of the Hebrew text show different attitudes toward female sexuality. Unlike the LXX translators, neither Aquila nor Symmachus attempted to shame Sarah. Rather, they portrayed her, like her Hebrew counterpart, as a sexual Jewish matriarch. The Targumim, on the other hand, were less forthright than the Palestinian revisions of the LXX; in general, however, they are also less shaming than the LXX. Thus, the translations and interpretations made within the land seem to have had no problem with the physical aspects of female sexuality. However, those done in the Diaspora downplay the physical nature of Sarah's thoughts and focus instead on the outcome.

Interpretive activity, which was hidden in the LXX and only part of the targumic process, was the raison d'être of the so-called "Re-Written Bibles."[40] These texts paraphrase and often expand upon the biblical stories; in so doing, they also implicitly comment on them. *Jubilees*, a rewritten account of the stories between Genesis 1 and Exodus 16, retells them in an effort to focus on the basic elements of Judaism that were understood to make Jews distinct from and superior to Gentiles. Thus, the author whitewashes any perceived blemishes of the Jewish ancestors and portrays them as models of Torah obedience. As in the biblical account, Sarah's first words in *Jubilees* are her instructions to Abraham, "Go into Hagar, my Egyptian maid. It may be that I will build seed for you from her" (15:22).[41] This retelling, like that of the LXX, shows that the motive for Sarah's plan is, at least in part, to build seed for her husband. Unlike the LXX, however, it allows Sarah to retain her subjectivity. Her domestic duty to bear a child for her husband and her own upgraded gendered status are not mutually exclusive.

The *Jubilees* account of the story of Sarah's laughter similarly removes some of her questionable attributes. As in Genesis, she laughs when she hears that she herself would give Abraham a son. But there is no indication in *Jubilees* that her laughter suggests either mistrust in God's abilities or skepticism about Abraham's. In fact, all the physical aspects of the Genesis story—Abraham's old age, Sarah's withered state, and her thoughts of pleasure—are missing. The primary focus of the story is her laughter itself, thus allowing the wordplay on Isaac's name to be retained.

Extant in a portion of a scroll discovered at Qumran Cave 1, the Genesis Apocryphon is a retelling of Genesis from the birth of Noah to the promise to Abraham in 15:4. The scroll was written in Aramaic and likely dates to the first century BCE.[42] Unlike *Jubilees*, which emphasizes the importance of obedience to a retributive God, Genesis Apocryphon stresses the providence and power of God. The biblical characters are more glorified than whitewashed. Because the scroll leaves off at Genesis 15:4, we have no indication of how the author might have treated Sarah's thoughts of pleasure. However, the author's unapologetic attitude toward female sexuality in his expansion of the story of Lamech (Gen 4:23-24), when he twice has Lamech's wife refer to the sexual pleasure [עדינתי] she achieved from him, suggests that he would likely have allowed Sarah hers.[43]

Pseudo-Philo's *Biblical Antiquities* retells the biblical history of Israel from the time of Adam until the death of Saul. Written in Palestine in the latter half of the first century CE,[44] *Biblical Antiquities* emphasizes the qualities of good leaders, their absolute faithfulness to God, and their obedience to Torah—all of which were important messages to Jews in Palestine, particularly around the time immediately before or after the destruction of the Temple. Pseudo-Philo uses these characteristics to create heroic roles for some of the male biblical figures. However, he is not so creative when it comes to women.[45] With Betsy Halpern-Amaru, I maintain that women are included in *Biblical Antiquities* only when they serve Pseudo-Philo's theological agenda by functioning as passive instruments or active agents of God. All the strong female characters are defined, in one way or another, through motherhood, especially motherhood made possible through God's miraculous opening of their barren wombs.[46]

Pseudo-Philo's three brief references to Sarah exemplify this motif. He relates the entire story about her surrogacy plan in one sentence, "Since Sarai was sterile and had born no children, Abram then took Hagar his maid and she bore him Ishmael" (8:1b). Unlike the biblical Abraham, whose skeptical laughter results from his and Sarah's mutual old ages (Gen 17:17), the *Biblical Antiquities* patriarch questions God only because of Sarah's sterility, referring to her as "that womb that is closed up" (23:5). God reiterates his promise to Abraham to give him offspring "from the one who is closed up" (23:7) and later gives him Isaac by forming him "in the womb of her who bore him" (23:8). Sarah obeys God's command to give Isaac back to God in the seventh month. As a result of Sarah's obedience, "Every woman who gives birth in the seventh month, her son will live, because upon them I summoned my glory and revealed the new age" (23:8). To Pseudo-Philo, Sarah is known primarily for her barrenness and the later paradigmatic conception and birth of Isaac.

The "real" Philo, a Hellenistic Jew writing in Alexandria in the early part of the first century CE, interpreted the Hebrew Scriptures in a way that demonstrated their complementarity with Platonic philosophy. In his allegorical commentaries, Philo ignores the historicity of the biblical characters and depicts the patriarchs as ideal figures who possess piety, hospitality, tact, kindness, courage, and self-control. Abraham, for example, personifies virtue from study, Isaac from nature, and Jacob from practice (*Jos.* 1). Furthermore, all three major patriarchs are embodiments of God's cosmic laws. The matriarchs, like the patriarchs, represent types or lessons for Philo's readers. He portrays Hagar as the middle stage of education; i.e., the school disciplines or encyclical studies, in contrast to Sarah, who is the preferred higher education of philosophy or wisdom. Philo regards Sarah, like other biblical women, as a virgin whose "conceiving and bearing might be not so much through union with a man as through the providence of

God" (*Quaes. Gen.*3.18). This not only allows Philo to emphasize God's miraculous powers, but also enables him to dissociate both the patriarchs and the matriarchs from sexuality, which from a Platonic worldview represents the inferior baser senses rather than the superior godly intellect.

The internal and external apologetic for Judaism that began with the LXX translation and continued in the interpretive texts of the rewritten biblical literature reached its peak with the late first century CE writings of Josephus. Citing the LXX as his precedent, Josephus undertook the writing of *Jewish Antiquities* "in the belief that the whole Greek-speaking world will find it worthy of attention" (*Ant.* 1§5).[47] His twenty-volume *Jewish Antiquities* provides a history of the Jews from creation to the period just prior to the war with Rome. Like Philo, Josephus represents the major biblical heroes, for example, Abraham, Joseph, Moses, David, and Solomon, as model Hellenistic Platonic-like philosopher-kings who exemplified the four cardinal virtues of wisdom, courage, temperance, and justice; the spiritual attribute of piety; and the external qualities of good looks and laudable ancestors. Josephus does not go as far as Philo, whose allegorical interpretation enabled him to portray the patriarchs as personifications of these virtues. Instead, Josephus emphasizes their paradigmatic humanity and transforms them "into a reflection of the Hellenistic ideal of the virtuous wise man, especially as seen in the popular ethics of the first-century Graeco-Roman world."[48]

Josephus likewise emphasizes the unsurpassed virtue of the matriarchs and portrays them and other biblical women in ways that enhance their image in the eyes of his Greco-Roman audience. In his retelling of the story of Sarah's plan, Josephus deprives Sarah of her creativity by relating that Sarah only carries out the surrogacy scheme that is divinely conceived. Furthermore, like the LXX, Josephus reports that the surrogacy is intended so that Abraham, not Sarah, would have children through Hagar. Josephus also upgrades Sarah's behavior in his retelling of the story of her laughter. Sarah does not laugh at the messengers' prediction that she would be a mother; she merely smiles [μειδιᾶσαι] and states that her age would make childbearing impossible (*Ant.* 1§213). Josephus's Sarah, like LXX Sarah, behaves like an appropriately shameful woman by reflecting on the impossibility of bearing a child, rather than on the possibility of having pleasure when trying to do so.[49]

By the time Sarah makes her appearance in the New Testament, she has been domesticated and is remembered only for her miraculous motherhood. For Paul, she symbolizes the mother of the "children of the promise," who are the true descendants of Abraham (Rom 9:8-9; Gal 4). The author of Hebrews mentions Sarah in his hero list only as a way to demonstrate an aspect of Abraham's faith; namely, that he believed in God's power of procreation despite her barrenness (Heb 11:11-12). The worst insult to Sarah's character comes in the New testament book of 1 Peter. There we read that, like the other holy women "who used to adorn themselves by accepting the authority of their husbands," Sarah "obeyed Abraham and called him lord" (1 Pet 3:5-6, NRSV). The Petrine writer conveniently overlooks Abraham's obedience to Sarah (Gen 16:3), and, although he correctly writes that Sarah did refer to Abraham as "lord," she did so in the context of his possible failure to provide her pleasure (18:12).

The domestication of Sarah, begun in the LXX with the denial of her sexuality, is extended further by New Testament writers, for whom Sarah serves as a model of female obedience and motherhood. Thoughts of pleasure and feelings of desire gave way to motherhood as the defining characteristic of a woman who would provide her husband honor. However, Sarah has the "last laugh" because we always remember the story of Sarah's laughter. Now we can remember that her laughing thoughts might be about the pleasure she is about to have—perhaps for the first time in her life.

NOTES

[1] Here, and throughout this paper, I use the combined term "YHWH/God" for Israel's deity when I refer to him as a character in the biblical texts. Although these texts distinguish between יהוה (κύριος) and אֱלֹהִים (θεός), these distinctions are not significant for my arguments. I am not concerned with the theological aspects of the divine character, but rather with the social aspects of human characters. Furthermore, I use the masculine pronoun intentionally when referring to YHWH/God, since I maintain that YHWH/God is a male deity.

[2] As I will explain more fully later, the Septuagint is the third century BCE translation of the Hebrew scriptures into Greek.

[3] Unless otherwise noted, all translations of the biblical text are mine. My source for texts in Hebrew is the Masoretic Text (hereafter MT) as it appears in the *Biblia Hebraica Stuttgartensia*. My source for the Greek is the eclectic text reconstructed by

John Wevers, *Genesis* (vol. 1; Göttingen Septuagint; *Septuaginta: Vetus Testamentum Graecum, Auctoritate Academiae Scientiarum Gottingensis* (Göttingen: Vandenhoeck & Ruprecht, 1974).

[4] Scholars typically cite ancient Near Eastern legal texts as evidence for the practice of infertile wives providing their husbands with concubines to bear children. Nahum Sarna, *Genesis* (JPS Torah Commentary; Philadelphia: Jewish Publication Society, 1989), 119, for example, refers to the nineteenth century BCE laws of Lipit-Ishtar and the laws of Hammurabi as attestations of the practice of concubinage. Although neither text provides a precise parallel, both show that surrogacy was practiced before the time of the biblical ancestors.

[5] J. Goody, *Production and Reproduction: A Comparative Study of the Domestic Domain* (Cambridge Studies in Cultural Anthropology 17; Cambridge: Cambridge University Press, 1976), 86-98. For a discussion of the significance of this type of inheritance to the Sarah-Hagar story, see Naomi Steinberg, *Kinship and Marriage in Genesis*, (Minneapolis: Fortress, 1993), 6-7.

[6] A word that appears only once in a particular form in the biblical text.

[7] Robert Alter, *Genesis: Translation and Commentary* (New York: W.W. Norton, 1996), 79.

[8] Alter, *Genesis*, 130.

[9] See, for example, *On the Seed*, 4-9, 12. This understanding seems to conflict with the procreative theory of monogenesis, which regards the woman as a fertile field into which a man plants his seed. Although some ancient writers such as Aristotle (e.g., *On the Generation of Animals*, 1.727b.6-11, 728a.31-33) thought the woman was only a passive partner in reproduction, others such as Pythagoras maintained that women also emit seed. Yet, the mere existence of female seed does not negate the monogenetic theory; for a discussion and analysis of the ancient debate between these two schools of thought, as well as the modern scholarly debate supporting one or the other, see David Halperin, "Why is Diotima a Woman?" in *Before Sexuality: The Construction of Erotic Experience in the Ancient Greek World*, David Halperin et al., eds. (Princeton: Princeton University Press, 1990), 278-89. Ann Hansen comments on the renewed interest in Greco-Roman gynecological treaties in the last fifteen years and, like Halperin, evaluates scholarly contributions. She expands the discussion to include an analysis of the social conditions that produced and resulted from the different approaches taken by medical writers to sex and reproduction (Ann Hansen, "The Medical Writers' Woman," in *Before Sexuality*, 309-37). Galen, for example, acknowledged that the woman emitted seed, but asserted that her seed was inferior and less generative than that of the man (*On the Usefulness of the Parts of the Body*, 14.10-11). Soranus, the prominent first century CE gynecologist, denied the woman's seed a role in conception, since it is excreted outside the uterus (*Gynecology* 1.12).

[10] In his *Gynecology*, Soranus wrote that the uterus "at certain times dilates, as in the desire of intercourse for the reception of semen" (1.10). He goes on to say:

> the best time for fruitful intercourse is when menstruation is ending and abating, when urge and appetite for coitus are present, when the body is

neither in want nor too congested and heavy from drunkenness and indigestion, and after the body has been rubbed down and a little food been eaten and when a pleasant state exists in every respect. Just as without appetite it is impossible for the seed to be discharged by the male, in the same manner, without appetite it cannot be conceived by the female… neither can the seed be taken up or, if grasped, be carried through pregnancy, unless urge and appetite for intercourse have been present (1.36-7).

[11] Many generations earlier, back in the primeval garden, YHWH/God realized that the first woman and her husband had eaten from the one tree that he had declared off limits (Gen 3:11). He needed to teach these now knowledgeable human beings a lesson. Rather than following through with his earlier threat of death (Gen 2:16-17), YHWH/God punished them with life, but a life characterized by hardship, toil, and pain. The man, as the prototype for all men after him, would labor in hardship to produce food from the ground (Gen 3:17-19), while the woman, as the prototype for all women after her, would labor in pain to produce children (Gen3:16). YHWH/God sentences Eve by saying, "I will greatly increase your pain and your conceptions; in pain, you will bear sons. While your desire [תְּשׁוּקָתֵ֣ךְ] will be to your husband, he will rule you." Thus, desire for her husband serves as some type of compensation for the pain that she would later experience. The Greek translation of Gen 3:16, however, denies the woman her compensatory desire. Her response to her husband is only a "turning" [ἀποστροφή].

[12] George Savran, *Telling and Retelling: Quotation in Biblical Narrative* (Indiana Studies in Biblical Literature; Bloomington: Indiana University Press, 1988), 26, notes that in Gen 18:13 God quotes Sarah more freely than is usual in quoted direct speech. Nevertheless, he maintains that God is "still being essentially truthful." Although God ostensibly addresses his question about Sarah's laughter to Abraham, he really is addressing Sarah. Following Rashi, Savran claims that God's rephrasing of Sarah's question is meant to reprove her for denigrating her husband (73). He further maintains that God's quoted direct speech points to both his omniscience and his omnipotence, i.e., "he who can hear all can also contravene the laws of nature" (93). Although I agree with Savran's analysis of the function of God's speech, I disagree that God is being essentially truthful. On the contrary, I maintain that God's rephrasing of her internal musings is a complete reversal of Sarah's implied critique of Abraham.

[13] In his comment on Gen 18:12, Alter, *Genesis*, 79, likewise recognizes the potential threat to Abraham's masculinity:

> The dangling third clause hangs on the verge of a conjugal complaint: how could she expect pleasure, or a child, when her husband is so old? The Lord, having exercised the divine faculty of listening to Sarah's unspoken words, her silent laughter of disbelief, reports them to Abraham, tactfully editing out (as Rashi saw) the reference to the patriarch's old age and also suppressing both the narrator's mention of the vanished menses and Sarah's allusion to her withered flesh—after all, nothing anaphrodisiac is to be communicated

> to old Abraham at a moment when he is expected to cohabit with his wife
> in order at last to beget a son.

[14]Leonard Greenspoon, "The Use and Abuse of the Term 'LXX' and Related Terminology in Recent Scholarship," *BIOSCS* 20 (1987): 21-29, notes that the scholarly use of the term "Septuagint" and its standard abbreviation, LXX, is inconsistent. The term is often used to refer to the entire Greek Bible, while in other places it is used only to refer to the Greek translation of the Pentateuch. The latter is probably more accurate, inasmuch as the abbreviation LXX represents the seventy (or seventy-two) translators to whom the *Letter of Aristeas* attributes the translation of the Pentateuch. Since my examination deals primarily with the pentateuchal book of Genesis, my use of the term Septuagint/LXX is appropriate.

[15] John Wevers, "The Earliest Witness of Jewish Exegesis," in *The Frank Talmage Memorial Volume* (vol 1; eds. F. Talmage and B. Walfish; Haifa and Hanover: Haifa University Press and University Press of New England with Brandeis University Press, 1993), 127. Wevers, in *Notes on the Greek Text of Genesis* (SSC 35; ed. L. Greenspoon; Atlanta: Scholars Press, 1993), further argues that when there are differences between the Hebrew and Greek texts, one should not automatically assume a different parent text. He goes on to say, "Through such details a picture of the attitudes, theological prejudices, even of the cultural environment of these Jewish translators gradually emerges" (xxi).

[16] Stafan Olofsson, *LXX Version: A Guide to the Translation Technique of the Septuagint* (CBOTS 30; ed. T. Mettinger and M. Ottosson; Stockholm: Almqvist & Wiksell, 1990), 2.

[17] J. M. G. Barclay, *Jews in the Mediterranean Diaspora: From Alexander to Trajan (323 BCE - 117 CE)* (Edinburgh: T & T Clark, 1996), 2-3.

[18] Barclay identifies three levels of assimilation in Alexandrian Judaism. Highly assimilated Jews were those who were fully integrated into the political and religious affairs of state. Jews who represented a medium level of assimilation had significant ties with the non-Jewish world, but also attempted to preserve some aspects of their distinct Jewish identity. Those whose social contact with non-Jews was minimal experienced a low level of assimilation. Although Barclay recognizes that there is little agreement among social scientists on the definition of assimilation, he defines it for his book as "social integration into non-Jewish society," 103.

[19] Sarah Pomeroy, *Women in Hellenistic Egypt: From Alexander to Cleopatra* (Detroit: Wayne State University Press, 1984), 121; V. Tcherikover, *Hellenistic Civilization and the Jews* (trans. S. Applebaum; Philadelphia: Jewish Publication Society, 1959), 350.

[20] Louis Feldman, *Jew and Gentile in the Ancient World: Attitudes and Interactions from Alexander to Justinian* (Princeton: Princeton University Press, 1993), 45-69.

[21] Sherry Simon, *Gender in Translation: Cultural Identity and the Politics of Transmission* (New York: Routledge, 1996), 135.

[22] Wevers, "An Apologia for Septuagint Studies," *BIOSCS* 18 [1985], esp. 16-19, Victor Tcherikover, "The Ideology of the Letter of Aristeas," *HTR* 51 [1958]: 59-85,

and others have argued that the details regarding the High Priest, the six learned men from each of the twelve tribes of Israel, and the unanimity of approval for the LXX in the *Letter of Aristeas* represent the attempt of its author to show that the Greek translation was as authoritative as the Hebrew text. Harry Orlinsky, "The Septuagint and its Hebrew Text," in *The Hellenistic Age* (vol. 2, *Cambridge History of Judaism*; ed. W. D. Davies and L. Finkelstein; Cambridge: Cambridge University Press, 1989), esp. 534-48, argues that this Letter was written by Jews for Jews, not as an apologetic document, but to attest the divinely inspired nature of the LXX.

[23] David Gilmore, "Introduction: The Shame of Dishonor," in *Honor and Shame and the Unity of the Mediterranean* (American Anthropological Association 22; ed. D. Gilmore; Washington, D.C.: American Anthropological Association, 1987), 8-11.

[24] The verb's imperfect tense implies not a simple past action, but rather a continuous or habitual action or state.

[25] εἶπεν δὲ Σαρα πρὸς Αβραμ ἰδου συνέκλεισέν με κύριος τοῦ μὴ τίκτειν εἴσελθε οὖν πρὸς τὴν παιδίσκην μου ἵνα τεκνοποιήσῃς ἐξ αὐτῆς ὑπή κουσεν δὲ Αβραμ τῆς φωνῆς Σαρας.

[26] This verb is second singular, in reference to the masculine Abraham.

[27] John Skinner, *A Critical and Exegetical Commentary on Genesis* [ICC 1; New York: Charles Scribner's Sons, 1910), 301.

[28] Many feminist theorists warn about the dangers of false universalizing, in this case, the automatic connection of women and childbearing. However, they do allow for the particularity of specific historical contexts. See, for example, Nancy Fraser and Linda Nicolson, "Social Criticism with Philosophy: An Encounter between Feminism and Postmodernism," *Feminism/Postmodernism* [Thinking Gender; ed. L. Nicholson; New York: Routledge, 1990), esp. 34-35. In the specific cultures represented by the social worlds of the Hebrew and Greek texts, childbearing was considered a woman's right as well as her duty.

[29] Wevers, *Notes*, 252.

[30] Perhaps γέγονεν could allude to the other meaning of γίγνομαι, to give birth.

[31] The question of authorial intent, or in this case translation intent, is moot since it never can be answered definitively. As Anneli Aejmelaeus rightly notes, the intention of the translator can be read only from his translation ("Translation Technique and the Intention of the Translator," in *VII Congress of the IOSCS*, ed. Claude E. Cox, SBLSCS 31 [Atlanta: Scholars Press, 1989], 30). The LXX domestication of Sarah, if not intentional, at the very least reflects an unconscious denial of her sexuality. Perhaps the translator was attempting, in David Wigtil's words, "to reproduce for the new audience the same vision of reality which the translator saw in the text. The content of the writing is merely secondary to the real truth as it might appear in the original text, or as it appeared to the translator from the original" ("The Independent Value of Ancient Religious Translations" [*ANRW* 2.16.3, 1986], 2054). In this case, the "same vision of reality" in the LXX text would represent the "real truth" that Sarah, as the foremother of Diaspora Jews, should model the values deemed most appropriate for these Jews in their new environment.

[32] Demosthenes, *Against Neaera*, 122.

[33] "Περὶ γυναικὸς ἁρμονίας," 142-45 = Stob. 4.28.19.

[34] Semonides, frag 7 (Diehl).

[35] Sidney Jellicoe, *The Septuagint and Modern Study* (Oxford: Oxford University Press, 1968), 75. In this context, Jellicoe cites C. F. D. Moule's earlier characterization, in *Faith, Fact, and Fantasy* (London, 1964), 106, of the Christian appropriation of Hebrew scripture as "one of the most remarkable take-over bids in history."

[36] Wevers's translation, *Notes*, 252.

[37] Wevers, *Notes*, 252.

[38] See, for example, Philostratus' report (*Vitae Sophistarum* 1.25.7) that Polemo was raised to a pitch of excitement over the conclusions to his argument (περὶ τάς ἀκμὰς τῶν ὑποθέσεων).

[39] Roger Le Déaut maintains that, as a literary genre, targum is different from midrash (based on the Hebrew דרשׁ, "to seek or interpret") because it is primarily a translation, not a commentary, and its major purpose was liturgical ("Targumim," in *The Hellenistic Age*, 563). Renee Bloch, on the other hand, believes that interpretation, particularly in the Palestinian Targumim, was primary ("Midrash," in *Dictionnaire de la Bible, Supplément* [Paris: Letouzey, 1957], 5:1278). All, however, agree that each Targum must be evaluated on its own terms.

[40] This term was coined by Geza Vermes, *Scripture and Tradition in Judaism: Haggadic Studies* (Leiden: E. J. Brill, 1961), 95, 124-26.

[41] All translations from the book of *Jubilees* are those of O. S. Wintermute in *The Old Testament Pseudepigrapha*, ed. J. H. Charlesworth (Garden City, New York: Doubleday & Co., 1985).

[42] John Fitzmyer, *The Genesis Apocryphon of Qumran Cave 1* (Rome: Pontifical Biblical Institute, 1966), 14-17.

[43] With Fitzmyer, I maintain that the noun used for pleasure, עֲדִינָתִי, is the Aramaic form of the Hebrew עֶדְנָה (*Genesis Apocryphon*, 77-8). See also Gary Anderson, "The Garden of Eden and Sexuality in Early Judaism," in *People of the Body: Jews and Judaism from an Embodied Perspective* (SUNY Series, the Body in Culture, History, and Religion; ed. H. Eliberg-Schwartz; Albany, New York: State University of New York Press, 1992), 60-61.

[44] Most scholars agree that *Biblical Antiquities* was written around 70 CE. See, for example, Louis Feldman, "Josephus's *Jewish Antiquities* and Pseudo-Philo's *Biblical Antiquities*," in *Josephus, the Bible, and History* (ed. L. Feldman and G. Hata; Detroit: Wayne State University Press, 1989), 80, and George W. E. Nickelsburg, "*Jewish Writings of the Second Temple Period: Apocrypha, Pseudepigrapha, Qumran Sectarian Writings, Philo, Josephus* (CRINT Section 2; vol. 2, *The Literature of the Jewish People in the Second Temple and the Talmud*; Assen: Van Gorcum, 1984), 109. For a discussion of the arguments for dates before and after the destruction of the Temple, see Howard Jacobson, *A Commentary of Pseudo-Philo's* Liber Antiquitatum Biblicarum: *With Latin Text and English Translation* (AGJU 31; Leiden: E.J. Brill, 1996), 199-209. All translations of *Biblical Antiquities* are Jacobson's.

[45] Jacobson, *Pseudo-Philo*, 251, also suggests that Pseudo-Philo's virtual omission of the stories of the matriarchs in the beginning of his account is one indication that he is not going to be particularly favorable to women in what follows.

[46] Betsy Halpern-Amaru, "Portraits of Women in Pseudo-Philo's *Biblical Antiquities*," in *Women Like This: New Perspectives on Jewish Women in the Greco-Roman World* (SBLEJL; vol. 1; ed. Amy-Jill Levine; Atlanta: Scholars Press, 1991), 106.

[47] Unless otherwise noted, this and all other English translations of *Jewish Antiquities* are those of H. St. J. Thackeray in the LCL edition (Cambridge: Harvard University Press, 1930).

[48] Louis Feldman, "Mikra in the Writings of Josephus," in *Mikra: Text, Translation, Reading and Interpretation of the Hebrew Bible in Ancient Judaism and Early Christianity* (CRINT Section 2; vol. 1, *The Literature of the Jewish People in the Period of the Second Temple and the Talmud*; ed. M. J. Mulder; Assen/Maastricht: Van Gorcum, 1990), 486. See also Carl Holladay, *Theios Aner in Hellenistic Judaism: A Critique of the Use of This Category in New Testament Christology* (Missoula: Scholars Press, 1977), 67-68.

[49] At this and other points, Josephus appears to be following the image of Sarah in the LXX. Since he does not explicitly cite his biblical sources, it is impossible to know whether he was merely paraphrasing the LXX or similarly changed the story as reported in the Hebrew text in order to censor Sarah's thoughts of sex.

Nice Jewish Girls:
Liquor, Sex, and Power in Antiquity

Charles David Isbell

A popular bumper sticker on the campus of Louisiana State University features a ridiculous-looking person holding up a huge mug. The caption reads: "BEER: Helping ugly people have sex since 1862." Although biblical literature does not ban the use of alcohol or teach total abstinence, it is certainly fair to say that the majority view is at least cautionary and perhaps even negative. On the positive side, wine can bring pleasure (Jugs 9:13, Ps 104:15) even to the point of banishing sorrow (Prov 31:6-7) and may be acknowledged as a legitimate part of a sacrificial meal.[1]

On the negative side, drinking to intoxication was a disgrace on the order of "harlotry," according to the prophet Hosea (Hos 4:11, 18). And drunkenness was perceived as a sin most likely to be committed by rulers like the hapless Israelite king Elah (1 Kgs 16:9), the Syrian Ben-Hadad (1 Kgs 20:16), the profligate Persian Ahasuerus (Esth 1:10), or by a wealthy but foolish person like Nabal (1 Sam 25:36). In fact, habitual drunkenness—along with stubbornness, rebellion, and gluttony—could form the grounds for capital charges brought by parents against an insubordinate son (Deut 21:18-20).

Isaiah tied drunkenness to the moral confusion of spiritual leaders such as priests and false prophets (Isa 28:7-13), or simply to the greed of the wealthy (Isa 5:11-12, see also Isa 56:11-12). The Book of Proverbs offers quite a practical argument against excessive drinking by reference to the inevitable hangover, complete with hallucinations, delusions, bleary eyes, and bruises on the body, whose cause cannot be remembered (Prov 23:29-35)! Even as righteous a man as Noah serves as an example of the evils of drinking to excess (Gen 9:20-27).

Talmudic opinion holds that a drunken person is forbidden to conduct a service, concluding that if a person prays in a state of drunkenness, his prayer is an abomination (*Ber. 31b*). Furthermore, judges must not render decisions after drinking wine (*'Erub. 64a*), and the judges of the Sanhedrin had to abstain from wine whenever they heard of a capital case (*Sanh. 5:1*; and see also *Sanh. 42a*). In fact, as a precautionary measure, judges were forbidden to eat dates because of their possible intoxicating effects (*Ketub. 10b*).

While we moderns view the use of alcohol as a weapon typically used by males to lure females into trouble, the Bible offers four classical examples of Jewish women who used alcohol as a weapon against men, either to achieve personal power or status or to perform acts of heroism on behalf of the Jewish community when it faced a dire crisis. In each case, a hapless and unsuspecting male was bent to the will of a powerful and purposeful female who used wine as a major part of her arsenal.[2] Indeed, these four examples teach us how appropriate the observation of ben Sira was: "Wine has been the undoing of many" (Sir 31:30).

THE DAUGHTERS OF LOT

In the narrative of Gen 19:31-38, Lot is seduced by his two daughters. In order to succeed with their seduction, they ply their father with wine to such excess that he was unable to realize he was having intercourse with his own daughters. Their purpose in so duping their father has nothing to do with modern ideas about sex. Rather, for them intercourse was the necessary means for procreation; their intentions are described quite specifically in the text as the desire to establish a family. Pointedly, the text twice attests that the daughters sought to acquire "seed" from their father (Gen 19:32, 34), a word pregnant (!) with meaning elsewhere in Genesis to describe the future descendants of mighty Abraham. In short, the daughters of Lot were anxious to attain for themselves the biblical form of immortality normally reserved for men, and wine was the tool they used to accomplish their aim. It gave them power over the man in their lives, allowing them to play on his lack of self-control so as to control their own destinies.

As noted, the narrative twice states that Lot was an ignorant dupe of the two females, remaining ignorant when each of his daughters entered his bed and when she rose to leave (Gen 19:33, 35). What is also of more than passing interest is that the text itself nowhere condemns the daughters for their actions. Readers do learn that these improper liaisons produced people who became terrible enemies of the Israelites, namely, the Moabites and the Ammonites, among whom were Balak and Bil'am (Num 22-24), Eglon the obese (Judg 3), and later King Mesha (2 Kgs 3:6-27). But the Genesis text seems to take for granted that both the motivation and the method of the daughters should be understood and accepted, even though the final result produced unforeseen and negative consequences.

RUTH

The story of Ruth has become one of the most beloved in the Bible for several reasons. First, it is beautiful narrative art that can be read and appreciated quite apart from the normal struggles of the professional exegete to determine its date, author, and meaning as a biblical text. Second, it ends in the most perfect way possible, securing for the heroine a place of wealth along with the prestige of a permanent place in the ancestry of David. Third, it towers over some of the more troublesome exclusivist and chauvinistic passages of biblical literature: it teaches "how great is the reward that accrues to those who perform deeds of kindness" (*Ruth Rab.*2.14), while *Ruth Rab.* 3.5 invites readers to "come and see how precious in the eyes of the Omni-present One are converts." In addition, it draws the highest praise possible from the rabbis, being listed first, ahead even of Psalms, among the Writings (*b. Ber.* 14b).

Given its universal acceptance and the joy with which it has been read and studied, it is instructive to note how purposeful the actions of the heroines Ruth and Naomi are. Ruth, who is the quintessence of a modest young woman throughout chapters one and two, becomes openly calculating in chapter three—and she does so under the careful and detailed guidance of her mother-in-law. Naomi articulates the goal of their involvement with Boaz in 3:1. The Jewish Publication Society's TANAKH captures the correct sense of the Hebrew: "I must seek a home for you," while the New American Standard Bible is also correct in its rendering: "Shall I not seek security for you?" In the world of their day, a home, complete with husband and children, was the only conceivable path to security for a female member of society. Naomi also reveals to Ruth where Boaz can be found (3:2) and instructs her to "bathe, anoint yourself, dress up, and go" (3:3).

Ruth also receives explicit instructions from Naomi to wait until Boaz has finished eating and drinking to approach him. This will be no ordinary chat between a shy maiden and her beau. It will be nothing less than a brazen proposal of marriage, made by the woman! The wording of 3:4 leaves no doubt about Naomi's instructions. Ruth must observe the place where Boaz lies down, and then she must "uncover his feet."

We notice that the text is concerned to assure us that Ruth's lying at the "feet" of Boaz will not become public knowledge; plainly there is more going on here than meets the eye of the casual reader.[3] It is not really necessary to employ other biblical examples to show the meaning of "feet" in Ruth, for the conclusion of the story itself cinches the point. When Boaz is startled awake by the presence of a woman lying at his "feet," she proposes to him, boldly instructing him: "spread your robe" over me (3:9). This is no less than a formal act of espousal.[4]

Of particular interest is the specification by Naomi in 3:3 that Ruth must wait until Boaz has finished eating and drinking before setting their joint plan into motion. This is highlighted by the notation in 3:7 that the heart of Boaz was "merry" after having eaten and drunk, before Ruth made her move.[5] Boaz may well have been a righteous man willing to act in Ruth's behalf, but clearly an appropriate ingestion of wine helped smooth the path of romance. Once again it is significant that there is no condemnation of Ruth for the employment of alcohol in order to obtain her goal. Much like the case of the daughters of Lot, neither the motivation nor the methods of Ruth and Naomi require justification or explanation from the creator of the story.

ESTHER

The familiar story of Esther is intriguing on many levels. We note first that the banquet given by King Ahasuerus for the ordinary citizens of the capital city lasted a mere seven days. Although this compares nicely with the report of King Ashurnasirpal's hosting 69,574 guests for a ten day banquet, it is scarcely comparable with the 180 day bash held for the nobles and provincial princes that begins the book (Esth 1:3-4).[6] Further, this biblical description of a lengthy celebration involving heavy drinking is attested in classical sources, one of which notes that Persian monarchs regularly entertained as many as 15,000 guests.[7]

In such a context, it is not difficult to understand why the rabbis believed that Vashti, the king's consort, had been summoned to appear naked before Ahasuerus and his buddies. The Talmudic discussion of this passage clearly portrays Vashti as an immoral woman who had forced nice Jewish girls to work naked on Shabbat, and speculates that she herself would have had no hesitation about appearing naked except that God had smitten her with leprosy and she was ashamed of her body. A simpler and perhaps more plausible explanation appears in *Esth. Rab. 2.13*, which tells how Vashti did not wish to appear wearing only a crown in front of a group of drunken Persians (see Esth 1:10-12).

While it is clear that alcohol and drunkenness figure prominently in the cultural backdrop of the story, there is a specific phrase that links this story to the incident between Ruth and Boaz. The order of Ahasuerus that Vashti be summoned to appear was given only "when the heart of the king was merry with wine" (1:10). Perhaps the narrative is trying to alert us to the fact that not even a Persian monarch would make such a demand of his wife if he were sober.

Of greater interest is the function of alcohol in describing the activities of Esther, the nice Jewish girl. The narrative, which is too familiar to require retelling here, describes Haman leaving the first banquet given by Esther "pleased of heart" (Esth 5:9), a description that calls to mind the condition of Boaz in Ruth 3:7, as well as of Haman's own king in Esth 1:10. And just as Ahasuerus had needed wine to screw up enough courage to make an outlandish demand on Queen Vashti, both banquets hosted by Esther employed wine to prepare the way for her requests of the king. At the first banquet, she pointedly waits to make her request until after the wine has been drunk (Esth 5:6), while regarding the second banquet, we are told specifically that "the king and Haman came to drink with Esther" (Esth 7:1). Even more significant is the fact that each banquet is described as "a wine banquet" (in Esth 5:6 and 7:2).

But there is also a subtle difference between the use of wine by Ahasuerus and by Esther. Ahasuerus had used wine to bolster his own courage in the presence of his macho buddies. Esther is never described as the one doing the drinking, but rather as the clever person who used wine to soften up the king for her request, surely knowing his drinking habits well enough to believe that such a ploy would be successful. Moreover, we note a third time that there is a complete absence of biblical condemnation or even special notice taken of the use of alcohol by the heroine for a noble purpose. Once again a female outsmarts and gains power over a male. Once again, her motives are viewed positively, while her methods are merely chronicled in prosaic fashion.

JUDITH

The example of Judith is an intriguing extension of our theme. Even though the Book of Judith stands outside the canon of Hebrew Scripture,[8] its Jewish character can scarcely be denied. For one thing, the town around which the action of the book is centered is unknown in any historical record; its significance surely lies in its name: Bethulia, or "virgin." Clearly the symbolism of "virgin Israel" under attack by godless enemies would not have been missed by early readers. The same symbolism adheres in the name of the heroine: *Youdith*, "the Jewess," whom the Assyrian monster wanted to ravage. That we are dealing with symbolism rather than history is certain, as James C. VanderKam notes with remarkable understatement: "Anyone familiar with Assyrian, Babylonian, and Persian history is likely to be baffled by the opening of the book."[9]

Regardless of the book's date, which scholars have set as early as the Persian period in the fifth century BCE or as late as the Maccabean Period in the second century BCE, the narrative artistry of the author shines brightly and serves as the basis for understanding the theological argument. As the book opens, seven tedious chapters chronicle the dastardly plots of the "Assyrian" King Nebuchadnezzar living in Nineveh [*sic*] and his evil general Holofernes to besiege and conquer the city of Bethulia. Only in chapter eight are we finally introduced to the heroine of the story. Judith is a beautiful, pious, and wealthy widow, who, we will learn, is also brazen and crafty. When the citizens of Bethuliah determine to surrender to the besieging enemy unless God can save them within five days, Judith volunteers to take matters into her own hands. Once she has decided that something must be done to oppose the evil Assyrians, she embarks on an incremental plan of action. Her first step is to meticulously prepare her appearance:

> She removed the sackcloth she had been wearing, took off her widow's garments, bathed her body with water, and anointed herself with precious ointment. She combed her hair, put on a tiara, and dressed herself in the festive attire that she used to wear while her husband Manasseh was living. She put sandals on her feet, and put on her anklets, bracelets, rings, earrings, and all her other jewelry.[10]

Thus arrayed, Judith and her maid entered the war camp of the enemy, where her dazzling beauty immediately brought her to the attention and into the very presence of General Holofernes, to whom she asserted, apparently without blinking or blushing, that she would never lie to the great general! Whereupon, she began—with scarcely a pause for breath—to weave a pack of lies that one can only stand back and admire. Pretending to honor both the general and his king,

Nebuchadnezzar, she explained that her Jewish brothers and sisters were preparing to eat *treif* [unkosher food] because of the exigencies of the siege to which they were being subjected. She had fled, she assured Holofernes, rather than partake of it. In light of the grave sin being committed by her Jewish brothers and sisters, she promised the Assyrian general that the God of the Jews would punish His own people and allow them to be defeated without the loss of a single Assyrian life.

Holofernes was so pleased with her report and so stricken by her beauty that he invited her to stay for supper. To underscore her commitment to *kashrut* [kosher food], she refused the Assyrian food, retiring outside the camp to partake of the meal that her maid had brought along in a picnic basket. We soon learn that even this apparently innocent action has a double meaning: over the following three days, Judith sets about establishing a pattern that would permit her to leave the Assyrian camp each evening for supper and each midnight or early morning for prayer.[11]

By the fourth day, Holofernes was totally enthralled with, and completely captivated by, the beautiful heroine. The narrator makes clear the general's intention to seduce Judith, having him tell "the eunuch who had charge of his personal affairs" (Jud 12:11) that "it would be a disgrace if we let such a woman go without having intercourse with her" (Jud 12:12).

To this end, he sent the eunuch Bagoas to invite Judith "to enjoy drinking wine with us" (Jud 12:13). Dressed in her finest, Judith arrived at the tent of Holofernes, whose passion was once more aroused by her beauty, and who invited her to "have a drink and be merry with us" (Jud 12:17). Judith responds: "I will gladly drink, my lord, because today is the greatest day in my whole life" (Jud 12:18). She knew, of course, what she meant, but Holofernes no doubt assumed that her excitement centered on the anticipation of having sex with him. Judith plays this assumption to the hilt. She munches on her simple kosher fare and does in fact take a drink of wine so that Holofernes can observe. The sight of his beautiful prey drinking made Holofernes so excited that, "he drank a great quantity of wine, much more than he had ever drunk in any one day since he was born" (Jud 12:20). All the servants were dismissed, "but Judith was left alone in the tent, with Holofernes stretched out on his bed, for he was dead drunk" (Jud 13:2).

Before we recount the final act of this heroine, it should be observed that the beheading of an adult male is physically quite difficult. A recent

report on the development of the guillotine in eighteenth century France
noted that supporters of the new machine were looking for a more
efficient way to take the life of condemned criminals, specifically seeking
to avoid the ghastly sight of muscular, male executioners forced to strike
numerous times at a neck in order to sever the head.[12] Thus, when the
text tells us that Judith severed the head of the Assyrian general with
only two whacks (Jud 13:8), we are supposed to be impressed. Even
more impressive than the sheer physical feat is the icily calm manner in
which Judith acts afterward. Rolling the body of the drunk general
onto the floor, she wraps his head in the canopy and gives it to her
maid, who pops it into the trusty picnic basket. Under cover of the
routine they had established each night, in plain sight of the Assyrian
soldiers, Judith and her maid boldly walk out of the camp with the
basket and the head firmly in hand. Under such auspicious
circumstances, who could doubt that a great victory would now be
achieved by the once frightened male soldiers in the besieged Jewish
army?

CONCLUSION

Our survey of four Jewish heroines yields surprising conclusions. The
women we observed in action were not demure and weak, but rather
tough in mind and body. In order to accomplish a necessary task, they
did not hesitate to use their sexuality and beauty or the notorious
stupidity of men in the presence of such beauty. Nor did they shrink
from employing alcoholic inducements to achieve their goals. The
daughters of Lot did what they set forth to do: they achieved immortality
by the only means at their disposal. Ruth was not content to settle for
the existence of a powerless young widow, but set her sights on a rich
husband and proposed to him. Esther manipulated the most powerful
male on earth into doing just what she wanted. And Judith, the
quintessential Jewish woman, stepped forward with the courage that all
the men in her city lacked and acted with a level of shrewdness and
bravery that Hollywood itself could not resist.[13]

It might be possible to argue that portrayals of women who used
liquor and sex to achieve power reinforces a negative stereotype of women
as sneaky, tricky, or underhanded. However, I do not believe that such
a stereotype fits any of the narratives examined here. Instead, I believe
that these stories depict women who acted well within the boundaries
set for them by societies in which they were seldom full and equal

partners. In my judgment, these women simply learned well the rules by which men play, and then applied those rules as or more successfully than the men. They remained well within those rules, using them to achieve power in situations where societal norms might otherwise have conspired to keep them weak, dependent, and vulnerable. In addition, just as modern society tends to view a woman who drinks at wrong times and in unsafe contexts as somehow "loose" or "easy," so these ancient heroines adopted the view of their own society that men who drank foolishly or to excess were "easy" to conquer. Thus, they used their knowledge of reality to do what had to be done.

The women we have examined are not realistic historical figures, which makes them all the more remarkable. It speaks volumes that ancient audiences thought such women believable and acceptable, that Jews of an earlier era would have found their deeds worthy of legend and fame, and that indeed they were celebrated by having their stories immortalized in literature that came to be deemed sacred by the entire community. It is safe to assume—is it not?—that the women singled out for such special notice had many a sister, unknown to us and unheralded in the literature, who gave her own measure of courage and strength to Israel whenever she was needed.

NOTES

[1] Note that Deut 14:26 allows a tithe of agricultural produce to be converted into money with which to purchase wine.
[2] Delilah is never said to have used wine to seduce Samson and obtain his secret (see Judg 16). This is especially interesting in light of his vow as a Nazirite.
[3] In fact, the expression "feet" is often used in biblical narrative as a euphemism for the penis. We may note in particular 2 Sam 11:8, where David orders Uriyyah to "wash your feet," followed by 11:11, where Uriyyah refuses to go home "to eat and drink and lie with my wife." See also Judg 3:24, 2 Kgs 18:27, Isa 6:2.
[4] As TANAKH correctly notes, citing Ezek 16:8.
[5] Note Ps 104:15; see also Judg 9:13.
[6] See D. J. Wiseman, "A New Stela of Ashshur-Nasir-Pal II," *Iraq* 14 (1952): 24-44.
[7] So Ctesias. Ctesias, the Greek physician of Artaxerxes II, was believed unreliable by Plutarch. See *La Perse, L'Inde* (trans. R. Henry; Paris, 1947). For a modern evaluation of Ctesias as a historian, see E. A. Yamauchi, *Persia and the Bible* (Grand Rapids: Baker, 1996), 79. For a graphic description of a Persian banquet, see Xenophon, *Cyropaedia*

8:4.1-27. Herodotus (1.126; 9.80) notes the Persian preference for drinking wine from expensive vessels.

[8]It is considered canonical in Roman Catholic, Orthodox, and Slavonic "Old Testament" scriptures.

[9]James C. VanderKam, *An Introduction to Early Judaism* (Grand Rapids: Eerdmans, 2001), 73.

[10]Jud 10:3-4. Translation is the New Revised Standard Version.

[11]See her meetings with Holofernes in Jud 11-13. On the historical and literary structure of the book, see VanderKam, *Introduction to Early Judaism*, 72-75, and Daniel J. Harrington, *Invitation to the Apocrypha* (Grand Rapids: Eerdmans, 1999), 27-43.

[12]August 8, 2001, The History Channel.

[13]See Dan W. Clanton, Jr.,'s chapter in this volume, "Judy in Disguise: D. W. Griffith's *Judith of Bethulia*."

Traditions about Miriam
in the Qumran Scrolls

Sidnie White Crawford

The literature of Second Temple Judaism (late sixth century BCE to 70 CE) contains many compositions that focus on characters and events known from the biblical texts. The characters or events in these new compositions are developed in various ways: filling in gaps in the biblical account, offering explanations for difficult passages, or simply adding details to the lives of biblical personages to make them fuller and more interesting characters. For example, the work known as *Joseph and Aseneth* focuses on the biblical character Aseneth, the Egyptian wife of Joseph, mentioned only briefly in Gen 41:45, 50.[1] This work attempts to explain, among other things, how Joseph, the righteous son of Jacob, contracted an exogamous marriage with the daughter of an Egyptian priest. In an elaborate scene, Aseneth rejects her ancestral religion and converts to the worship of the God of Israel (10:2-17:10).

Further Second Temple period compositions focus on other biblical characters, most of them from Israel's hoary past: the patriarchs and matriarchs Abraham and Sarah, Isaac and Rebekah, Jacob, Leah and Rachel, and their descendants. The collection of manuscripts recovered from the caves surrounding Khirbet Qumran, popularly known as the Dead Sea Scrolls, contains a wealth of previously unknown literary compositions from the period of the Second Temple, many adding to our knowledge of the traditions surrounding these familiar biblical characters. It is especially pertinent, given the theme of this volume, to note that there is new material concerning female biblical characters to be gleaned from the fragmentary remains of the Qumran collection.

This paper focuses on two or three Qumran texts that mention the biblical character Miriam, the sister of Moses and Aaron, who, with her brothers, was a leader of the Israelites during the sojourn in the wilderness. Miriam appears in seven passages in the Hebrew Bible. In Exod 15:20-21 Miriam, identified as a prophet, is portrayed as leading

the Israelite women in a victory celebration following the rout of the
Egyptians at the Reed Sea:

> Then the prophet Miriam, Aaron's sister, took a tambourine in
> her hand; and all the women went out after her with
> tambourines and with dancing. And Miriam sang to them: "Sing
> to the LORD, for he has triumphed gloriously; horse and rider
> he has thrown into the sea."[2]

As it stands, Miriam's song is only a repetition of the first verse of Moses'
Song of the Sea (Exod 15:1); one might ask if Miriam sang anything
else.

Numbers 12:1-15 contains the story of Miriam and Aaron's
complaint against Moses, with Miriam's subsequent punishment with
a form of skin disease:

> While they were at Hazeroth, Miriam and Aaron spoke against
> Moses because of the Cushite woman whom he had married
> (for he had indeed married a Cushite woman); and they said,
> "Has the LORD spoken only through Moses? Has he not spoken
> through us also?" And the LORD heard it...Suddenly the LORD
> said to Moses, Aaron, and Miriam, "Come out, you three, to
> the tent of meeting." So the three of them came out. Then the
> LORD came down in a pillar of cloud, and stood at the entrance
> of the tent, and called Aaron and Miriam; and they both came
> forward. And he said, "Hear my words: When there are prophets
> among you, I the LORD make myself known to them in visions;
> I speak to them in dreams. Not so with my servant Moses; he is
> entrusted with all my house. With him I speak face to face—
> clearly, not in riddles; and he beholds the form of the Lord.
> Why then were you not afraid to speak against my servant
> Moses?" And the anger of the LORD was kindled against them,
> and he departed. When the cloud went away from over the
> tent, Miriam had become skin-diseased, white as snow. And
> Aaron turned towards Miriam and saw that she had skin disease.
> Then Aaron said to Moses, "Oh, my lord, do not lay sin upon
> us for a sin that we have so foolishly committed. Do not let her
> be like one stillborn, whose flesh is half consumed when it
> comes out of its mother's womb." And Moses cried to the LORD,
> "O God, please heal her." But the LORD said to Moses, "If her
> father had but spit in her face, would she not bear her shame
> for seven days? Let her be shut out of the camp for seven days,

and after that she may be brought in again." So Miriam was shut out of the camp for seven days; and the people did not set out on the march until Miriam had been brought in again. (Num 12:1-2, 4-15; NRSV with modifications).

It should be noted that although Miriam is punished in this passage, she is clearly a leader of the people; it is implied in verse 6 that she is a prophet of visions and dreams, and her skin disease and subsequent quarantine cause the journey through the wilderness to be delayed seven days (verse 15). Miriam's skin disease is then recalled in Deut 24:9.

The death of Miriam is recounted in Num 20:1: "The Israelites, the whole congregation, came into the wilderness of Zin in the first month, and the people stayed in Kadesh. Miriam died there, and was buried there." In the verse immediately following the notice of Miriam's death, the narrative notes that the wells dry up and the people have no water; while there is no necessary connection between these two events, later tradition creates one.[3] Miriam also appears in genealogical notices in Num 26:59 and 1 Chr 5:29 (Eng. 6:3), where she is identified as the daughter of Amram and Jochebed and the sister of Aaron and Moses. Finally, Micah, the eighth century prophet, lists Moses, Aaron and Miriam as the leaders of the Exodus from Egypt (Mic 6:4).

In addition, Exod 2:4-8 portrays an unnamed sister of Moses watching over him after his mother sets him adrift on the Nile. Although later tradition identifies this unnamed sister as Miriam (for example, *Jubilees* 47:4-9), some scholars have speculated that the tradition that identifies Moses, Aaron, and Miriam as siblings is a later P tradition, and that originally Miriam was a leader in her own right, unrelated to Moses.[4]

These few passages provide a tantalizing glimpse of a female leadership figure, a prophet whose actual role may have been far greater than recorded. Ilana Pardes suggests that "there must have been other traditions [about Miriam] which were not included in the canon."[5] It is always difficult to determine what the biblical accounts, some of which may be quite ancient (for example, Exod 15:1-18, the Song of the Sea), may have left out when they were redacted into their present form; but whether or not traditional material about Miriam was excluded from the books that now make up the biblical canon, the short passages concerning Miriam were ripe for interpretation and expansion, with the potential of forming a traditional body of material about Miriam.

In a few fragmentary manuscripts from Qumran we seem to have the oldest record of such traditions.

The first Qumran manuscript to contain fresh information about Miriam is 4Q365, one of a group of manuscripts known collectively as 4QReworked Pentateuch.[6] 4Q365 is dated paleographically to c. 75-50 BCE, but includes much older material. It contains an expanded and altered text of the Pentateuch or Torah. 4Q365 changes the text of the Torah from the received text with which we are familiar by means of rearrangements, some omissions, and additions. These alterations were deliberate and usually had an exegetical purpose. One such addition occurs in the fragments that contain Exod 15. Fragments 6 of 4Q365 preserve the remains of two columns. Column I begins with Exod 14:12 and breaks off in the midst of 15:20-21, the verses concerning Miriam's victory song at the Reed Sea: "And [Miriam the prophet, the sister of Aaron] took [the tambourine in her hand and] she lead a[ll] the women after her with [tambourines and with dancing. And she answered…]"[7]

The verse presumably was completed at the bottom of column I (not preserved). The next verse that we expect, 15:22, does not appear until the beginning of line 8 in column II. In the seven preceding lines we find the very fragmentary remains of a poetic composition, presumably an expanded version of the song that Miriam sang at the Reed Sea. The preserved words are as follows:

1. you despised [
2. for the majesty of [
3. You are great, a deliverer [
4. the hope of the enemy has perished, and he is for[gotten
5. they perished in the mighty waters, the enemy [
6. And extol the one who lifts up[, a r]ansom you (feminine plural) gave [
7. [one who d]oes gloriously

As can be seen by the feminine plural imperative in line 6, this song is being addressed to a group of women, evidently those following Miriam in 15:20. The subject of the song is God, who is praised for destroying an enemy who must be the Egyptians. Several of the lines contain words or phrases that have already appeared in Moses' song, the Song of the Sea: the words "majesty" and "gloriously" in lines 2 and 7, from a Hebrew root that is also used in Exod 15:1, 7; and the "mighty waters," found in line 5 and also 15:10. All this evidence allows us to say with confidence that these lines are the remnant of a Song of Miriam, part of a body of traditional material that has contributed to the longer text of 4Q365. Perhaps this Song grew up in answer to the question raised above, "What did Miriam really sing?" It certainly parallels other songs of triumph sung by biblical women; for example, Deborah in Judg 5, Hannah in 1 Sam 2:1-10, and Judith in Jdt 16.[8] Miriam's role in the victory celebration at the Reed Sea is the subject of some discussion in Second Temple literature; for example, Philo, the Alexandrian Jewish philosopher of the first century CE, states that Moses and Miriam formed separate men's and women's choirs (*Moses* 1.180), although in another work he says that there was a single choir, with the men being led by Moses and the women by Miriam (*De Vita Contemplativa* 87).[9] However, this Qumran fragment is unique; nowhere else in Second Temple Jewish writings do we find an actual record of Miriam's song. This song cements Miriam's status as a leader of the Israelites; since she is also called a prophet in verse 20, it could be argued that the song is the product of divine inspiration.

The second work from Qumran that mentions Miriam focuses on her prophetic gifts and her membership in the family of the first high priest, Aaron. 4QVisions of Amram is an Aramaic text found in six or seven fragmentary manuscripts, which was composed, according to its editor, in the early second century BCE.[10] The text is part of a trilogy of testaments from the ancestors of the high priestly family: Aramaic Levi, the Testament of Qahat (or Kohath, the son of Levi), and the Visions of Amram (the grandson of Levi and father of Aaron).[11] Miriam appears in the Visions of Amram as the daughter of Amram and Jochebed, the grandson and daughter of Levi respectively (Exod 6:20 and Num 26:59), and thus a member of the Levitical priestly house.

Miriam is first mentioned in the opening lines of the text, when her father Amram arranges her marriage:

A copy of the writing of the words of the visions of Amram, son of Kohath, son of Levi, all of which he declared to his sons, and which he commissioned to them on the day of his death, in the one hundredth and thirty-sixth year, that is the year of his death, in the one hundredth and fifty-second year of Israel's exile in Egypt. And then it came to him and he sent and called Uzziel, his youngest brother, and he gave him Miriam his daughter as a wife, she being thirty years old. And he made a marriage feast for seven days.[12]

Miriam is here identified as the daughter of Amram, as she is in at least some parts of the biblical tradition. However, the biblical texts make no mention of Miriam's husband; thus we have preserved here an extra-biblical tradition. Uzziel appears in Exod 6:18 and Num 3:19, as well as the pseudepigraph *T. Levi* 12, as the youngest brother of Amram. It is surprising to find Amram arranging for his daughter to marry her uncle, since uncle-niece marriage was clearly forbidden in the Qumran community. According to the Damascus Document, in a context that condemns the sexual activities of those outside its community:

> And each man marries the daughter of his brother or sister, whereas Moses said, "You shall not approach your mother's sister; she is your mother's near kin." But although the laws against incest are written for men, they also apply to women. When, therefore, a brother's daughter uncovers the nakedness of her father's brother, she is near kin (CD 5:9-11).

This prohibition is also found in the Temple Scroll, col. 66: "A man shall not take the daughter of his brother or the daughter of his sister, for this is abominable." The same prohibition is also found in 4QHalakhah[a], 12. The prohibition against uncle-niece marriage is quite clear in these documents. Moreover, it is based on the biblical prohibition of aunt-nephew marriage, found in Lev 18:12-14:

> You shall not uncover the nakedness of your father's sister; she is your father's flesh. You shall not uncover the nakedness of your mother's sister, for she is your mother's flesh. You shall not uncover the nakedness of your father's brother, that is, you shall not approach his wife; she is your aunt.

This negative commandment is reiterated in Lev 20:19: "You shall not uncover the nakedness of your mother's sister or of your father's sister, for that is to lay bare one's own flesh; they shall be subject to punishment." According to the interpretation found in the Damascus Document and implied in the Temple Scroll and 4QHalakhah[a], what is expressly forbidden for men (to marry an aunt) is equally forbidden for women (to marry an uncle).[13] Thus Miriam's marriage, according to the regulations of the Qumran community, is illegal. It is thus remarkable that they would preserve several copies of a text that so blatantly supported uncle-niece marriage.[14]

However, the explanation may lie in the circumstances of the marriage of Miriam's parents, Amram and Jochebed. According to Exod 6:20 and Num 26:59, Jochebed was the daughter of Levi and the sister of Kohath, therefore Amram's aunt! In other words, Amram himself contracted a marriage that was explicitly forbidden according to the terms of the Torah given to his son Moses on Mt. Sinai. This anomaly was not ignored everywhere in the tradition; *Aramaic Levi* amplifies the terse notice in Exodus and Numbers by stating that Jochebed and Amram were born on the same day. Thus, Miriam's marriage to Amram's youngest brother is parallel to Amram's marriage to Levi's youngest daughter. Both marriages are endogamous, something applauded throughout the patriarchal history.[15] Nonetheless, the forbidden quality of Amram's marriage to Jochebed forces the author of *Jubilees*, otherwise a polemicist in favor of endogamous marriage, to pass over this particular marriage in silence.[16] Later rabbinic tradition argues that before the revelation at Sinai only maternal relationships were considered, and that Jochebed was only the half-sister of Amram's father Kohath, through their father Levi, but that they had different mothers.[17]

A similar type of apologetic may be at work in the Qumran community, which tends to excuse the peccadilloes of the ancients on the basis of ignorance of the Law. For example, the Damascus Document excuses the fact that David had many wives, seemingly in direct contradiction to Deut 17:17 ("He [the king] shall not multiply wives for himself"), by saying "but David had not read the sealed book of the Law which was in the ark, for it was not opened in Israel from the death of Eleazar and Joshua, and the elders who worshipped Ashtoreth. It was hidden and not revealed until the coming of Zadok" (CD 5:2-4). The same argument could be applied both to Amram and Jochebed and to Miriam and Uzziel; both couples did not know the Law and therefore could not be expected to follow it. Thus the Qumran community could preserve such seemingly contradictory documents. This, however, points to a different interpretive tradition than *Jubilees*, also preserved by the community, which argues vehemently that the patriarchs and matriarchs did observe the Law.

The second mention of Miriam in the Visions of Amram comes in 4Q546, 12, 3-4: "and he clung to Aaron to be [ ] and the secret of Miriam he made for th[em..."[18] The Hebrew word for "secret" has a divine connotation; thus, Miriam's secret had been revealed to her by God. As E. Puech notes, there are several extra-biblical traditions according to which Miriam is the recipient of divine revelation;[19] since she is called a prophet in Exod 15:20 and in Num 12:2 makes the claim that God has spoken to her, the growth of this extra-biblical tradition is not surprising. In the *Biblical Antiquities* of Pseudo-Philo, Miriam has a prophetic dream concerning the birth of Moses (9:10).[20] In rabbinic tradition, Miriam is the recipient of divine revelations.[21] This fragment seems to be part of that extra-biblical tradition, although unfortunately we cannot be certain what the "secret of Miriam" was. Puech suggests that it is a revelation concerning the birth of Moses and his mission, in the same tradition as Pseudo-Philo.[22]

4Q547, 9, 10, another manuscript of the Visions of Amram, has a brief mention of Miriam, unfortunately in a broken context. Amram appears to be narrating his return to Egypt from the land of Canaan, perhaps followed by the birth of Miriam, the oldest of the three siblings.[23] Nothing more can be ascertained from the fragment.

The last manuscript containing a mention of Miriam is 4Q549. This Aramaic manuscript was originally catalogued by Jean Starcky as a separate work entitled "Composition mentionnant Hur et Miriam." In his *DJD* edition, however, Puech argued that 4Q549 is not a separate work, but a seventh manuscript of 4QVisions of Amram. In support of his argument, he notes that the characters mentioned by name are either part of the family of Amram, for example, Miriam, Aaron and Sitri, or are associated with Moses and Aaron, for example, Hur. Further, he finds in fragment 2 elements of the genre "testament": a meal, an announcement of the anticipated death of the patriarch, and a reunion with his sons and other male relatives. Finally, fragment 1 mentions Egypt, the setting for 4QVisions of Amram.[24] Robert Eisenman and Michael Wise, however, have argued that there is no connection between this text and 4QVisions of Amram because in this text Miriam is married to Hur rather than Uzziel.[25] As we shall see, the text itself does not clearly identify the spouse of Miriam. The lines in question read as follows:

8. ten, and he begat from Miriam, a relative? [[26]
9. and Sitri. *blank* And Hur took [for a wife...
10. and he begat from her Ur, and Aaro[n...
11. from her four/fourteen sons [

These lines are clearly giving the genealogical record of the family of which Miriam and Aaron are a part; that is, the family of Amram. We are already familiar with Miriam and Aaron from the biblical text and the fragments presented above. Sitri, according to Exod 6:22, is the son of Uzziel. In 4QVisions of Amram, Miriam is the wife of Uzziel and, by implication (but not biblically), the mother of Sitri. The juxtaposition of lines 8 and 9 here, with the unnamed husband begetting children from Miriam and Sitri's name in the next line, may yield the understanding that Miriam is the mother of Sitri. Hence, her unnamed spouse must be Uzziel, in agreement with manuscripts 4Q543, 545 and 546, 4QVisions of Amram.[27]

The character Hur, presented as taking a wife and fathering Ur in lines 9 and 10, appears in the biblical text in two different contexts and is in fact probably two different characters. The first Hur debuts in Exod 17:10-12, where he and Aaron prop up Moses' hands during the battle against the Amalekites. In Exod 24:4 Moses leaves Aaron and Hur in charge of the people when he goes up on the mountain. Although Hur's genealogy is not given in either of these passages, his association with Moses and Aaron suggests that he is a Levite.

There is a second series of passages concerning Hur. This Hur is the grandfather of Bezalel, the chief craftsman of the tent sanctuary, and is a Judahite (Exod 31:2, 35:30, 38:22; 2 Chr 1:5). In 1 Chr 2:19-20 Hur is a son of Caleb by his second wife Ephrath. There would seem to be no necessary connection between these two Hurs; however, the later tradition identifies the two characters and further puts Miriam into relationship with Hur.

Josephus, the late first century CE Jewish historian, knows a tradition in which the Hur of Exod 17:10-12 is married to Miriam (*Ant.* 3.53-54). He also identifies the two Hurs with one another, since he states that Bezalel is the grandson of Miriam (*Ant.* 3.105). Another tradition, however, identifies Miriam with Ephrath, the second wife of Caleb in 2 Chr 2:19, thus making her the mother of Hur, the grandmother of Uri, and the great-grandmother of Bezalel (*Tg. Chron.*, *Sifre* to Num 78, *Sotah* 11b-12a, *m. Rab.* to Exod 1:17, among others). Is 4Q549 part of either of those traditions?

The Hur found in line 9 must be identified with the biblical Judahite Hur, since he is the father of Ur in line 10, and Ur is clearly part of the Judahite ancestry of Bezalel: "Bezalel son of Uri son of Hur, of the tribe of Judah" (Exod 31:2). It might then be possible to argue that Hur is the unnamed husband of Miriam in line 8 above. We would thus have a text in line with the tradition of Josephus, which identifies the Judahite Hur with the Hur of the battle against the Amalekites and relates him to Moses and Aaron through his marriage to Miriam.[28] However, two elements militate against this solution. First, the pattern of the text seems to follow this order: Male person marries female person and begets a certain number of sons who are listed by name. Given that pattern, it is most likely that Miriam is the mother of Sitri. Since we know that Sitri is the son of Uzziel and is nowhere related to Hur, it follows that the unnamed husband of Miriam must be Uzziel. Further, there is a *vacat* [blank space] in the middle of line 9, after Sitri's name and before the mention of Hur's marriage. This implies that there is no relationship between the two groups of people. Therefore, it seems most likely that 4Q549 is part of the tradition known to 4QVisions of Amram, in which Miriam is married to Uzziel; Hur (identified with the Judahite Hur) is mentioned here because of his connection with Aaron (line 10), not Miriam. This conclusion strengthens Puech's argument that 4Q549 is a seventh manuscript of 4QVisions of Amram.

In sum, these few fragments have added much to our knowledge of the body of traditions surrounding the biblical character Miriam. Miriam's reputation as a prophet is visible in the creation of the Song of Miriam in 4Q365 and the mention of the "secret of Miriam" in 4QVisions of Amram. Miriam's status as an important member of the family of Amram is emphasized through her presence in the genealogical material in 4QVisions of Amram. Finally, a new tradition has been discovered concerning Miriam's marriage to Amram's brother Uzziel, pointing to a process that was neither static nor unified, but grew in different directions among different groups of Jews in the Second Temple period.

NOTES

[1] C. Burchard, "Joseph and Aseneth," in *The Old Testament Pseudepigrapha* (vol. 2; ed. J. Charlesworth; Garden City, NY: Doubleday, 1985), 177-248.
[2] ll biblical passages are taken from the New Revised Standard Version.
[3] See, for example, J. Kugel, *The Bible as it Was* (Cambridge: Harvard University Press, 1997), 364.
[4] D. Setel, "Exodus," in *The Women's Bible Commentary* (expanded ed.; eds. C. Newsom and S. Ringe; Louisville: John Knox Press, 1998), 36.
[5] I. Pardes, *Countertraditions in the Bible: A Feminist Approach* (Cambridge: Harvard University Press, 1992), 11.
[6] For a complete discussion of these manuscripts, see E. Tov and S. White, "4QReworked Pentateuch," in *Qumran Cave 4, VIII; Discoveries in the Judaean Desert* XIII (eds. H. Attridge et al.; Oxford: Clarendon Press, 1994), 187-352. 4Q365 is discussed on 255-318.

[7]Here and elsewhere in translations of the Dead Sea Scrolls, material in brackets has been supplied by the editor of that fragment.

[8]G. Brooke, "A Long-Lost Song of Miriam," *BAR* 20 (1994): 62-65.

[9]Kugel, *The Bible as it Was,* 350.

[10]E. Puech, "Visions de 'Amram," *Qumrân Grotte 4, XXII; Discoveries in the Judaean Desert* XXXI (Oxford: Clarendon Press, 2001), 285.

[11]Puech, "Visions de 'Amram," 283. For a discussion of the family of Levi, see also R. Kugler, *From Patriarch to Priest: The Levi-Priestly Tradition from Aramaic Levi to Testament of Levi* (Atlanta: Scholars Press, 1996), 111-18.

[12]4Q543, 1, 1-7, parallel 4Q545,1A I, 1-6, and 4Q546, 1, 1-4. The text is taken from Puech, "Visions de 'Amram," 292-93, 333-35, and 353-54; the English translation is based on his French translation. For other English translations, see M. Wise, et al., *The Dead Sea Scrolls, A New Translation* (San Francisco: HarperCollins, 1996), 433-36, and F. García Martínez and E. Tigchelaar, *The Dead Sea Scrolls Study Edition* (vol. 2; Leiden: Brill, 1998), 1084-95.

[13]Rabbinic tradition did not forbid uncle-niece marriage, but in fact actively encouraged it on the grounds that since it was not expressly forbidden in the Torah, it was approved (*b. Yebam.* 62b). See M. Broshi, "Anti-Qumranic Polemics in the Talmud," *The Madrid Qumran Congress: Proceedings of the International Congress on the Dead Sea Scrolls, Madrid, 18-21 March 1991* (vol. 2; eds. J. Trebolle Barrera and L. Vegas Montaner; Leiden: Brill, 1992) 596.

[14]Also Wise et al., *The Dead Sea Scrolls*, 434.

[15]A. Caquot, "Les Testaments Qoumraniens des Peres du Sacerdoce," *Revue d'histoire et de philosophie religieuses* 78 (1998): 20.

[16]B. Halpern-Amaru, *The Empowerment of Women in the Book of Jubilees* (Leiden: Brill; 1999), 123.

[17]*b. Sotah* 58b.

[18]Puech, "Visions de 'Amram," 364-65.

[19]Puech, "Visions de 'Amram," 300.

[20]D. Harrington, "Pseudo-Philo," in *The Old Testament Pseudepigrapha* (vol. 2; ed. J. Charlesworth; Garden City: Doubleday, 1985), 297-378.

[21]L. Ginzberg, *The Legends of the Jews* (vol. 3; Baltimore: Johns Hopkins University Press, 1939, 1998), 256.

[22]Puech, "Visions de 'Amram," 399.

[23]Puech, "Visions de 'Amram," 390.

[24]Puech, "Visions de 'Amram," 399.

[25]R. Eisenman and M. Wise, *The Dead Sea Scrolls Uncovered* (New York: Penguin Books, 1992), 152.

[26]Puech, "Visions de 'Amram," 402-03, restores the Hebrew and translates it "une parente." Caquot, "Les Testaments Qoumraniens des Peres du Sacerdoce," 25, restores the Hebrew, "a father's sister, paternal aunt," but suggests that here it means something like "kinsman on the father's side." Eisenman and Wise, *The Dead Sea Scrolls Uncovered*, 94, suggest a proper name, Ab[?. Abegg, in Wise et al., *The Dead Sea Scrolls*, 437, reads

"a peopl[e?", the same letters as Puech but understanding it differently. García Martínez and Tigchelaar, *The Dead Sea Scrolls Study Edition*, 1097, have the same reading, but translate "aunt(?)".

[27]Puech, "Visions de 'Amram," 404; Caquot, "Les Testaments Qoumraniens des Peres du Sacerdoce," 25.

[28]Eisenman and Wise, *The Dead Sea Scrolls Uncovered,* 93-94.

Women and Passover Observance: Reconsidering Gender in the Study of Rabbinic Texts

Marjorie Lehman

I join many feminist scholars in the field of Talmud and Rabbinics who are grappling with how to study women and Jewish law.[1] I am a proponent of the need to resist the tendency to view rabbinic texts as misogynist, oppressive, and therefore objectionable—or, sympathetic, enlightened, and therefore redeemable. Such labeling, I believe, diminishes our ability to see the complex nature of the male elite who authored and transmitted them. We contribute far more to the field of Jewish feminist studies when we resist producing overarching theories that generalize what lies before us. In other words, we should not reduce the rabbis to one-dimensional beings. Rather, we should be truer to the human condition and its complexities by recognizing the struggles, countenancing the contradictions, and upholding the ambiguities in rabbinic texts.[2] Elizabeth Shanks Alexander, in reviewing feminist scholarship in the field of Talmud, correctly summarizes this method as follows:

> The texts are not read as if they were a transparent window onto a historical reality that existed in rabbinic times, but rather as documentary traces of the struggle to create a particular version of Jewish culture. What is innovative in this method of reading rabbinic texts is that it resists the temptation to accept the program the texts themselves propose, even though this program has been accepted without question by many generations of Jewish readers.[3]

Both Daniel Boyarin[4] and Miriam Peskowitz[5] have made significant contributions to the field of Jewish feminist studies by employing this methodology to illuminate those contestations out of which rabbinic culture grew.[6] Boyarin examined women and sexuality while Peskowitz analyzed the use and meaning of women's spindles. In this essay, I

GLOSSARY OF TERMS

Amora (Amoraim, pl., amoraic, adj.)—A rabbi who lived after the completion of the *Mishnah*.

Baraita (baraitot, pl.)—A tannaitic source that was not included in the Mishnah. Many baraitot were eventually compiled into a collection called the Tosefta. The Babylonian Talmud as well as the Jerusalem Talmud quote baraitot that can be found in the Tosefta as well as those that can not be found in the Tosefta.

Jerusalem Talmud (also referred to as the *Yerushalmi* or Palestinian Talmud)— The Jerusalem Talmud was compiled in Palestine. A parallel work, the Babylonian Talmud (*Bavli*), was compiled in Babylonia. Both are arranged to look like commentaries on the Mishnah.

Mishnah (*mishnayot*, pl.)—An early rabbinic collection containing six orders or sections arranged topically. The traditional belief is that the Mishnah was redacted, arranged, and revised around the beginning of the third century by Rabbi Judah ha-Nasi. Each order is broken down into tractates and each tractate is divided into individual units called *mishnayot*. The Mishnah also serves as the primary text for the Babylonian Talmud and the Jerusalem Talmud; they were both redacted and arranged in accordance with the topical arrangement of the Mishnah.

Stammaim (stammaitic, adj., Stamma, sing.)—The redactors of the Talmud who compiled and arranged earlier *tannaitic* and *amoraic* source material as well as authored its anonymous portions. They are responsible for giving the Talmudic *sugya* its shape.

Sugya (*sugyot*, pl.)—A Talmudic passage.

Tanna (Tannaim, pl., tannaitic, adj.)—A rabbi who lived during the time when the Mishnah was being compiled. All rabbis mentioned in the Mishnah are Tannaim.

explore women and festival observance in the legal texts of the Babylonian Talmud. I have chosen this category of law to seek a fuller understanding of the rabbis and gender precisely because women are always mentioned when festival rituals are discussed, seemingly without concern for molding a coherent image of them. Moreover, the commandments defining holiday observance cross the boundary between Temple/synagogue and home—that is, between the public and private spheres of rabbinic society—and therefore provide insight into the sociocultural challenges confronting the rabbis with respect to women.

In this paper I offer one portion of a larger research project: an analysis of the legal texts dealing with the role of women in Passover ritual as presented in tractate *Pesachim* of the Babylonian Talmud. I begin the consideration of what can be gleaned about gender when discrepancies in these particular rabbinic texts are acknowledged. Although my claims are somewhat tentative, I believe that this paper will convince readers not only of the need for a larger analytical study of women and festival observance, but also of the significance of the method employed.

BACKGROUND
Mishnah Qiddushin 1:7 exempts women from all positive ritual commandments governed by time.[7] The history of scholarship on this mishnah runs in two familiar directions. Some scholars redeem the rabbis by describing them as compassionate. They perceive the rabbis as generous men who wished to rid women of a dual responsibility to God and family. These scholars interpret *m. Qidd.* 1:7 as offering women religious sanction to value familial duties as foremost.[8] On the other end of the spectrum are those who condemn the rabbis for being exclusionary.[9] Women, they claim, are being demeaned; exemption turns them into second-class citizens. Undeniably, *m. Qidd.* 1:7 supports both positive and negative depictions of the rabbinic view of women. However, no scholar has yet attributed the existence of this broad and even contradictory range of interpretive opinion to the ambiguous nature of the principle itself. In other words, the reason for the wide array of opinion is that the term "exemption" itself is vague. On the one hand, women are given the autonomy to abstain from performing a set of sacred commandments. This privilege, offered as it is within the confines of a religion that is defined by the performance of commandments, seems to grant women free choice.[10] On the other hand, the very same

principle undermines this authority. By exempting women, rather than requiring them to observe a set of laws, they emerge as "other." Men are the norm; women fall outside the norm and are "less than" men because they are not commanded in the same way. The principle thus reflects and fosters gender asymmetry because men must abide by a set of rules that women are not required to perform. Therefore, through this single principle the rabbis simultaneously give power to women by enabling them to fulfill positive time-bound commandments if they so choose, and strip them of control by devaluing them as full-fledged members of a religious system defined by the fulfillment of commandments. The mishnah argues against what it seems to promote.

However, we need to ask why the Tannaim are not more definitive in their treatment of women and ritual law. Why do they choose to "exempt" women, thereby creating a legal category that is far vaguer than if they had "required" or "prohibited" women from positive time-bound rituals?[11] The picture becomes even more complicated when we consider that women are required to perform the majority of festival rituals.[12] Women are, for instance, exempt from hearing the shofar, shaking the lulav, and sitting in the sukkah,[13] but are required to perform all the commandments associated with the observance of Passover, to bring *bikkurim* [first fruits] on Shavuot,[14] to hear Kiddush,[15] to light Hanukah candles,[16] to hear *Megillat Esther* on Purim,[17] to fulfill the commandment of the *simchah* offering brought on each of the three pilgrimage holidays,[18] and to be present for *hakhel* [the public teaching of the Torah which was to occur on Sukkot every seven years].[19] Women also seem to have participated in the water libation ceremony, *Simchat Beit Hoshoevah*, which was celebrated during the holiday of Sukkot.[20] In this regard, the exemption of women from certain commandments as delineated in *m. Qidd.*1:7 breaks down altogether.[21]

To return to the example of Passover: since women are required to perform all of the rituals associated with the rabbinic Seder, women are not "other," but equal participants. The lines demarcating husband and wife, son and daughter, dissolve. Of course, some scholars have dismissed Passover ritual as an exception to *m. Qidd.*1:7 and have attributed the discrepancy to the fact that the Seder is celebrated at home, in private.[22] But how would these same scholars explain sources requiring women to perform the Passover sacrifice, the rite of the *simchah* offering, *hakhel*, and the bringing of *bikkurim* in celebration of Shavuot— all of which are public Temple rituals? And, for those who might dismiss even these requirements because they are obsolete in the wake of the destruction of the Temple, how would they justify that women are obligated to hear the Megillah? Certainly, this reading is public, requiring as it does a male quorum of ten.

While I, like others, have been frustrated by the inconsistency generated between *m. Qidd.*1:7 and the list of rituals required of women, I would suggest that we reconsider this mishnaic principle and view it as an outgrowth of the rabbis' uncertainty regarding women. Perhaps their decision to design a weak legal principle reflects their desire to generalize about what is not susceptible to generalization. Certainly, each ritual (or category of festival rituals) presents them with a different set of challenges. For example, a semi-private hut constructed to celebrate the holiday of Sukkot and open to any passerby forces the rabbis to deal with the threat of women in public spheres, while the eating of matzah, which is prepared by women and eaten in the privacy of the home, prompts them to wrestle with the role of women within the desired family structure. These social concerns become even more complicated when considered against the backdrop of biblical events, including the Exodus from Egypt and the Israelite sojourn in the desert that define the observances of Passover and Sukkot respectively, events that were believed to have occurred to a community of men and women. No doubt, the fact that every festival ritual is considered and reconsidered in Talmudic and post-Talmudic literature testifies to the indeterminate nature of this exemption. It also shows that the dictum found in *m. Qidd.*1:7 resolved little.[23] We must now follow the model set by these rabbis and analyze each ritual example (or category of festival rituals) individually. My goal is to unearth the tensions that underlie the texts written about women and festival law by beginning with a discussion about women and Passover observance.[24]

METHODOLOGY

I now turn to the legal material dealing with women found in tractate *b. Pesachim*. This discussion is configured to reflect my reliance upon a source critical methodology. Such an approach assumes it is possible to differentiate between various historical layers of text and thereby write the history of Talmudic law. By distinguishing between the tannaitic material (our earliest layer), the later amoraic sources, and the contributions of the final editors, the Stammaim, we can detect transitions or reorientations in the rabbinic mindset. Although I agree with critics of this method who question our ability to separate strata of material by "objective means," I do believe that source critical studies are useful.[25] This method forces us to study the Talmud for what it is—a document that represents many viewpoints authored over the course of several centuries. The method assumes and presumes that the Talmud is multi-vocal. Its implementation can thereby distance us from generalizing about the rabbis.

WOMEN AND PASSOVER OBSERVANCE: THE TANNAITIC SOURCES[26]

Mishnah Pesachim is virtually silent regarding the role of women in Passover ritual. This silence may simply reflect the fact that the rabbis are relying on the universality of the principle, delineated in *m. Qidd.* 1:7, that women are exempt from all positive time-bound commandments. *M. Pesach.* 2:5 and 2:6 ("These are the things by [which] a man [*adam*] fulfills his obligation [to eat matzah/*maror* (bitter herbs)] at Passover") also make sense within this framework. Since women are exempt from eating matzah and *maror*, these *mishnayot* do not make reference to them. *M. Pesach.* 10:1-9, where the details of Seder ritual are outlined, also does not mention women. Not surprisingly, *m. Pesach.* 3:4 mentions women, but only in their roles as the bakers of bread/matzah.[27] In this mishnah, women are cited for their specific domestic contributions to the observance of Passover. Women emerge as distinct from their fathers, husbands, and sons, who are required to eat the matzah baked properly by their female relatives. But, none of these sources offers definitive guidance regarding women's participation in the ritual of matzah and *maror*.

Additional ambiguity surfaces around the commandment of the Passover offering. *M. Pesach.* 8:1 describes the case where a woman is included in the offering made both by her husband and by her father during her first year of marriage. This mishnah offers her a choice: she can consider herself part of whichever ritual offering she so desires. While I am struck by a text that grants women some choice, we are left wondering what this source says about the role of women in the Passover sacrifice.[28] Does this source presume that women are required to eat the sacrificial meat and hence that fathers and/or husbands must automatically include them in their offerings? Do women take on passive participatory roles when they are required to perform a ritual because their fathers and husbands assume the responsibility for them? Or, does the fact that the Mishnah offers women a choice suggest that they are exempt from this ritual?[29] Is it not true that women, when they are exempt, make decisions about their inclusion or exclusion from a particular ritual? And so I ask: Does this mishnah include or exclude women, or both?[30]

Non-mishnaic tannaitic (or *baraitan*) material[31] contains far more discussion on the subject of women's participation in Passover rituals than that found in *m. Pesach.* In fact, the tannaitic *baraitot* found within the *sugyot* of *m. Pesach.*, as well as those found in the Tosefta, contain support for, as well as discomfort with, the inclusion of women in the performance of Passover rituals, as the following *baraita* shows:

> The Passover offering, and matzah, and *maror* are obligatory on the first night, but are voluntary from then onwards. Rabbi Shim'on objects: In the case of men—[they are] obligated [to perform these rituals]; in the case of women—[the performance of these rituals] is voluntary.[32]

However, what is striking and distinctive about the *baraitan* material, in contrast to the Mishnaic treatment of women and Passover law, is that we find references that clearly require women to perform Passover rites. Women are required to eat matzah and *maror*,[33] as well as to drink four cups of wine.[34] In addition, they are not only described as the bakers of matzah,[35] but their role in the removal of *chametz* [leavened food forbidden on Passover] is illuminated as well. According to a *baraita* found on *b. Pesach.* 4a, women ought to be believed when they claim that their household *chametz* has been burned,[36] and, according to *b. Pesach.* 87a, women are relied upon for *chametz* removal in instances where their husbands are unable to return home before the onset of Passover.[37] Women are even given the power to offer their own sacrifices and to protest being included in their husbands' sacrifices.[38] One *baraita*, in particular,[39] offers an interesting anecdote describing a group of sisters as more zealous than their brothers in their commitment to offering the Passover sacrifice.

The array of tannaitic perspectives on whether or not women should be included in the requirements of Passover highlights the fact that making halachic determinations regarding women is neither simple nor straightforward. Judith Hauptman has logically argued that a certain circle of Tannaim required women to perform the rituals of Passover because they, more than others, viewed women as integral to the structure of rabbinic society.[40] Such arguments, while oversimplified to some degree, correctly accentuate what emerges directly from the tannaitic source material: there is no consensus on women and Passover law during the tannaitic period. For me, the question is not why some Tannaim seem to possess a more "proto-feminist" outlook and so require women to perform the rituals of Passover while others do not, but why there is no unified position. What makes the issue of women and Passover ritual so complex? What are the factors that promote the eruption and preservation of conflicting halachic opinions regarding women and Passover?

SOCIOCULTURAL CONSIDERATIONS: THE DOMESTIC ROLE OF WOMEN

Analyzing the observance of the holiday of Passover through a sociocultural lens has moved me closer toward an understanding of why tannaitic sources preserve a gamut of opinion on the role of women. Few institutions are more valued in rabbinic society than the family. In a utopian sense, the rabbis want the family[41] to embody a patriarchal and androcentric social order, paralleling what they hope for in rabbinic society at large. Therefore, in the ideal family gender identities are clear—women are housewives and men are everything else.[42] However, the observance of Passover simultaneously confirms and challenges this ideal social order. Indeed, it is difficult to establish definite gender identities, even in a male-authored cultural system.

In the case of Passover the rabbis confront a festival defined by a set of rituals that are, by their very nature, dependent upon domestic activity.[43] A *chametz*-free house, kosher matzah, the availability of properly fermented wine completely protected from the touch of the gentile, and even the preparation of the meat of the Passover sacrifice are dependent on the degree of perfection with which household duties are executed. Each and every Passover ritual is related to food; therefore, women, in their social position as keepers of the home, contribute and even control the manner in which such observances are executed.[44] Indeed, the tannaitic sources make several references to the role of women specifically in the preparation of matzah and the removal of *chametz*. One could also argue that *m. Pesach.* 8:1 includes women in the eating, but not the offering, of the Passover sacrifice because of their connection to the preparation of the sacrificial meal. In this way, women cross the line from keepers of the home to keepers of ritual. They are relied upon and entrusted to ensure that Passover is observed properly.

Therefore, the spectrum of tannaitic opinion on women's participation in these rituals may very well reflect the ongoing debate over whether women's contributions to the performance of Passover necessitate their inclusion in them. If a ritual enjoins the actions of women and also sanctifies their domestic role in the household, should they be required for its performance? The rabbis may have been aware that by institutionalizing women's contributions to Passover observance through law, they shift the balance of power and place women beside them at the Seder table (or at an imaginary sacrificial altar). Presumably, they also realize that the very same legal decision may generate a preferred religious outcome. That is to say, by obligating women to observe Passover rituals they can not only be assured of Passover rites that are better executed, but also more formally involve a larger portion of the population in the commandments that are key to rabbinic self-definition. The conflicting viewpoints suggest to me that the observance of Passover rituals essential to confirming a relationship with a commanding God, coupled with a desire to promote a particular social order within the family, thrust the rabbis into a quandary regarding what to do about women. I now turn to the amoraic and stammaitic sources in order to shed more light on the challenges faced by the rabbis in their struggle to define the role of women in the celebration of Passover.

THE AMORAIC SOURCES

On the surface, it appears as though the discordant positions evident in the tannaitic sources are resolved during the amoraic period in favor of the inclusion of women.[45] The Amoraim require women to offer the Passover sacrifice,[46] to eat matzah and *maror*,[47] and to drink four cups of wine.[48] Unlike the Tannaim, the Amoraim entertain the question of why women are required to perform these rituals. They seem aware of the fact that the principle found in *m. Qidd.*1:7, exempting women from all positive time-bound commandments, has been undermined. A statement attributed to the Amora, Rabbi Yehoshua ben Levi, regarding the four cups of wine indicates that women should be required to perform this rite at the Seder because they, too, were redeemed from Egypt along with men. Rabbi ben Levi's statement is the first to associate the inclusion of women in any of the rituals of Passover with the biblical events that define this festival. His statement is also a reminder to us that events of the past are not gender specific and therefore suggests that women should participate in rituals that commemorate such significant circumstances. Therefore, women seem to become active participants in the drama of Passover observance.

However, the involvement of women is circumscribed. They are required to perform only the rituals that fall within the domestic sphere. Thus, wives[49] and daughters,[50] as *b. Pesach.* 108a informs us, "need not" recline[51]—the one ritual unrelated to food preparation.[52] This exemption attests to the fact that legal decisions can concretize sociocultural anxieties. In other words, by exempting wives and daughters from the ritual of reclining, the rabbis may be exhibiting their discomfort with wives who perform the same rituals as they do. Reclining symbolizes the freedom of the Israelites from slavery; to abstain from reclining signifies that "freedom" does not mean the same thing for everyone. Wives who do not recline willfully acknowledge their secondary status in relation to those who are required to participate fully in all Passover rites (i.e., men).[53] Indeed, it seems that the Amoraim are encouraging wives to adhere to a particular familial-social pecking order rather than choose to embrace rituals designed to commemorate biblical events that also have meaning for them. Hence, the active participation of wives in Passover ritual can be tempered by their refusal to recline at the table of their husbands. Indeed, this legal position maintains the male-topped familial hierarchy and highlights the fact that husband/wife and father/daughter relationships are central to sustaining this social structure. Further, according to the Talmud, single, divorced, and widowed women, who pose far less of a threat to the internal family structure, are required to recline at the Passover table.

Admittedly, two additional issues emerge from tractate *Pesachim* to complicate my argument. First, "prominent women" are required to recline. This means that there is a group of married (or unmarried) women who contest the social structure and are recognized for it. Rabbinic law acknowledges rather than ignores their distinctiveness.[54] Second, we must again confront the fact that most women are exempt and not, more simply, prohibited from reclining. Of course, an exemption does not ensure that women will refrain from reclining. Therefore, it would seem that the exemption reflects a degree of tentativeness in the voices of the Amoraim. Such an exemption may underscore a sense of internal conflict over how women should observe together with men at a celebratory ritual meal. Should women participate as housewives (and second-class citizens) exemplifying a well-defined social position by refraining from reclining beside their husbands? Or, given their shared collective past, should they become equal participants? The Amoraim offer no clearer vision of the rabbinic attitude toward women than their predecessors, the Tannaim. The tensions exhibited in the tannaitic material are also present in the legal decisions of the amoraic source material.

The stammaitic material also confirms rather than challenges this position. While sociocultural anxiety surfaces through the presence of conflicting viewpoints regarding Passover material during the tannaitic material and in the legal decisions of the Amoraim, it emerges through yet another means during the stammaitic era. I now turn to this body of material.

THE STAMMAIM

The Stammaim, who are known for their contribution of molding a set of received sources into a final *sugya*, regularly adapt earlier material so that often a different message or legal position emerges.[55] It is interesting then that in the case of women and Passover law the Stammaim adopt a conservative stance toward the amoraic source material. In other words, they preserve the legal decisions of the Amoraim despite the mishnaic principle exempting women from all positive time-bound commandments. The Stammaim do not refashion earlier legal material about Passover to reflect the principle found in *m. Qidd.* 1:7.[56] For example, the *sugya* that discusses the inclusion of women in the ritual of drinking four cups of wine possesses surprisingly little stammaitic material. It is as if the Stammaim received a smaller *sugya* and were reticent to tamper with its sources. In the case of reclining and the role of women, the Stammaim add no expansive material. With respect to matzah, *maror*, and the Passover sacrifice, these redactors weave a more characteristically stammaitic argumentative web around the amoraic decisions, but nevertheless support them.

In addition, they devote no literary space to grappling with the dictum found in *m. Qidd.* 1:7 when they discuss the Passover sacrifice, matzah, *maror*, wine, and reclining.[57] It has been silently trumped. In fact, the Stammaim preserve an overall legal tension in their decision to support the required participation of women in most of the rituals associated with Passover and leave us wondering why these laws became an exception to the rule found in *m. Qidd.* 1:7. They opt to preserve an inconsistency despite their power to reorient source material transmitted to them. What are we to glean from the conservative redactional choices of the Stammaim, given that on so many other occasions they assume the freedom to manipulate the very nature of their source material?[58] What can we unearth from this about the men who are represented by the editorial layer of tractate *Pesachim* or perhaps even about the women of whom they spoke?

I would like to propose that the literary freedom of the Stammaim was hampered by the fact that in their day many women were performing the rituals associated with Passover observance.[59] In other words, the consensus reached during the amoraic period to include women in the performance of Passover ritual may have been a direct result of a widespread level of observance on the part of women that the Stammaim could not easily undo. This may also explain why the issue of reclining became so significant. A balance needed to be struck between the existing reality and the sociocultural concerns generated by women's participation. Indeed, it remains unclear to me whether a class of women took upon themselves the requirements of Passover and the law was designed to reflect this fact, or whether the rabbis were responsible for prompting women's active participation. The sources withhold the answer from us. Unfortunately, the Stammaim do not send us a clear message regarding the forces motivating the legal decisions of their predecessors. Precisely because I also cannot resolve the issue of whether determinations regarding the participation of women emanate from the actions of women or from a group of men possessing the legal authority to impose requirements upon them, it is impossible for me to offer a vivid image of the attitude of the rabbis toward them.

CONCLUSION: CONSIDERATIONS ABOUT RABBINIC JUDAISM AND GENDER

What may we conclude from this analysis? Throughout this paper I have cautioned against drawing definitive conclusions regarding the rabbis' attitude toward women. I have argued that to label the rabbis as enlightened or exclusionary is reductive. Such terms oversimplify the complexity of the societal and religious factors at work in making determinations about women and festival law. When faced with incongruous texts or ambiguous legal principles, we need to ask, "What types of conflicts and struggles do these sources represent?"

Undoubtedly, rabbinic culture fostered gender asymmetry. Women are "other." However, despite their "otherness," women never fall short of evaluation and reevaluation. Every positive time-bound ritual is examined individually. In fact, no uniform position regarding the observance of women is offered. Instead, women are, at times, required to perform certain festival rituals and at other times exempt. Consequently, in this area of law women are never passed over, never ignored. Rather, legal generalizations made about them, like that found in *m. Qidd.*1:7, are rejected.[60] This means that women are not viewed in isolation; the rabbis do not look upon them as an entirely separate category about whom they can speak in a single fashion. The world of women is part of the world of men, created within it and influenced by it.

Therefore, each ritual decision made regarding women has a direct and distinct impact upon the men who make them. If, for example, wives are required to recline at the Passover Seder, a male-centered family structure is threatened. At the same time, the exemption of women dilutes the universal meaning of Passover; the causal relationship between the freedom of the Israelites from Egypt and the rituals of Passover observance is undermined. In this case, when women observe the rituals of Passover, they test the boundaries of desired social conventions; when they do not, they question the very definition of a religious system defined by commandments signifying biblical events that have meaning for them as well. This is precisely what allows us to label the rabbis as gendered.[61] We should not imagine them only as elitist men who wish to exclude women from ritual life or, alternatively, as enlightened when exemptions are trumped and women become obligated. Rather, what enables us to conceptualize the rabbis as gendered is their continuous consideration of women at each legal turn. Through their discussions about women and Passover ritual in particular, the rabbis offer us an image of their society. It is a society defined by a system of complex relationships between men, women, and God. As responsible interpreters of this culture, we need to use Talmudic source material to describe this set of relationships and the issues that make them so complicated. Unearthing "positive" and "negative" depictions of women is less important than understanding the cultural tensions that gave birth to this complex set of relationships. Today, we need to study women of the rabbinic era as the rabbis studied them—as integral members of the society in which they lived and acted to observe God's commandments. Extant rabbinic sources that support both "positive" and "negative" depictions of women testify to the web of issues faced by the rabbis when they made ritual determinations regarding women.

ACKNOWLEDGMENTS

I acknowledge Carole Balin for acting both as my colleague and friend in guiding me toward the completion of this paper. I also offer sincere thanks to my research assistant, Ilana Kogen.

NOTES

[1] For a comprehensive review of scholarship in the field of Jewish women's studies, see Tal Ilan, "Introduction," in *Jewish Women in Greco-Roman Palestine* (Peabody: Hendrickson, 1996). See also Charlotte Elisheva Fonrobert and Tal Ilan, "Feminist Interpretations of Rabbinic Literature: Two Views," *Nashim* 4 (2001): 7:14.

[2] I am influenced here by the reading of rabbinic texts in Miriam B. Peskowitz, *Spinning Fantasies: Rabbis, Gender, and History* (Berkeley: University of California Press, 1997), 45.

[3] Elizabeth Shanks Alexander, "The Impact of Feminism on Rabbinic Studies; The Impossible Paradox of Reading Women into Rabbinic Literature," in *Jews and Gender: Studies in Contemporary Jewry XVI* (ed. Jonathan Frankel; Oxford: Oxford University Press, 2000), 110.

[4] I agree with Daniel Boyarin that we need to read our literary texts as "(failed) attempts to propose utopian solutions to cultural tensions." See his extensive discussion in *Carnal Israel* (Berkeley: University of California Press, 1993), 15 ff. See also Aryeh Cohen's review and critique of Boyarin in *Rereading the Talmud: Gender, Law and the Poetics of Sugyot* (Atlanta: Scholars Press, 1998), 89-121.

[5] Peskowitz goes further in her analysis than I, to the extent to which she contextualizes the sources that she analyzes in the culture of Roman Palestine. Her ability to reach outside the texts and use archeological data to interpret rabbinic sources is also beyond the scope of my reading here. I focus on the rabbinic texts alone and offer an analysis that represents a preliminary stage in a larger study on women and festival observance.

[6] I agree with Boyarin, *Carnal Israel,* 15, that we can detect in rabbinic discourse a hegemonic view that influenced later generations and a countervailing (less dominant) position. In the texts that he analyzes, Boyarin correctly shows how the rabbis expend their energy to suppress tensions and to offer us a dominant view. Therefore, our goal is to uncover the cultural anxieties and expose the resulting contestations. In the rabbinic texts describing the role of women and Passover observance, I have found that even the dominant legal view reflects the socio-cultural challenges facing the rabbis. See the section below where I discuss the amoraic source material.

[7] See also Saul Lieberman, ed., *Tosefta Kifshuta* (New York: JTSA, 1967), *t. Qidd.* 1:10 and *b. Qidd.* 33b-34a, where a version of this *baraita* is quoted and analyzed alongside *m. Qidd.* 1:7. This *baraita* offers us a list of commandments that are positive time-bound rituals from which women are exempt. The festival rituals included in this list are sukkah, *lulav*, and shofar. A stammaitic addition to the *baraita* notes three

exceptional rituals required of women. They are matzah, *hakhel,* and the *simchah* offering. No reference is made on *b. Qidd.* 33b-34a to any of the other positive time-bound rituals required of women; see the more comprehensive list later in this paper. This raises the following question: Why does this Talmudic *sugya,* which functions as a comment upon *m. Qidd.* 1:7, not grapple with so many of the other festival commandments required of women? See Jay Rovner's thorough analysis of this Talmudic *sugya,* "Rhetorical Strategy and Dialectical Necessity in the Babylonian Talmud: The Case of Kiddushin 34a-35a," *Hebrew Union College Annual* 65 (1994): 193-94, where he offers one reason why the discussion may have been limited to these three festival requirements. (Note that all subsequent references to the Tosefta will be to Lieberman's edition.)

[8]From as early as the fourteenth century, scholars were concerned about whether women should focus on the domestic needs of their households rather than on fulfilling ritual requirements; see *Abudarham Hashalem* (Jerusalem: Usha Press, 1340/1963), 25. See also more contemporary scholars, including Noam Zohar, "Ma Bein Ish L'ishah," *Et La'asot* 1 (Summer 1988). See also Shmuel Safrai, "Mechuyavutan shel Nashim Bemitzvot Bemishnatan shel HaTannaim," *Bar Ilan Yearbook for Jewish Studies and Humanities* 26/27 (1994): 227-36; there he states that determinations made regarding the exemption of women from certain rituals are dependent upon the domestic demands of their households. That the Tannaim commanded women to perform certain positive time-bound rituals merely reflects what women felt capable of performing in the wake of their domestic obligations. According to Safrai, the dictum found in *m. Qidd.* and the exceptions to it reflect the existing social reality. See also Saul Berman, "The Status of Women in Halachic Judaism," *Tradition* 14 (1973): 5-28.

[9]Judith Baskin argues that any classification of women as "different from" automatically implies that they are "less than." See "The Separation of Women in Rabbinic Judaism," in *Women, Religion, and Social Change* (eds. Y. Y. Haddad and E. B. Findly; Albany: SUNY Press, 1984), 3-18, and "Rabbinic Reflections of the Barren Wife," *Harvard Theological Review* 82:1 (1989): 101-14. See also Jacob Neusner, *A History of the Mishnaic Law of Women* (Leiden, 1980), 97, where he states that the Mishnah sees men as "normal" and women as "abnormal"; and Judith Romney Wegner, *Chattel or Person? The Status of Women in the Mishnah* (Oxford: Oxford University Press, 1988), 153.

[10]See Judith Hauptman's discussion of *m. Qidd.* 1:7 in *Rereading the Rabbis: A Women's Voice* (Boulder: Westview, 1997), 227-228. Although Hauptman candidly acknowledges the negative societal repercussions of exempting women from positive time-bound commandments in *m. Qidd.* 1:7, she utilizes *m. Qidd.* 1:8, which prohibits women from performing various cultic practices, in order to read the exemption principle in a positive light. She argues that exempting women from a set of rituals points to a positive change in rabbinic law as compared to biblical/cultic law, in that women can observe these laws if they so choose. This stands in contrast to the sacrificial prohibition found in *m. Qidd.* 1:8, which clearly prohibits women from the

performance of cultic rituals. On the other hand, Ilan, *Jewish Women in Greco-Roman Palestine*, 184, argues that the destruction of the Temple brought about a "sharp reduction in women's participation in religious rituals."

[11]It appears that even the Amoraim struggle with why women are exempt from certain rituals and required to perform others. Surely this difficulty prompts Rabbi Yochanan to make the following statement in response to *m. Qidd.* 1:7 and its parallel *baraita*: "We do not learn from general rules even if the exceptions are listed." See *b. Qidd.* 34a.

[12]See Hauptman's analysis of *m. Qidd.* 1:7 in *Rereading the Rabbis*, 221-43. She correctly acknowledges that the rabbis were struggling with the issue of women and ritual law. In her view, this struggle represents a positive development in rabbinic attitudes toward women (238). I, however, would like to propose that rabbinic contestations are not necessarily positive or negative.

[13]See *b. Sukkah* 28a-b. In this *sugya* the issue of women's exemption from the commandment of sukkah is considered. The *sugya* creatively disassociates the observance of the ritual of sukkah from other festival rites that women are required to perform (for example, Passover rites and the Yom Kippur ritual of *innui* [afflicting one's self]). See also the following parallel sources, *b. Sukkah* 27a and *b. Qidd.* 34a-b.

[14]*m. Bik.* 1:5. Wegner, *Chattel*, 149, comments that women are exempt from the ritual of *bikkurim*. She translates the words in *m. Bik.* 1:5, "*vahaeeshah...mevi'in*" as "and women... may bring [the first fruits]." However, the observance of this ritual is contingent upon possessing fruit trees grown on one's own property, as it says, The first fruits of your land" (Exod 23:19). Women are, therefore required to bring "first fruits" when they own land. They are, however, exempt from reciting the liturgical declaration drawn from Deut 26 when they perform the ritual of bringing *bikkurim*. In contrast, no mention is made of the role of women in this ritual in the Tosefta.

[15]*b. Ber.* 20b.

[16]*b. Shabb.* 23a.

[17]See *m. Meg.* 2:4 and *b. Meg.* 4a. *M. Meg.* 2:4 reads: "All are eligible to read the Megillah except a deaf person, a mute person, or a minor person." Although women are not specifically mentioned, they seem to be included in the general category of those eligible. In contrast, *t. Meg.* 2:7 exempts women from reading the Megillah. In *b. Meg.* 4a, the Amora, Rabbi Yehoshua ben Levi, indicates that women are required to perform this mitzvah because they were part of the miracle.

[18]*T. Hag.* 1:4, *b. Hag.* 6b, *m. Pesach.* 10:4, *b. Pesach.* 109a, *b. Sukkah* 27b. The commandment to offer the *simchah* sacrifice is derived from Deut 16:14 and is intended to fulfill the requirement to rejoice on Pilgrimage holidays. However, the nature of this commandment changed following the destruction of the Temple. A *baraita* found on *b. Pesach.* 109a informs us that wine became the medium through which one expressed joyousness and replaced the meat of the sacrificial offering. *B. Sukkah* 27b suggests that a celebratory atmosphere was created and the requirement of *simchah* fulfilled when men remained at home during Pilgrimage holidays.

[19]See Deut 31:10-12, which states, "Every seventh year, the year set for [the] sabbatical year [of the land], at Sukkot....Gather the people—the men, women, children...that they may hear [the Torah] and so learn to revere the Lord your God and to observe faithfully every word of this Teaching." See also *b. Qidd.* 34a and *b. Hag.* 4a.

[20]Although some might argue that *Simchat Beit Hashoevah* is not a Sukkot ritual per se, I include it here because of its extensive treatment in the fifth *perek* of *Massekhet Sukkah*, *b. Sukkah* 50a ff. See also 51b regarding women. For a more extensive discussion regarding the development of this ritual see, Jeffrey Rubenstein, *The History of Sukkot in the Second Temple and Rabbinic Periods* (Atlanta: Scholars Press, 1995), 68 and 131 ff.

[21]Consider also that the commandments to have children and to study Torah are positive precepts not governed by time, yet women are exempt from them (*b. Qidd.* 34a).

[22]See Wegner, *Chattel*, 145-167, where she draws a distinction between the public and private spheres of Jewish communal life and indicates how this demarcation influenced legal decisions made regarding women. In contrast, Miriam Peskowitz, in "'Family/ies' in Antiquity: Evidence from tannaitic Literature and Roman Galilean Architecture," in *The Jewish Family in Antiquity* (ed. S. J. D. Cohen; Atlanta: Scholars, 1993), 26-34, argues for the need to reevaluate the division of rabbinic society into a "public" realm," which is viewed as predominantly male, and a "private" realm, which is viewed as female.

[23]See David Kraemer's discussion of *m. Ber.* 20b in light of *m. Qidd.* 1:7 and the exemption of women from positive time-bound commandments in "Critical Readings and Religious Insight: New Readings in the Bavli," *Conservative Judaism* 42 (1990) 3: 52-53.

[24] In his article, "Rhetorical Strategy and Dialectical Necessity," 198-203, Jay Rovner discusses the tannaitic origins of the Qiddushin principle of exemption. The general pattern that he detected in the tannaitic midrashic collections was for exemptions to be dealt with on a "case by case" basis rather than as an entire category of law. As such, women were exempt from certain rituals, including *re'iyah*; see Saul Horowitz and Israel A. Rabin, eds., *Mekhilta d'Rabbi Ishmael* [*Mekhilta Mishpatim 20*] (Jerusalem: Bamberger and Wahrmann, 1960); on Exod 23:14, see Louis Finkelstein, ed., *Sifrei 'al SeferDevarim: im hilufe girsa'ot ve-he'arot* (New York: Jewish Theological Seminary of America, 1993), sect. 143 (196). However, women were required for *simchah*; see *Sifrei Devarim*, sect. 138, (193), on Deut 16:11; *t. Hag.* 1:4. Additionally, he points out that exemptions were treated in accordance with scriptural references to these commandments and were not grouped together under the general rabbinic principle found in *m. Qidd.* 1:7.

[25]For a good summary as well as critique of Talmudic source criticism, see A. Cohen, *Rereading the Talmud*, 7-42. See also Richard Kalmin, *Sages, Stories, Authors, and Editors in Rabbinic Babylonia* (Atlanta: Scholars Press, 1994), 2.

[26]See Judith Hauptman's excellent comparison between the mishnaic and *baraitan* material dealing with women and Passover observance in "Nashim Bemassekhet

Pesachim," *Atarah Lechayim: Mechkarim Besifrut Hatalmudit Veharabbanut Likhvod Professor Chayim Dimotrovzky* (ed. D. Boyarin; Jerusalem, 2000), 69ff. She thoroughly describes the array of legal positions extant during the tannaitic period.

[27] A woman's role in the preparation of bread is a cause for concern, as noted on *b. Pesach.* 37a, because woman might "tarry over it and cause it to turn to leaven."

[28] Hauptman, "Nashim Bemassekhet Pesachim," 69, also argues that *m. Pesach.* 8:1 is not explicit in its treatment of women and the requirement of the Passover offering.

[29] The parallel *baraita* states that women must eat the sacrifice made by their fathers if Passover is the first pilgrimage holiday that they celebrate following their marriage. However, on the remainder of Passover holidays they may choose to eat the sacrifice made by either their father or their husband (*b. Pesach.* 87a).

[30] Additionally, *m. Pesach.* 7:6 notes that certain types of *temay'ot* [ritually impure males] are not disqualified from offering and eating the Passover sacrifice. However, the *niddah* [menstruant] and the *zavah* [the ritually impure female who sees blood at times other than her period] cannot participate in this Passover ritual (*m. Pesach* 9:4). It also remains unclear whether women should make up for a missed opportunity to participate in the Passover sacrifice with the observance of *Pesach Sheini*, as *m. Pesach.* remains silent on this issue. However, *m. Chal.* 4:11 states that women are not required to offer a sacrifice on *Pesach Sheini*. By comparison, *Pesach Sheini* is incumbent upon any man who is *tamei* [impure] on Passover (*m. Pesach.* 9:1). Also note that in *t. Pesach.* 8:1, *niddot* and *zavot* are required to observe *Pesach Sheini* in contrast to the position offered by the Mishnah. See also Hauptman, "Nashim Bemassekhet Pesachim," 72-75, for a thorough discussion of women and *Pesach Sheini*.

[31] Note that some of this *baraitan* material appears in the Tosefta and some does not.

[32] *b. Pesach.* 91b. This *baraita* indicates, through the opinion of Rabbi Shim'on, that there was no monolithic position regarding women's Passover observance during the tannaitic period. Also take note of the *baraita* quoted earlier on 91b, where Rabbi Shim'on is found disagreeing with the *Tanna kamma* and Rabbi Yossi on whether women are required to offer the Passover sacrifice. See the parallel source in *t. Pesach.* 8:10, including the anecdote about Rabbi Yosef Hakohen that is used to prove that women are not required to bring the Passover offering in celebration of *Pesach Sheini*. In fact, this *baraita* is also ambiguous. On the one hand, the anecdote functions to exempt women from *Pesach Sheini*. On the other hand, Rabbi Yosef Hakohen brings his entire household to Jerusalem in order to observe this ritual. See also Saul Lieberman's textual correction, *t. Kifshuta, Moed* (New York: Jewish Theological Seminary of America, 1955-88), 627.

[33] *t. Pesachim* 2:22, *b. Pesach.* 91b.

[34] *b. Pesach.* 108b-109a.

[35] See the *baraita* quoted on *b. Pesach.* 48b and the parallels in *t. Pesach.* 3:7 and 3:8.

[36] Rashi comments here that women are believed when they testify on the fourteenth of Nissan that their husbands did *Bi'ur chametz* the previous night—see *b. Pesach.* 4a. However, the *baraita* does not eliminate the possibility that women performed this rite. It reads as follows: "all are believed regarding *bi'ur chametz*, even women, even

slaves, even minors." The Palestinian Talmud, *y. Pesach.* 1:1; 27b, offers a similar position to that found in the Babylonian Talmud. However, an additional amoraic statement, attributed to Rabbi Yermiah (in the name of Rabbi Zeira), indicates that women are not necessarily careful when checking for *chametz.* Despite this, women are believed when they make claims about its removal.

[37] According to *m. Pesach.* 3:7, men are allowed to mentally nullify *chametz* in the event that they find themselves en route to performing another ritual. Their participation in this rite makes them unable to return home in time to complete the process of *chametz* removal. The parallel *baraita, t. Pesach.* 3:12, lists the same set of circumstances under which a man might find himself in conflict over whether to return home to remove the *chametz* he had forgotten. The main difference between *m. Pesach.* 3:7 and *m. Pesach.* 3:12 is that the *baraita* does not offer men the opportunity to annul the leftover leaven mentally. Rather, the *baraita* states that men need not return home. I attribute this difference to an understanding, on the part of the *baraita,* that men leave their homes prior to the completion of *chametz* removal because the women of their households take upon themselves much of the responsibility for performing this rite properly. They do not have to be concerned about returning home or even about completing the process of *chametz* removal mentally because their mothers, wives, and daughters automatically assume the role.

[38] See *b. Pesach.* 88a. Also note that in contrast to *m. Pesach.,* women who are *niddot* and/or *zavot* during Nissan are specifically commanded to observe *Pesach Sheini* (*b. Pesach.* 93a; *t. Pesach.* 8:1). However, there is *baraitan* material that matches the position of the Mishnah and prohibits women from *Pesach Sheini* (*t. Pesach.* 8:10 and *b. Pesach.* 93a), the position of Rabbi Shim'on.

[39] *b. Pesach.* 89a; *b. Ned.* 36a.

[40] Hauptman, "Nashim Bemassekhet Pesachim," 65.

[41] For a more extensive discussion of the family during the tannaitic era, see Peskowitz, "'Family/ies' in Antiquity."

[42] See Peskowitz, "'Family/ies' in Antiquity," 60-66, and her discussion of women in rabbinic society who were paid laborers and worked outside of the domestic and household sphere. Despite stereotyped views of men as producers and women as consumers Peskowitz is able to show that this was not the case for all Jewish women living in Roman Palestine. See also Alexander, "Impact of Feminism," 111, for a summary of Peskowitz.

[43] There are many instances in Talmudic literature where the domestic contribution of women to the proper observance of various rituals is recognized. See *m. Pesachim* 3:4 on baking matzah. See also *m. Shabbat* 2:6, where women are warned against transgressing three rituals: *niddah* [family purity law], *hafrashat challah* [the separation of the challah], and *hadlakat haner* [the lighting of the lamp before Shabbat]. The threat of dire punishment noted in this mishnah seems to be related to the fact that women are primarily responsible for their husbands' proper observance of these rituals. See Wegner, *Chattel,* 155. See also tractate *b. Beitzah* 17a, *b. Beitzah* 29a, *b. Beitzah* 33a, and, *b. Beitzah* 37a, where women are specifically commanded to execute

certain laws in a specific way because they are seen as entirely responsible for food preparation.

[44]See *b. Yoma* 66b, which defines "wise women" as those who are wise with the distaff. This source acknowledges that a degree of wisdom was necessary for certain domestic chores, a type of wisdom that men did not necessarily possess.

[45]Note that the amoraic source found on *b. Pesach.* 90a is less inclusive of women than the remainder of amoraic material found in this *massekhet*. The Amora, Rav Adda bar Ahava, comments on the mishnah that speaks of a woman who is a *zavah* on the night the Passover sacrifice is offered. She will, however, be *tahor* in time to eat the sacrificial meat. According to the mishnah, one can slaughter the Passover offering for a *zavah* on the eighth day that she is free of discharge. Even though this *sugya* cites a *baraita*, informing us that one can slaughter the Passover offering for a *zava* on the seventh day free of discharge, admittedly a more lenient position, Rav bar Ahava interjects and suggests that the *baraita* be emended to match the position of the Mishnah. As a result, the more exclusive position of the Mishnah is adopted over that of the *baraita*, making it more difficult for *zavot* to participate in the Passover offering. It therefore appears that Rav bar Ahava did not feel comfortable with the leniency of the *baraita* and chose to align himself with the Mishnah.

[46]Statements attributed to the Amora Rava confirm that women are to be included in the Passover sacrifice. Such statements allow wives to protest the sacrificial offerings of their husbands; adult daughters and maidservants can do the same (*b. Pesach.* 88a-b). Rava also permits women to join together in groups in order to offer sacrifices (*b. Pesach.* 91a-b). This seems to represent an amoraic preference for the involvement of women in this rite. However, three other *sugyot* that discuss the role of women in the Passover sacrifice are far less clear about this issue. A mishnah on *b. Pesach.* 79a, delineating the circumstances under which the Passover sacrifice is made despite the impurity of certain members of the community, indicates that the status of the majority of the population determines whether the sacrifice can be offered. The problem introduced by the Stammaim concerns whether women can be counted as "pure" members of the group in order to make up a majority. The decision depends upon whether women are required to offer the Passover sacrifice. The *sugya* offers no clear-cut conclusion. In the second *sugya*, *b. Pesach.* 91b, the *Tanna kamma* and Rabbi Shim'on disagree about whether women are required to offer the Passover sacrifice. This argument is also left unresolved. In the third *sugya*, *b. Pesach.* 93a, a disagreement regarding *Pesach Sheini*, and the Passover sacrifice offering that is key to its observance, is left undecided as well.

[47]Rabbi Eleazar is quoted in two *sugyot* as stating that the requirement placed upon women to eat matzah is biblical rather than rabbinic, thereby equating women and men in the performance of this commandment (*b. Pesach.* 43b and 91b). Also note that on *b. Pesach.* 43b, Rabbi Eleazar is recorded as the Tanna, Rabbi Eliezer. The majority of available manuscripts indicate that the attribution is to the Amora, Rabbi Eleazar; see *Mesoret Hashas* to *b. Pesach.* 43b.

[48]*b. Pesach.* 108a-b.

[49]See manuscript evidence that supports the inclusion of the phrase "*eitzel ba'alah.*" The presence of such a phrase suggests that only wives sitting alongside their husbands are exempt from reclining. Rabbenu Asher (Rosh) insists that divorced and widowed women are therefore required to recline. See also Rabbenu Hananel, who argues more generally that all women, except prominent women, are exempt.

[50]See *b. Pesach.* 108a, where mention is made of the fact that sons are required to recline, but daughters are not mentioned. This suggests that daughters, like wives, are exempt.

[51]*b. Pesach.* 108a uses the term *tzrikha* ["women alongside their husbands *need not* recline"] in its discussion of reclining, instead of the more familiar word *patur* [exempt].

[52]Although the statement regarding reclining is not an attributed statement and may appear on the surface to be stammaitic, the parallel discussion regarding this ritual is amoraic in the Palestinian Talmud (*y. Pesach.* 10:1, 37a). This suggests that the issue was discussed prior to the stammaitic period. Additionally, the Talmudic technical term, *eetmar*, which generally precedes amoraic material, introduces the entire discussion on reclining (*b. Pesach.* 108a). A portion of stammaitic material, which discusses the nature of the initial amoraic statement attributed to Rav Nachman regarding reclining and the commandment of four cups of wine, may have been inserted into the larger discussion prior to returning to address the halakhah regarding women and reclining. (I thank Judith Hauptman for alerting me to the fact that the statement concerning women and reclining could very well be amoraic.)

[53]See Rashbam, *b. Pesach.* 108a.

[54]In the parallel source in *y. Pesach.* 10:1, 37b, no distinction is made between "prominent women" and "average women." In addition, the amoraic source is far more vague than the Babylonian source, as it states:

> Rabbi Simon said in the name of Rabbi Yehoshua ben Levi, "[Matzah] that is equal to the amount of an olive [and] through which a man fulfills his obligation on Passover—must be eaten while reclining." Rabbi Yosi came before Rabbi Simon and asked, "Even a slave before his master; even a wife before her husband?" And he responded: "This is as far as I have heard."

It is unclear to me whether Rabbi Simon is acknowledging Rabbi Yosi or dismissing his query. Interpretations of this source found in the commentaries to the Palestinian Talmud, *P'nai Moshe* and *Korban Haeidah*, reflect the position of the Babylonian Talmud and mute the apparent ambiguity.

[55]Jay Rovner, "Rhetorical Strategy and Dialectical Necessity" 182.

[56]See *b. Pesach.* 43b, where mention is made of the dictum, "Women are exempt from all positive time-bound commandments." Nonetheless, reference to this exemption is not used to question the inclusion of women in the requirement to eat matzah. Rather, it functions, albeit oddly, to ensure that women are included in the prohibition against eating *chametz*. *Chametz* is a negative commandment that, according to *m. Qidd.* 1:7, women are required to perform. I have, therefore, discounted it here.

[57]The Palestinian Talmud offers a general rule explaining the reason why a positive time-bound commandment like matzah is incumbent upon women despite the well-

known exemption found in *m. Qidd.* 1:7. The source reads, "Positive [time-bound] commandments are more stringent [and therefore incumbent upon women] when they are derived from negative commandments" (*y. Pesach.* 8, 35:4). Although the requirement to eat matzah is derived from the negative commandment to abstain from eating *chametz* in both the Babylonian and Palestinian Talmudim, there is no reference made in the Babylonian Talmud to a general rule. See *b. Pesach.* 43b and 91b, where the equation between matzah and *chametz* is made.

[58]Christine Hayes in her article, "Halakhah le-Moshe mi-Sinai in Rabbinic Sources: A Methodological Case Study," in *The Synoptic Problem in Rabbinic Literature* (Providence: Brown Judaic Studies 326), 64, has also argued that "we simply do not see uniform and universal homogenization of earlier sources or a consistent attempt to replace the polyphony of the sources with the univocality of a single authorship." See also Kalmin, *Sages, Stories, Authors*, 11.

[59]See Boyarin, *Carnal Israel*, 181, and his reference to Saul Lieberman: "The late Saul Lieberman [notes that] the presuppositions of a Talmudic statement are a more reliable index to social reality than the manifest content of its statements." Therefore, it becomes necessary to read between the lines of our texts in order to unearth the motivations of their author(s).

[60]However, the rabbis never admit outright that they are rejecting the dictum.

[61]I am indebted to Joan W. Scott for prompting me to rethink the sense of the word "gender." See "Gender: A Useful Category of Historical Analysis," *American Historical Review* 5 (1991): 1055-56.

Weaving Women's Words:
Gendered Oral Histories for the Study of American Jewish Women

Jayne K. Guberman

"Everyone has a story," the renowned anthropologist Barbara Myerhoff taught us, and those stories "told to oneself or others can transform the world."[1] This simple but profound insight, learned as a child from her immigrant grandmother, informed Myerhoff's life work and research among an elderly Jewish population in Southern California during the 1970s and 1980s. It also epitomizes a transformation in how we have come to think about women's oral narratives over the past several decades.

Storytelling has always been a part of the way women transmit personal and family history from generation to generation, impart values and knowledge, and create community. A feature of both leisure and work culture in traditional societies, women's stories have taken on new meanings in recent decades as oral history has become an increasingly important tool for the "historically voiceless" to affirm the importance of their own experiences and to create a record of multiple voices and perspectives from which a more inclusive historical narrative can be constructed.

Over the past twenty-five years, historians, anthropologists, folklorists, and others have explored the unique characteristics of women's oral narratives for generating new kinds of historical and literary materials on women and for creating intergenerational encounters that validate women's experiences. As Carolyn Heilbrun reminds us, oral history is good for women because through it they can explore and construct "new narratives" that let them tell their life stories in ways that are expressive of their actual experiences.[2]

Nonetheless, the practice of women's oral history remains an intriguing challenge. A quarter of a century after the National Women's Studies Association first brought two dozen feminists together to discuss their work in this uncharted realm, methodological and substantive issues continue to confront scholars who turn to oral history for access to the "muted channels of women's subjectivity."[3] The complexities of what was once thought to be an easy fit between the feminist principle of "research by, about, and for women" and the dialogic methodology of oral history have become more apparent. How, scholars have asked, does women's oral history deal with issues of shared authority between the narrator and the interviewer? Who, in the final analysis, shapes the narrative by controlling the conversational flow and determining what topics are discussed? And whose voice ultimately prevails in creating the "approved transcript," the final product that will represent the narrator's experience in the world?

The Jewish Women's Archive (JWA) has wrestled with these issues for more than three years as we conceptualized and launched a national oral history project, *Weaving Women's Words*.[4] The project's aim is to record the life histories of a diverse group of Jewish women born in the early decades of the twentieth century. In capturing their reflections on what it meant to each of them to be an American Jewish woman over a century of momentous change, we hope to create a body of resources that will deepen our understanding of the profound, though often unacknowledged, impact Jewish women have had within their families, their local communities, and the larger society. As we conclude the transcribing, editing, and processing of the first sixty interviews from our pilot sites in Baltimore and Seattle, I would like to reflect on one of the key issues that has emerged in creating these gendered life histories of Jewish women: the topic guide as a locus of negotiation between the various participants in the oral history encounter.

I begin with some background on the use of oral history in the study of American Jewish women and the genesis of *Weaving Women's Words*. Over the past several decades, coinciding with the rising interest in women's narratives in a wide variety of academic disciplines, communities and organizations have sought to document the unique experiences of Jews in different parts of the country. Jewish museums and historical societies have been among the leaders in using oral history to document local and regional Jewish history and culture. Many of these projects were started in the late 1960s and 1970s as efforts to tell the grassroots story of the late-nineteenth and early-twentieth century immigration and settlement that brought Jews to remote towns, villages, and rural communities, as well as growing urban centers, across the country. Focusing on a particular period, event, or topic, several such projects have collected hundreds of interviews from the pioneer generation, capturing their recollections of the early years of communal Jewish life. Women's stories, although not the focus of the project, have often been part of this invaluable record. In addition, national organizations like the American Jewish Committee, Hadassah, and the National Council of Jewish Women, have initiated oral history projects that focus on Jewish women of achievement, women's recollections of organizational history, and regional Jewish history.

Four years ago, JWA conducted an initial survey of institutional repositories across the country in an effort to ascertain how many oral histories existed of Jewish women and what their focus had been. A summer of intensive research by Keren McGinity, the first JWA Fellow, identified more than fifteen hundred oral histories of Jewish women in close to sixty repositories.[5] These represent an invaluable resource for communities and scholars alike, enriching our knowledge of Jewish life in the United States and, in particular, of everyday life. But further probing by McGinity about the goals of oral history projects and the ways in which their subjects were selected resulted in the preliminary conclusion that virtually none of them were specifically designed with a focus on preserving Jewish women's histories from a gendered perspective.

Extensive digging through the archives at the University of Washington and key repositories in Baltimore by subsequent JWA Fellows confirmed these impressions. When Pamela Brown Lavitt, our JWA Fellow in Seattle and one of our *Weaving Women's Words* oral historians, listened to numerous oral histories and read through transcripts from the Jewish Archives Project housed at the University of Washington Archive, it became apparent that interviewers rarely asked questions about the lives, experiences, and role of women. "Instead," she reported:

> interviewers pushed for information about their mothers and fathers, male partners, counterparts, and relations, especially if they were rabbis, businessmen, or community leaders. Interviews of women leaders in the philanthropic, synagogue, and Jewish community were often asked to detail their lives according to organizational involvement and history, rather than reflect upon their experiences running these organizations and how it affected their personal lives.[6]

In sum, she concluded, "women's unique perspectives and biographical reflections were often glossed over."[7] Furthermore, existing oral histories tended to reflect a concern with capturing Seattle and Northwest history from the perspective of older, long-term residents, organizations, synagogues, and community leaders. Of several hundred oral histories in the collection, there were few if any interviews with "everyday" Jewish women. In Baltimore, the report of JWA Fellow Carolyn Eastman, who surveyed a number of archival institutions for their holdings on Jewish women, corroborates Lavitt's findings in Seattle. "As rich as the [oral history collections] are in discussing Jewish identity," she concluded, "only very rarely do the subjects specifically discuss their lives as women or their own understanding of gender roles."[8]

It was in this context that the Jewish Women's Archive, just a year after its founding, made its first foray into the realm of collecting oral narratives of American Jewish women. With its mission to "uncover, chronicle and transmit the rich legacy of Jewish women and their contributions to our families and our communities, our people, and our world," JWA believed that oral history was an important vehicle both for creating new records about American Jewish women's history and for helping women feel validated as historical actors whose lives have mattered. In 1996, JWA embarked on a pilot oral history project, *Women Whose Lives Span the Century*, a community-based effort to record the life histories of Jewish women over the age of 80 in Temple Israel, one of the oldest Reform synagogues in Boston. Building on the success of this project, in the year 2000 JWA launched *Weaving Women's Words* in Baltimore and Seattle, the first stage in a national initiative to collect the oral histories of women born in the first quarter of the twentieth century in communities across the country.

The choice to focus on life histories rather than on women's major achievements allowed us to select a group of narrators who represent a broad range of backgrounds and affiliations in both the Jewish and secular communities. In Baltimore, for example, the narrators include a shoe saleswoman and the first Jewish woman to serve in the Maryland legislature, the owner of a real estate firm and a noted woman judge on the Circuit Court, a Hebrew school teacher and an obstetrician/gynecologist who was the first woman admitted from the Johns Hopkins undergraduate college to its medical school. In Seattle, they have included several of the matriarchs of the Sephardic community, the third largest in the United States, allowing us to explore the evolution of relationships between Sephardim and Ashkenazim over the course the twentieth century. Narrators have been married, widowed, divorced, and single;

they have been parents, grandparents, and great-grandparents; a few have been childless. Their Jewish identities and affiliations have ranged from secular to orthodox, and their activism and community involvement have occurred within the context of Jewish organizations as well as the larger society.

In conceptualizing the interviews for *Weaving Women's Words,* we wanted to create a structure that would encompass this diverse array of life experiences. Recent scholarship also taught us that "women see the world from their vantage point, which may not mesh with the dominant world view and definition of reality."[9] Gendered life histories, we believed, would offer a broad and flexible structure for the interviews that would encourage the narrators to construct richly textured narratives of themselves in the world. At the same time, the focus on women's perspectives would lead to a better understanding of how women were active agents in shaping their own lives in the context of societal and familial expectations and constraints.

From the outset, then, creating a comprehensive interview topic guide that would allow women to narrate their life histories from the vantage point of the full range of their experiences was a primary goal. The topic guide was designed to probe three interrelated themes in the construction of Jewish women's identity: the impact of gender on personal choices and outcomes, the experience of being Jewish, and the importance of place and region in shaping identity and experience. To explore these themes, interviews were structured around ten major topics to elicit stories and memories of key facets of women's lives and to invite the narrator's reflections on the events, choices, and forces that shaped her world. The ten topics include: family, education, work (both paid and unpaid), community service, leisure and culture, sexuality and health, religion, home and place, women's identities, and the impact of historical and world events. Working within these broad parameters, oral historians and narrators were free to structure the interview around the most salient areas in each narrator's life. At the same time, the existence of categories such as women's friendship networks and the culinary aspects of domestic Judaism were meant to invite recollections and reflections in areas that women do not usually think of as noteworthy or historically significant.

In most cases, the broad focus of the interviews resulted in a richly interwoven text that creates relationships between diverse associations in women's lives and embedded reflections on abstract issues in the particularities of time and place. We hear in these interviews the ways in which Jewish women's lives combined domestic and outside work, in both volunteer positions and in paid employment. Our first readings of the transcripts that came into our office highlighted the fluidity of women's lives in this pivotal generation, as many women moved from committed volunteer positions to paid work in the same organizations. In some cases, this led to significant careers. This is the case for Inge Weinberger, who was born in Germany and came to Baltimore via Bolivia during World War II. She worked with refugees at HIAS (Hebrew Immigrant Aid Society) for many years as a dedicated volunteer before being asked to assume the position of executive director. Today, a widow in her eighties, she continues to work four days a week for the organization, having officially retired in 1990. The work of Laurie Zabin, another Baltimore narrator, on behalf of Planned Parenthood, first locally and later nationally and internationally, grew out of a similarly committed volunteer position with the organization. Her work as a "professional volunteer" led to a position as executive director of Planned Parenthood's first community family planning clinic in East Baltimore and from there to doctoral work and a distinguished career at the Johns Hopkins School of Public Health.

The inclusive nature of life history interviews has also led to vivid portraits of the ways in which women combined motherhood and work in this generation. In Ruth Finkelstein's interview, for example, we hear stories about the development of her career as a beloved Baltimore physician, beginning with her studies at the Johns Hopkins University, where she was the first woman admitted from the undergraduate college to the medical school. As a woman unable to get training as a surgeon, Dr. Finkelstein worked in a post-partum clinic in Baltimore early in her career. This led to her lifelong interest and active involvement in the field of contraception and family planning, including the provision of assistance and counseling to her female patients who were unable to obtain legal abortions prior to Roe v. Wade. The life history approach also allowed us to hear about the influence of Finkelstein's father on her choice of career and the fear of disappointing him that drove her to continue in the face of tremendous bias against women medical students and physicians. We hear about the support of her husband, a manufacturer's representative in Baltimore, in opening her own clinic, and her decision to move from obstetrics to gynecology after the birth of her two children so that she would be available to them after school hours. She speaks about the division of parental responsibilities, where she took it for granted that her husband would not get up in the middle of the night to take care of his own children so that she could go out to deliver another woman's baby, and about the household help which allowed her to pursue a career in medicine.

But beyond the richly textured descriptions of women's complex lives, the very broadness of the topic guidelines ultimately posed dilemmas for both narrators and oral historians, bringing to the fore questions of emphasis and focus. On the one hand, we delighted in the diverse genres of women's expressive culture that we were able to collect, such as that of Louise Azose, our oldest narrator at age 97 and one of the matriarchs of the Seattle Sephardic community, who sang traditional women's love songs and lullabies in Ladino. On the other hand, we became increasingly aware of the ways in which traditional women's genres can become points of tension and negotiation in how the narrators wanted to be represented, reminding us, as Sherna Gluck and Daphne Patai point out, that "the typical product of an interview is a text, not a reproduction of reality."[10]

Of all the areas of women's expressive culture in the interviews, both the most common and the most contentious involved conversations around food and Jewish women's culinary traditions. The doctoral research of Marcie Cohen Ferris, one of our Baltimore oral historians, provides an interesting foil to the *Weaving Women's Words* interviews, precisely because her specific agenda in talking to women throughout the South was on Jewish culinary traditions.[11] In *Weaving Women's Words*, by contrast, food has proven to be an interesting locus of tension. Most narrators spoke at various points in their narratives about food and its meaning in their lives. We hear Becky Benaroya, a philanthropist and a doyenne of Seattle society, describe at length her family recipes for Sephardic specialties such as burekas, baklava, and apio, a typical Passover dish. And we hear another Seattle narrator reminisce about the lessons learned regarding tolerance and diversity in an immigrant neighborhood classroom, when she incurred her teacher's displeasure by bringing in a home-baked challah rather than the courser bread assigned by the teacher. In these cases, the narrators talked readily about culinary traditions, the complex roles that food played in their live, and its meaning for them as Jewish women.

But what also became apparent in a few narrators' reactions following their interviews and in their negotiations with JWA and members of the local Community Advisory Boards is that these women felt unfairly represented. In a life history in which they had been invited to dwell on food-related memories, they felt these reminiscences came at the expense of "what I really wanted to talk about"; that is, more in-depth discussion of the substantive areas of their accomplishments and contributions in careers and community activism. Food, then, became a locus of negotiation, an area of women's traditional discourse where some narrators could retreat when they did not want to discuss certain aspects of their public or private lives. For other narrators, however, food talk became a diversion from discussion about what they considered to be the truly important areas of their lives.

These reactions remind us that in oral history, as Dennis Tedlock has suggested, "people tell what they want you to know about themselves."[12] This leads us to look for what the narrators reveal about themselves through the topics they are comfortable addressing, whether it is culinary traditions, their active involvement in community organizations, or the importance of a parent, grandparent, or teacher as a role model. But of equal importance, as Dana Jack notes, we need to attend to what is missing, what literary critics call the "presence of the absence" in women's texts.[13] An initial reading of the *Weaving Women's Words* interviews, rich in their descriptions of so many aspects of Jewish women's lives, reveals a great deal about how women of this pivotal generation want to be portrayed through their silences as well as their presence. Recollections of family conflict, for example, are largely absent from these texts. Indeed, the most common restriction we have received thus far as a condition for releasing a text is the deletion of a narrator's negative comment, sometimes very minor, about a family member or a less than flattering depiction of family relationships. We have heard little of the strains and disappointments in the relationships between spouses or parents and children. Only one narrator discussed marital infidelity, but then deleted all references to her numerous affairs during the editing process. In the case of the sole narrator who endured a difficult divorce, the narrative jumps from one marriage to the next with no explanations about the causes of the marital breakup and with only oblique reflections on how she coped during this traumatic period in her life.

In other cases, narrators have been reluctant to talk directly about a difficult, though defining, issue or event in their lives, and the oral historians have struggled to introduce these topics in ways that would not violate commonly accepted rules of social discourse. One of our oral historians, for example, raised the subject of a narrator's husband's trial and subsequent conviction and imprisonment, by asking: "Tell me—I know that there were obviously in later years—you had to go through some fairly, you know, real trials—here and at home. And I'm really curious to know what those taught you and what that experience was like for you, and how you came out of it on the other side." Though the narrator talked at length about the impact of her husband's trial and conviction on her own life and on her children, neither she nor the oral historian ever described what had happened or the issues involved.

In a second example, the oral historian asked a narrator about the rape of her adult daughter. Though the narrator had mentioned that this was a defining life event that she wanted to talk about in her interview, she was not in fact able to discuss the incident directly. Instead, the oral historian brought up the topic and prompted her by giving her the basic facts: "It was an intruder that came into the house?" and later, "It was a rape, wasn't it?" In response, the narrator was able to focus on the impact of this trauma on her own life and that of her family. In both of these examples, the narrators were able to talk about a critical life event mainly in terms of demonstrating their own resilience and the paramount importance of family ties.

As we come to the end of the initial period of processing the *Weaving Women's Words* interviews and begin to look to them as a valuable collection of women's texts for creating a more inclusive historical narrative, we are well aware, as many scholars have pointed out, that what is left out is sometimes more significant than what has been put in. And, as Carolyn Heilbrun urges us, we need to "search for the choices, the pain, the stories that lie beyond the 'constraints of acceptable discussion.'"[14]

In an email correspondence, Mary Marshall Clark, director of the Oral History Research Office at Columbia University, attributed the success of a major oral history project on the history of women journalists to the fact that "gender never became the dominant category."[15] It would have been insulting to women journalists, she wrote, pioneers in a male world, to ask them only about what it was like to be a woman in that context. "In other words, the project was really a project on the history of journalism—and because we were interviewing women we paid a lot of attention to the question of gender—but without reducing the potency of the larger story."[16]

Clark's message is in essence a commentary on what should be discussed in women's oral history. What difference does the interview topic guide make in terms of the narrative that is ultimately constructed, and how does it help define what are the expected and acceptable topics for discourse? How much, in other words, should women talk about cooking versus their accomplishments in the worlds of work and community activism? How do issues of class, ethnicity, place, and worldview play into both the creation of these texts and their interpretation? How do the rules of social discourse influence the choice of topics and appropriate questions in women's oral history? Finally, how, in the inter-subjective space of the oral history encounter, are the answers to these issues resolved? These are indeed the underlying questions as we begin to process and interpret the *Weaving Women's Words* interviews. As we work towards making them available on the JWA website and in local archives, we look forward to the collaboration of our readers to help identify the answers.

NOTES

[1] Barbara Myerhoff, *Number Our Days* (New York: Dutton, 1979), 20.

[2] Carolyn Heilbrun, *Writing a Woman's Life* (New York: Norton, 1988).

[3] Kathryn Anderson and Dana C. Jack, "Learning to Listen: Interview Techniques and Analyses," in *Women's Words: The Feminist Practice of Oral History* (eds. Sherna Berger Gluck and Daphne Patai; New York, London: Routledge, 1991), 11-26.

[4] Jayne K. Guberman serves as project director for *Weaving Women's Words*. For information on the Jewish Women's Archive, see online: http://www.jwa.org.

[5] See also Keren McGinity's chapter in this volume, "Immigrant Jewish Women Who Married Out."

[6] Pamela Brown Lavitt, "Final Report, Jewish Women's Archive: *Weaving Women's Words* Seattle Project" (unpublished, 2000), 10.

[7] *Ibid.*

[8] Carolyn Eastman, "Final Report, Jewish Women's Archive: *Weaving Women's Words* Baltimore Project" (unpublished, 2001), 15.

[9] Shelly Tenenbaum and Lynn Davidman, *Feminist Perspectives on Jewish Studies* (New Haven: Yale University Press, 1994), 11.

[10] Sherna Berga Gluck and Daphne Patai, "Introduction," in Gluck and Patai, *Women's Words*, 3.

[11] See Marcie Cohen Ferris, "Exploring Southern Jewish Foodways," in *Studies in Jewish Civilization 15: Food and Judaism* (Omaha: Creighton University Press, forthcoming).

[12]Ronald J. Grele, ed., *Envelopes of Sound: Six Practitioners Discuss the Method and Practice of Oral History* (Chicago: Precendent, 1975), 74.
[13]Anderson and Jack, "Learning to Listen," 19.
[14]Heilbrun, *Writing a Woman's Life*, 30-31.
[15]Correspondence with the author.
[16]*Ibid.*

Stories and Subversion

S. Daniel Breslauer

Since at least the nineteenth century, Yiddish and Hebrew stories have been fulfilling both a need for entertainment and a subversive purpose. They entertain by appealing to the suppressed desires and interests of their readers. They subvert by showing the validity of those desires in contrast to the conventional suppression under which the readers must suffer. Yiddish stories seem to address three levels of suppression in particular. The first is socio-economic. Life in the Eastern European town or shtetl was highly stratified. Workers were relegated to a lower class because of their relative ignorance and lack of leisure for study. At the other end of the scale were the rabbinic authorities. The ultimate power group within the community, they were marked by their learning as having had the leisure to study and become pious. These leading scholars expected and received both material and spiritual deference. The wealthy middle class gained prestige through patronage of the learned, rabbinic elite. Subverting this aspect of Eastern European Jewish life entails creating a sympathetic link between the poor and oppressed and the values of the intellectual and cultural elite. Empathy with the oppressed as examples of exalted values undermines the class stratification often accepted without thought.

This socio-economic class system was in turn reinforced by a power structure created within the family. The balance between husbands and wives and parents and children demanded the suppression of individuality for the sake of the survival of the family unit. A subversive story could liberate people whose loyalties had been wedded to kinship ties. The story would show how family often acts as an obstacle to personal development, how it detracts from rather than enhances human expression, and how the highest values are those for which one should sacrifice family. Such subversion represents a trans-valuation of the traditions of family life.

In addition, narratives of good familial relations were part of an entire complex of conventional models of social roles. The conventional narratives established a hierarchy imposed by tradition. Youth was subordinated to age; women were subordinated to men. The good of the whole was thought to follow from obedience to conventional ways of being male, female, Jewish, or Gentile. Subverting these conventional notions entails demonstrating the failures, suffering, and human cost they impose. This type of subversion makes a political point: the structures of society do not advance the cause of humanity but rather undermine that cause.

One of the best vehicles of such subversion is that of the romantic story. The figure of the Jewish woman plays an important symbolic role throughout Jewish literature. By studying how writers (usually male) portray women, one can trace responses to creativity and diversity in Jewish life.[1] David Biale shows how the European romantic ideal infiltrated traditional Judaism through rabbinic responsa; personal memoirs; and the evolution of the Yiddish chapbook, anonymous tales which "turned traditional practices into vehicles for romance."[2] These Yiddish stories used conventional practice as a backdrop for dramatic gender reversals in which, for example, a girl might disguise herself as a Yeshiva student to catch a glimpse of her future bridegroom. Tales of thwarted love, of erotic attractions, and feminine activism as well as passivity give evidence "of the infiltration of modern ideas of romantic love" in Jewish culture.[3] Biale shows how stories use tradition to subvert traditional values in these Yiddish tales.

With the rise of the Haskalah, the Jewish Enlightenment, stories often took on a more self-consciously subversive role. Biale points to Shmuel Yosef Agnon's story, "The Tale of the Scribe," as an example of how thwarted romance against the backdrop of traditionalism implicitly criticizes traditional piety. He also suggests that stories by Yiddish authors such as Shalom Aleichem celebrate the sexuality of marginal Jews to highlight the double curse of the Jewish middle class: "repressive Jewish tradition" and "nascent bourgeois respectability."[4]

Stories subvert more than just bourgeois ideology. Settling in the new agricultural community of the land of Israel, the *Yishuv*, young Jewish idealists were sacrificing all for their ideals. These *halutzim* [pioneers] dedicated themselves to Hebrew literature and to a single-minded devotion to building up the land. Even their personal erotic needs were to be subordinated to the task at hand. Zionism demanded loyalty and devotion from its followers that often seemed to leave no opportunity for romantic life or any alternative commitments. Young

Zionists often associated their ambivalence toward the strict erotic control of the movement with other types of control, such as that exercised over literary endeavors. The stories and novels of the period often portray a hero torn between his duties to the community and his heterosexual love.[5] The abandonment of strict loyalty to the mores of the group is sometimes accompanied by the reading of forbidden writings. By sneaking their reading of a Yiddish story in between duties to the *Yishuv*, these *halutzim* subvert the ascetic culture of their ideology. Rivka Mahnimit, a *halutza* of the Second Aliyah,[6] reports in her diary that she and her boyfriend would go off to a secret place, preferably the romantic location of a wheat threshing floor, and read the Yiddish stories of Yitzkhak Leib Peretz. Reading Yiddish was itself romantically subversive in the Hebraic atmosphere of the *halutzim*, as was indulging in personal eroticism.

TORAH, WORK, AND WIVES IN "DOMESTIC TRANQUILITY" BY PERETZ

That the couple chose the works of Peretz is particularly significant. Peretz himself tells a story showing the subversive power of fiction.[7] In his story "The Reader," Peretz describes a family enjoying the *oneg*, or pleasure, of the Sabbath night. The parents are sleeping after a week of labor. The children who usually sleep with them are in a different room so as not to awaken them. The eldest daughter, however, sits by herself poring over a romantic novel as the candle flickers out. Her red hair flows around her shoulders; her complexion is green from a diet made primarily of potatoes. In the book, however, she escapes to a world of separated lovers, of bandits, and of serpents lying in wait. As the candle sputters out she laments that she will not know how the story of the serpent ends. Here stories provide an escape and refuge from the drudgery of daily life in the Jewish village, of the shtetl.

Most of Peretz's writing is characterized by this approach to both the reality of Jewish life and the role of Yiddish literature in it. He was both sympathetic to shtetl life and critical of it. His writings are often meant to stimulate reform, and this reformist tendency is almost always a component in his presentation of women. While some nineteenth-century Yiddish authors caricatured women and others sentimentalized them, Peretz took a different approach. He has been hailed as one of the few writers of his time to see "woman in her human essentials."[8] To achieve full portraits, Peretz focuses different stories on different types of women. His stories include passive wives, shrewish ones, and those who are loving and caring. His portrayals, it can be argued, helped prepare for social reform of the treatment of women in the shtetl. His awareness of the entire complex of conditions in the shtetl, however, makes these narrative descriptions more complex than is often understood. Their appeal and sensitivity should be balanced against their polemical force.

His stories are accessible, plausible, and effective; their appeal and significance lie therein. Indeed, Esther Hauftzig, who transforms his tales into children's stories, testifies that the protagonists in his tale of "Peace at Home," a narrative to be examined in detail later, "were my first literary example of what equality of the sexes was all about." She also claims that Peretz anticipated the modern feminist movement.[9] As in the story of "The Reader," Peretz recognizes that while traditional Jewish religion afforded a man "many little avenues of escape from his burdens," women's possibilities were more restricted. Only modernity seemed to offer them the release that men had long enjoyed. Because of this inequality, Peretz uses his stories for several purposes. On one level he does indeed provide readers with exciting, romantic, and exotic alternatives to their daily lives. He melds mystical, poetic, and realistic elements into fascinating concoctions for his readers.

Beyond this talent for composing appealing fiction, Peretz also has a penchant for social criticism. He uses his stories to mobilize support for social change and reform. His tales depict the traditional world in dark colors, opposing traditional Jewish authority, the deadening poverty that both Jewish men and women suffered, and the call for patience through hope of reward in the next world. Finally, Peretz balances this rejection of tradition with a modernist affirmation that a this-worldly relationship based on "mutual care, respect, and responsibility" can substitute for the supernatural benefits once promised as a reward for Jewish suffering.[10] Clearly he sees his stories as subversive. In the name of love, respect, and companionship he undermined the traditionalism that had dominated Jewish personal and communal life. His stories focus on how that domination had affected women, men, and their mutual relationships. Exploring his tales shows the ways in which a narrative may use tradition and appeals to Torah to subvert traditional culture. Even the male protagonists have characteristics at odds with the dominant rabbinic culture and its concerns. This exaltation of nonrabbinic heroes subverts the tradition no less than does the positive view of women.

Peretz's story, "Domestic Tranquility" [*Sholem Bayis*], has been characterized as one in which "an unlettered shtetl porter is an eloquent advocate of women's rights."[11] The tale is far more complex.[12] Its title, sometimes misleadingly translated as "An Idyllic Marriage," is actually an ambiguous one. *Sholem bayis* is often used to justify a maneuver, slightly less than legal or completely legitimate, that is nonetheless necessary to prevent incivility between husband and wife. *Shabbat* 23b uses the term when discussing the commandment to light Hanukkah lamps: Jewish law forbids making use of these lamps for other purposes. On the Sabbath of Hanukkah a poor family may be faced with a difficult choice. If they can afford to light only one lamp, which should it be? The Talmud judges that they should light the Sabbath lamp, which may be used for such purposes as illuminating a kitchen, bedroom, or any other household necessity rather than the more restrictive Hanukkah lamp. The reason given for this choice is that it is done for *sholem bayis*, keeping peace in the family.

Other uses show that the phrase is employed to explain apparently mysterious lapses from absolute law. In Gen 18, divine angels announce that Sarah will bear a son. Sarah, overhearing this exchange, laughs because she thinks, "Can I get any pleasure now that my husband is old?" (Gen 18:12).[13] God, however, reports this differently. He tells Abraham that Sarah laughed because she thought that she was too old to bear children. Why did God change the truth? God's alteration of the facts, according to rabbinic interpretation, was motivated by a concern for *sholem bayis*. God was unwilling to tell Abraham something about Sarah that could cause friction between them. For the sake of domestic tranquility, even the divine bends the truth.

Peretz's story, if its title is correctly understood, tells how a couple negotiates its tranquility. It does not describe "an Idyllic marriage," but rather how two partners bend the rules in order to accommodate one another. Making the taking of liberties with laws and veracity the centerpiece of a good relationship subverts the traditional reverence for truth and obedience. The importance of negotiation, stressed by the title of the story, indicates that an absolute tradition is less important than the discovery of a *modus vivendi* by which partners in a marriage can relate to one another.

The tale, when looked at in detail, supports this supposition. Peretz tells of the porter Hayyim, who ekes out a living that just supports him, his wife Hannah, and their children. The names of these protagonists, while common ones, are also symbolic. Hayyim means "life." The hero is an "everyman" who struggles to make a living. His wife's name means "graciousness" and implies that she is bringing grace and beauty into his life. The relationship between these characters mirrors the relationship between the ideas they represent. Life needs graciousness; graciousness requires support. Men and women require one another. Maintaining their existence demands that each partner negotiate with the other to preserve the relationship they both need. A central scene in this short story pictures Hayyim standing below the window from which Hannah looks out at him. They are discussing how they will spend the money he earns. How will they choose among the various Sabbath necessities, since they do not have sufficient funds to purchase all of them? This scene of negotiation sets the tone for the tale as a whole. Both husband and wife share a similar piety, both are more comfortable using Yiddish than Hebrew, and both seek a way to balance religious duties and the realities of the life they must live.

The hero of this tale is a poor porter; his profession and his poverty are both important features of the story. These are common elements in stories by Peretz. He tends to favor simple heroes rather than scholars and saints. His sympathy rests with the common Jews, not the elite. Readers have often noted Peretz's "proclivity for manual labor" and the fact that his protagonists "almost invariably seek their livelihoods diligently, if sometimes ineffectively, through menial labor."[14] What may not be so easily grasped is that Peretz is very ambivalent about this kind of work. He recognizes its hardship, inefficiency, and inadequacy as a means of providing a dignified living.

In "Sholem Bayis," Hayyim's innate dignity contrasts with the indignities literally thrust upon him by his profession. Peretz exaggerates the grotesque and absurd nature of the porter's work. When engaged in his profession, the story relates, Hayyim was so bent under his load that it looked as if the burden were carrying itself. Nevertheless, Hayyim panted so loudly that his breathing could be heard far in the distance. His own appreciation of his poverty also evokes a type of humor. He praises Hannah for her patience with him, for bearing with the children's lack of clothes and shoes. His optimism is almost comic in its obliviousness to reality. While apparently sweetly sentimental, Peretz's portrait of his hero's determined good humor in the face of the indignities he must endure evokes a bitter irony; Hayyim expresses a type of gallows' humor that makes his condition faintly ridiculous rather than realistic.

Although he ridicules Hayyim's work, Peretz exalts his love and devotion to his wife, Hannah. The central theme in the short story is the redeeming power of such dedicated care. This care expresses itself through the playful dialogue that characterizes the relationship between Hayyim and Hannah. Immediately upon getting his payment, he runs to get a drink of water from the well and then goes to hand the small amount of money over to Hannah. When she appears at the window, he marvels that she always stays at home and never leaves. She chides him, telling him to leave because she has to tend to the welfare of the children. He asks lovingly about each of them and then leaves. It is clear from the interchange that he realizes she is tied to the home and that she accepts this as necessary for their family. His compassion and her sense of duty negotiate the harsh realities forced upon them by their circumstances.

Only on the eve of the Sabbath does the couple's exchange differ. Suddenly tradition, rather than work or poverty, makes its demands felt. Jewish law places certain restrictions on Sabbath life, and Jewish custom has expectations for Sabbath observance as well. Hayyim and Hannah negotiate to see how they can best fulfill the Sabbath commands on the basis of their meager income. This discussion occasions praise for Hannah, whose cooking skills can disguise even the lack of essential ingredients for her Sabbath pudding. What animates the relationship is the love and respect the two have for each other. Hayyim clearly marvels at his wife's ability to make do with what he can earn; she just as clearly cherishes his optimism and ability to accept what she can give. Just as she deprecates her own abilities at home, so he deprecates his own contributions. He laments that he is barely able to recite the basic Hebrew prayers of the Sabbath, the *kiddush* [sanctification of the holy day] and the *havdola* [the separation from the holy day and the beginning of the secular week]. She responds that he is a good provider. Mutual appreciation gives meaning to their lives. They can live with deprivation because they negotiate compromises that make sense to them. Neither the absolutes of work nor those of tradition spoil the flexibility and therefore amicability of the relationship.

The culminating event in the story occurs when Hayyim becomes anxious not about affairs in this life, but those of the world to come. In synagogue one of the *melamdim*, the teachers employed to teach very young children, expounds the Torah portion of the week for the ignorant working men. Usually the men are inattentive, but vivid descriptions of the horrors of *Gehenna* [hell] and the pleasures of paradise catch their attention. The teacher lists in detail the commandments that win a person a place in the world to come: primary among them is study. He describes in infinite detail the terrors awaiting those who are untutored and unlearned. The ignorant and impious cannot escape the terrors of hell. Moved to desperation by these descriptions, Hayyim approaches the teacher diffidently, calling him respectfully "rabbi," although this humble man hardly holds such a rank, to ask how he might earn paradise and escape hell. As someone who is also among the oppressed, this teacher responds with compassion and understanding. Hayyim is told, first, that he must study Torah. When he confesses that he is not a scholar, he is told to recite Psalms. He admits that his work leaves him no time for this. At least, the teacher says, recite your prayers with heartfelt devotion. Hayyim sadly admits that he cannot understand the Hebrew words he recites. Finally the teacher assures him of paradise through serving the students who learn Torah. Hayyim is instructed to bring water to the students in the House of Study and thereby earn the merit of paradise. Although happy, Hayyim worries about his wife who cannot share in this labor. The teacher assures him that the wives of the righteous go to heaven as the footstool of their husband's throne.

On returning home, Hayyim demonstrates his piety. He performs the *havdola* prayer (and his attention to the ritual suggests that while he does not understand it, his devotion is real). His wife also shows a deep Yiddish devotionalism as she reads in *Gott Fon Avrahom* [*God of Abraham*, a collection of Yiddish prayers and petitions]. The piety that the *melammed* said would earn him a place in the world to come is clearly evident despite the fact that neither he nor his wife knows Hebrew. Then Hayyim informs his wife of what the *melammed* told him to do and about his wife's place at his feet. His heart is moved by this subordination, and so he refuses to acquiesce to it. Hayyim breaks out with the cry, "I will not accept this!! You will not be my footstool. I will make room for you to sit with me on the throne." He concludes by claiming that even God will have to agree to this condition.

Here, for the sake of domestic tranquility, Hayyim is negotiating not only with his wife, but also with God. He has experienced the necessity of maintaining a balance of power so as to survive the perils of this world. He is unwilling to chance losing this balance in the world to come. Against Jewish tradition he takes his stand for egalitarianism, not because he is an eloquent advocate of woman's rights, but because to accept the traditional solution would jeopardize the only security he has managed to achieve—that of his relationship with Hannah. Taking grace away from life would be a curse not a reward. He cannot contemplate a heaven without the peace he has found on earth and so demands a change in tradition.

While one clear point of the story is the exaltation of the peace that Hayyim manages to establish in his domestic life, an equally clear objective of the tale is to devalorize the traditional alternatives of work and study. Peretz ridicules the world of Torah and learning no less than the world of labor. The detailed Sabbath requirements become primarily a vehicle for displaying the commitment of Hayyim and Hannah to each other. The synagogue is a place that cultivates superstitions. As Peretz portrays them, the *melammed*'s portraits of heaven and hell are simplistic and tailored to a simple audience. While the teacher does show sensitivity to Hayyim, his solution to the dilemma of the ignorant man is to have him serve the scholars. The class structure that enshrines the educated rabbi at the head of the community contrasts with the nobility of Hayyim's love of his wife. The reader cannot help but feel that Hayyim's egalitarian revision of the tradition shows a more exalted spirit than does the *melammed*'s male-centered view. While Peretz may well be providing a more balanced view of the Jewish women of the shtetl than his contemporaries do, he is also using this portrait of family negotiation for a polemical purpose. Neither this world with its ridiculous labors nor the world to come with its equally ridiculous rabbinic fantasies offers true relief to the burdened Jew. Instead close human relations, maintaining a balance of power that leads to domestic peace, and creating security at home provide the only true redemption. The supernaturalism in the story balances the grotesque naturalism describing Hayyim's work as a porter. Between these two stretches the negotiated tranquility established through the relationship between husband and wife. Peretz looks to this relationship as a substitute for and alternative to the promises of the tradition. Here Peretz offers a subversion of the socio-economic structure that divided Eastern European Jews according to a strict class system. His heroes transcend their class and reveal the inadequacies of such a system for understanding the true nobility of every human being.

SHMUEL YOSEF AGNON'S STORY OF THE PORTER AZRIEL MOSHE

Peretz and the Hebrew author S. Y. Agnon share a similar background, Polish Hasidism, the mystical folk movement of Jews in Eastern Europe. Several of their stories seem drawn from common sources—both tell about the discovery of a treasure on the Sabbath, and they both reflect on the power of the Straymel, the fur hat worn by Hasidic leaders.[15] Agnon tells a somewhat similar story to that of Peretz's "Sholem Bayis" about a porter called Azriel Moshe, who laments his lack of learning and scholarship.[16] Azriel Moshe is an orphan, who, without a parent to tutor him, has been forced to turn to menial labor to support himself. Although forced by fate into this lot, Azriel Moshe does not accept it gladly. His lack of learning never leaves his consciousness, and he meditates on his condition continually.

His name, like Peretz's hero, is clearly symbolic. This double name combines Israel's lawgiver, Moses, with a phrase that means "God is my helpmate." The true partner in his life is God, not any human being. Such an affirmation seems almost intentionally directed against Peretz's view, since it implies that God and not Azriel's actual wife is his true partner. Even if this element is not intended to oppose Peretz's tale, the story Agnon tells is, as a whole, a very different one, emphasizing piety and belief rather than realistic detail. Agnon's hero is not only a helpmate of God; he also bears the name of Israel's greatest prophet, by whom the Torah was delivered to the people. The importance of tradition, of literature, and of learning, rather than mere devotionalism, is exalted in this tale. The story of Azriel Moshe teaches the primacy of scholarly orientation rather than the fullness of life, as in the tale of Hayyim. Despite this different perspective, many similarities link the two heroes. Like Peretz's hero, Agnon's is also an ordinary Jew who shares the sensibilities and experiences of the Jewish masses.

Agnon's presentation of ordinary Jews, however, is touched with a sense of holiness conveyed by reverence for Torah. For Agnon, Torah and learning are at the heart of the holy. At the beginning Azriel is pious but ignorant. He asks God to give meaning to the prayers that he utters but cannot understand. From the very beginning, his hero has a special sense of Torah that lifts him beyond the ordinary. Azriel Moshe, unlike many of his fellow workers, recognizes the limitations of his earthiness. After prayer he goes to warm himself with a glass of spirits. As he does so, he comments that he is rewarding his body for the work of prayer and compares himself to a beast of burden like a horse or donkey. The others at the inn laugh at him, but they have misunderstood the depth of his piety. Azriel seeks to find an appropriate way of demonstrating his love of God, not for the sake of the world to come, but out of the natural love he feels for the creator. In the manner of other pious heroes, he promises God that he will work for him free of charge, but the offer has no realistic force to it. Very clearly, God has no possessions that Azriel can transport from one place to another. His simple piety still leaves Azriel far from the true holiness of Jewish life, a holiness that evokes respect rather than laughter.

Azriel's situation appears as the result of poverty and misfortune. He was an orphan, raised without training in Jewish learning, and is forced to maintain himself and his family by whatever he earns. He must spend his days in hard work just to afford life's necessities. In contrast to Peretz, Agnon portrays the labor his hero performs in starkly realistic terms, but sympathetically. Azriel Moshe has the physical abilities required for his trade, being prodigious in strength and work. Agnon's description of his hero's routine differs significantly from that given by Peretz for Hayyim the porter. For Agnon, earning a living is a holy act—it is accepting the yoke of work just as study is accepting the yoke of Torah. Azriel Moshe is pursuing a divinely instituted task as he carries out his labors. If Agnon laments the conditions of the worker, it is because Azriel Moshe's worth is not appreciated. The social system does not reward either his devotion or his skills. Despite his prowess, he must repair everyday to his corner of the market and wait for some passerby to hire him.

Even his ordinary acts sometimes have religious significance. When pallbearers need someone to carry a body to its burial place, Moshe takes on that task. Agnon uses such experiences to demonstrate the depth of his hero's piety. Thus, he describes in loving detail how Azriel carries the belongings of a wealthy scholar from place to place. The scholar cautions the porters to take special care with the holy books, and Azriel swears that he will protect the books. This oath foreshadows Azriel's future and his life-long dedication to the holy books of the Jewish tradition. At this point, however, he is merely thinking of transporting his load as safely and efficiently as possible. Nevertheless, his progress is delayed as he thinks about the treasures that are on his back. Agnon draws a poignant picture of the porter lost in thought as he bears his load. The stops and starts of this journey evoke respect and sympathy rather than laughter. Agnon's porter, unlike that of Peretz, does not strike an absurd or ridiculous pose when engaged in labor.

The central theme of Agnon's portrayal is Azriel Moshe's love of Torah. When given payment for this service, Azriel, unlike Hayyim, does not think first about his family affairs. His mind is still consumed with the holy works that he has just transported. He takes the few coins he has earned and immediately goes to a store to buy some chalk. He begins writing the names of all the sacred books he can remember on the walls of his house. Unfortunately, the chalk smears and over time becomes illegible.

At this point Azriel Moshe begins what will be his life's work. He buys paper and writing implements and draws up lists, chronologies, and even calendars in his manipulation of the names of the holy books and holy saints that he knows. To augment his collection, Agnon's porter decides on his own to spend time in the House of Study, and in so doing, he becomes familiar with the names of the sacred books and holy teachers. He learns to repeat those names and associate them with particular books. He writes lists of these sacred names and recites them to himself. Since Azriel Moshe has copied a calendar of the holy dates and festivals, he gains a reputation as an expert on when to observe the date of the passing of a loved one or another holy occasion. He invites scholars and students to his home, learns to imitate their ways, and becomes a changed person. Although he has been affected by the holy names he has memorized and has taken on many of the habits of a scholar, he remains a common man. Agnon comments: "Azriel had changed even in appearance so that one could not tell by looking at him that he was a simple fellow." This sentence has a double meaning— first, it clearly shows the effect on the hero of his devotion to scholars; secondly, it penetrates beneath appearance to insist that, after all, Azriel was still the simple person he had always been.

The difference between Agnon's porter and Peretz's should be clear. Despite his untutored state, Azriel Moshe does not need a *melammed* to teach him about Jewish law and lore. He possesses an innate way of understanding Torah once it becomes available to him. He does not even need the minimal instruction that Hayyim gets, but teaches himself through his association with scholars and scholarship. For Agnon the way to transcend poverty is through study and learning. Agnon does not mock the tradition but shows how even the most ordinary person can attain its glories.

The greatest change that has occurred is a domestic one. Agnon says far less about his hero's wife than does Peretz, but this silence, no less than what is reported, is significant. Although Azriel accepts "the yoke of earning a living," Agnon does not spell out the nature of his familial obligations. Indeed, he shows Azriel using his money either in the tavern to warm his insides or to buy writing material to create a list of sacred books. His life moves between his love of the holy and the duty of his labor; responsibilities beyond these do not come into play at all. This portrait is, alas, rather realistic. Memoirs and other evidence from shtetl life do indeed suggest that men often abandoned family life for the sake of Torah. Wives frequently bring cases against husbands who have left them and their children to go off and study with a great sage. Many women fell into the unfortunate category of the *aguna*, the woman whose husband has deserted her without giving her a valid divorce.

Peretz and Agnon both recognize that women suffering under such conditions might become shrewish or irascible. Agnon, however, treats the situation very differently than Peretz. Peretz, clearly sympathetic, draws a realistic picture of the angry wife.[17] Agnon uses the motif of the shrewish wife to show the power of Torah to change life. The first sign that Azriel's mastery of the holy names has changed him comes through his relationship to his wife. Agnon says: "Whenever his wife would vex him, he would occupy himself with the great names and not pay attention to her abuse." Agnon does not mention what her criticisms of Azriel might have been, whether or not they were justified, or even whether he should have responded. Instead he merely reports that Azriel, because of his newly discovered power, could remain silent in the face of his wife's arguments. Agnon then proceeds to note that since Azriel refused to answer her back, she ceased reviling him and established peace in the household. More than that, she began to respect him and boast about his newfound knowledge to her neighbors. Through her influence they began to come to him with their questions concerning when special days would fall. Thus, for Agnon, the importance of the wife lies in her transformation from being vexatious to becoming respectful and helpful.

Azriel's wife and family fade into the background. His love of learning and Torah outshines his concern for the people closest to him. Azriel Moshe, however, does develop in piety. The transformation that Azriel undergoes occurs through his association with sacred texts, even though he does not understand them. While the first stage of this transformation is noted in externals—his wife and neighbors give him respect—the fulfillment of the change requires personal dedication. From his original stage of self-denigration, Azriel advances by stages first to familiarity with the texts and finally to a loving commitment to them. The proof that he has truly changed and become an entirely different person comes when he is willing to give up his own life in defense of Torah and the holy books.

Azriel's city becomes the target for an anti-Semitic attack. Agnon reports that many Jews of the town fled to safety. He says nothing about Azriel's family or his concern for them. Instead, Agnon describes Azriel's frantic effort to save the holy books in the synagogue from the attack of the marauders. First, he checks on their welfare, then he tries to spirit them away to a safe hiding place. When that is no longer possible, Azriel Moshe stations himself in front of the synagogue. He will defend the books with his life. At first it seems as if he has accomplished the miraculous—the soldier dispatched to the synagogue flees in superstitious fear at the sight of this old man protecting the books. The captain of the troops, however, knows better than to be frightened away. He comes with reinforcements, and Azriel dies a martyr for the books that he had honored in his life.

Agnon supplies a supernatural ending that rewards Azriel for his self-sacrifice. After his death the prophet Elijah comes and brings him to the abode of Israel's martyrs, where he becomes a heavenly librarian because he has the names of all the holy books at his command. This fulfillment of Azriel's life-long desire represents the triumph of Torah over life. Azriel had been born an orphan and was denied training as a Jew. He transcends his beginnings and attains the highest status possible—association with the martyrs of Jewish history—through commitment to the holiness of sacred texts. Human life and family are merely a stage he passes through on his way to this ultimate achievement. Agnon, unlike Peretz, does not see salvation as an achievable goal in this world and its relationships with others. Redemption is possible, but only as a transcendent and transcending gift at the end of life. Agnon's purpose is a different subversion than that of Peretz. Agnon, as a creative artist, seeks to undermine that familial hierarchy which disseminates responsibility as duties of one member of a kinship group to another. He valorizes the special individual who transcends ordinary concerns and expectations. Agnon's treatment of his hero's wife is no less sensitive than Peretz's, but it transmits a different message: even family duties pale beside the duties of a creative artist. In a story that subverts ordinary expectations, Agnon suggests that the family eventually will recognize the primacy of the devoted individual.

TORAH, WORK, AND WIVES IN MARTIN BUBER'S *FOR THE SAKE OF HEAVEN*

Not only authors known primarily for their stories, but also philosophers and theologians tried their hand at epic narratives capturing life in the shtetl. The Jewish philosopher and political thinker Martin Buber offers such a literary tale. His epic novel, *For the Sake of Heaven*,[18] tells a long and sprawling tale with its central hero, Jaacob Yitzchak, called "The Yehudi," or "The Jew," undergoing a transformation subtly akin to that of the porters in the two previous tales. When writing this story, Buber had already gained a reputation for artistic presentation of literary works and for philosophical writing. Nevertheless, he claims that in this book he sought to evoke an authentic picture of Jewish life in Eastern Europe. He calls the tale a "chronicle," to emphasize its historicity despite its fictionalization. He even points to himself and his background as proof that he speaks with a genuine voice, declaring, "I am a Polish Jew....In the most impressionable period of my boyhood a Hasidic atmosphere made a deep impression on me."[19] He struggles to provide an honest and "just" rendering of the communities he describes.

His novel portrays a vast and variegated set of communities and personalities. The Hasidic atmosphere pervades, and Buber's hero (unlike those of Agnon and Peretz) is of the scholar class. He is a brilliant and spiritual disciple of the Seer of Lublin, whose religious life makes up the center of the book. Nevertheless, Buber never loses contact with ordinary people. The hero, Yaakov Yitzchak, titled the Holy Yehudi (the Holy Jew), lives among common people. His father-in-law and mother-in-law are laborers. Buber's portrait of Goldele, the Yehudi's mother-in-law, is realistic and not unsympathetic. She is a devoted wife and housekeeper, but also a shrewd and powerful woman. Goldele, Buber informs the reader, was the actual manager of the public house that belonged, in name at least, to her husband. She derived her sense of worth and power from her ability to understand affairs and people. The Yehudi thwarts her attempts to control his life; she finally has him banished from the household. "His wife," it is remarked, "had to bring him food."[20] Buber's hero does not fit in with the working class Jews among whom he lives, but Buber recognizes the needs of those Jews, as does the holy Yehudi himself.

Despite the difficulties in describing Yaakov Yitzchak as a common laboring Jew, Buber's hero has many traits in common with those of Agnon and Peretz. He is clearly a Hasidic master who studies Torah and practices spiritual exercises. His is the life of the spirit, not of the body. Nevertheless, Buber stresses again and again the difference between the Yehudi and his master, the Seer of Lublin, whose name he shares. The very title Yehudi is a generic name, as Yaacob Yitzchak gives up his individuality to take on the general term "Jew" as his description. When appointed to serve when the Seer was away, the Yehudi is frightened by the office he must assume, the Seer's shirt that he must wear, and the miracles that appear to occur through his means. He eventually gives the shirt to a poor beggar, who immediately disappears.[21] The Yehudi, not only by name but by deed, identifies with the ordinary Jew. If, as is central to the story, he has difficulty being accepted among his own family, the problem lies as much with the situation as with him. He wishes to be one of the people, even as the people misunderstand him. The Holy Yehudi is no less a member of Israel's masses than the heroes of Peretz and Agnon.

The theme of labor is introduced early in the tale, when the Yehudi tells how he apprenticed himself to a smith and learned to rise early, then apprenticed himself to a peasant and learned that he must use his strength to help others.[22] The first story that the Yehudi tells describes how he noticed that the fire of the smithy was already blazing when he rose in the morning. The Yehudi then made it a point to rise earlier thinking, "I cannot let that mere mechanic put me to shame—me who am striving after the life eternal." A rivalry began with each man seeking to rise earlier than the other. That rivalry finally taught him "that it is necessary to seek to understand what our fellows have at stake."[23] A second story relates how the Yehudi came upon a wagon that had been overturned and that blocked the road. The peasant asked him to help and, when he refused, saying he was unable to help, the peasant then accused him of being "unwilling" rather than "unable." When he finally did try pushing with the peasant, his work succeeded. From this, he learned that "no one knows whether he can do a thing until he has tried it."[24] These stories become parables for the spiritual struggle that the Yehudi undertakes. "The road of the world," Buber quotes the Yehudi saying, "is the road upon which we all fare onward to meet the death of the body." The encounters on that road are encounters with the *Shechinah* [the Divine Presence], the manifestation of God's indwelling presence.[25] The novel as a whole portrays the Yehudi's attempt to raise up the *Shechinah* and restore her to glory before he meets "the death of the body." That task is doomed, as the Yehudi knows.

The entire thrust of Buber's story is eschatological, focused on the coming of redemption to the Jewish people. The argument waged "for the sake of heaven," to which the title points, is between the Yehudi and his master the Seer of Lublin; it concerns the hastening of the messianic coming. The action reaches its acme at a Passover Seder, during which the Seer expects to cause the redemption to occur. The ritual meal has a very specific and detailed set of rules and regulations, to which the Seer adds his own. The Yehudi seeks to follow his master's rules so as to force the end of time by ritual means, but no sooner has he begun than his second wife, Schoendel Freude, interrupts and demands the honor due her. Her angry interruption critically interferes with the completion of the holiday service. That defective ceremony, combined with others, leads eventually to the Yehudi's death, as he attempts to achieve what his master desires. Unlike Hayyim he has no promise of heavenly bliss, and, unlike the case of Azriel Moshe, the reader cannot glimpse a beatific post-mortem glory accorded to him.

Buber, no less than Peretz, recognizes that a shrewish wife has been conditioned by her situation. Several passages in the novel show Buber's sensitivity to the plight of women in a traditional Jewish community. Women become the focus for resentment and passion precisely because they have been ignored, rejected, and abandoned. Buber, like Peretz, understands "the life circumstances that contributed to the irascibility of the shrew."[26] Buber displays great sympathy when describing the character of Schoendel Freude. While the wife of Agnon's hero becomes silent and respectful of her husband, Buber's Schoendel Freude falls into a more complicated silence. She is the Yehudi's second wife, taken as a levirate marriage after her sister, his first wife, dies (heartsick, according to some rumors, because her husband abandoned her to go to the Seer of Lublin). After the wife of his youth dies, Goldele comes to him to remind him of his duty to marry his wife's surviving sister.[27]

As a replacement for her sister, Schoendel Freude is aware of her secondary nature and is plagued by guilt and worry. This anxiety translates into impatience with the Yehudi as his hopes, aspirations, and dreams demand that he pay more attention to his duties than to her and their family. She scolds him, reproves him, and rebukes him continually. Her angry accusations leave him no peace. The Yehudi bears with her in silence again and again. Finally, he speaks reprovingly to her. When a disciple asks him to explain his change of behavior he replies, "Did you not observe how it throttled her that her scolding had no power over me? And so I had to let her feel that her words did strike me to the heart."[28]

Unlike Azriel Moshe's wife, Schoendel Freude requires an answer rather than silence. Nevertheless, she too eventually becomes quiet, in this case out of a sense of tragic responsibility rather than out of newfound respect. After her outburst during the Passover celebration contributed to the failure of the Seer's attempt to bring redemption, the Yehudi's wife was consumed by her guilt. Buber notes: "Since that unhappy *Seder* she had become strangely silent." She expresses her regret to the Yehudi saying, "I have been a bad wife to you," but her husband corrects her. She is a victim of the distorted reality of her times just as surely as her husband and the others in the story. Redemption must be postponed indefinitely, and the reality that substitutes for it is inevitably painful and tragic.

The tragedy of Buber's tale finds expression in a saying attributed to Rabbi Chaim Yechiel of Mogielnica: "One can kill a child in its mother's womb."[29] The theme of the novel is such a stillbirth; it suggests that those with the greatest potential for good, the scholars and saints, are also those with the greatest potential for evil. These leaders are the ones responsible for preventing the birth of that which would have redeemed the Jewish people. The ordinary Jews are not to blame; the scholars and sages bear the brunt of the charge that they have brought disaster to their own followers. The book is filled with sayings explicating the Torah, giving guidance about human life, and pointing the way to spiritual living. Nevertheless, the story also includes its scholarly villains. Rabbi Simon Deutsch had led the campaign against the Yehudi and slandered him repeatedly. After the Yehudi's death, the Seer of Lublin "turned to Simon Deutsch, who sat next to him. 'Rabbi Simon,' he said, 'You are a liar.'" The exalted teachers of Torah are not only enslaved to superstition, as Peretz would have it, but they are also obstacles that prevent the development of truth and peace.

Buber's tale instructs readers in ways of response when neither Torah nor the promises of salvation through natural life can be trusted. Where scholars are liars and where the experiences of daily life and the negotiations of domestic life provide no soothing balm, the best course of action is to accept things as they are. Buber makes this point by relating the tale of the death of Rabbi David of Lelov. Rabbi David laughed three times as he died: once because the opponents of the Yehudi were now getting rid of him as well: a second time because now no one other than the Yehudi would ever read the "Book of David" again; and finally, in his own words, "I laugh toward God, because I have accepted His world exactly as he made it."[30] The wisest use of reason and learning is not to change the world, to attain holiness, or to evoke righteousness, but rather as a way to become reconciled to life as it is. Buber's heroes purvey a political message—the conventional social structure inevitably and tragically creates suffering and conflict. Buber subverts acceptance of the status quo by showing the consequences of its definitions of male and female roles. If individuals were allowed just to live their lives rather than to force those lives into conventional molds, then much suffering could be avoided. His cautionary tale, therefore, undermines a satisfied self-assurance in the social conventions of Eastern European Jewish life. The conflicted relationships between men and women are symptoms pointing beyond themselves to problems in society itself.

THREE PHILOSOPHIES OF SUBVERSION

These three stories agree on several important points. Each goes beyond a simplistic understanding of labor. Work is more than simply that which (often ineffectually) seeks to sustain life. Work may be a grotesque joke, a chore to endure, or a metaphor for spiritual living. In any of these cases, labor takes on a special significance beyond its material success.

Secondly, all three agree that Torah has meaning even when it is not learned or understood in the traditional sense. Peretz makes Torah into a tissue of superstitions that has meaning only as a pretext for displaying conjugal affection. Agnon depicts a love of learning expressed through personal commitment to Torah, a love of the books more than a mastery of them, and a willingness to die even for that which one cannot understand. Buber scatters lessons of Torah throughout his novel. Nevertheless, he shows that learning Torah is never enough. One can be a great scholar and a great liar. Torah learning, then, is only a superficial indication of the nature of a person.

Finally, all three recognize that the world in which human beings live is often disappointing, conflicted, and painful. However, the three differ in their views of how to resolve the problem of life, each pointing to a different way in which to make life more bearable. Peretz takes relationships between people as central: they provide the redemptive force in life. If love redeems life, then Torah and labor are but distractions, secondary elements important only as vehicles to reveal redemptive caring. Torah itself is but the ideology of a certain leadership class, while work is a grotesque intrusion that must be transcended. For his part, Agnon emphasizes Torah. Both human relationships and labor find meaning and fulfillment through devotion to a transforming set of holy texts. The act of commitment to those texts, rather than just an understanding or learning of them, changes a person's entire life, both in work and in love. Buber looks skeptically at all the elements of life. Ethics consists of recognizing the tragedies of love, work, and Torah. A belief that redemption lies beyond the horizon, unattainable and illusory, cultivates a realistic approach that his story seems to endorse.

Finally, each perspective is subversive. After encountering Hannah and her relationship with Hayyim, Azriel Moshe and his quieted wife, or the Yehudi and Schoendel Freude, we can no longer look at the traditional valorization of Torah study in the same way. We cannot accept the class system that evaluates people such as Hayyim and Hannah based on their ability to have time to study. We can no longer unthinkingly affirm family values in the face of the transcendent values that a hero such as Azriel represents. We cannot remain silent in the face of political systems that inevitably pit the Yehudi against the needs of Schoedel Freude. The portrait of the women in each of these tales is significant as part of the subversive project each author envisions. The sacrifices of these women make a claim on us, as does the painful reality of the labor that all three heroes, including the Yehudi, must endure.

Which of these three approaches is the true one? In 1953, Buber provided a foreword to the new edition of his novel to explain why he wrote it. He declared that his aim was less ambitious than transmitting a true doctrine: "No way can be pointed to in this desert night. One's purpose must be to help men of today to stand fast...until the dawn breaks and a path becomes visible where none had expected it."[31] Only by subverting the places where we already expect a path can we hope for the surprise of the dawn. Stories, particularly these stories about Yiddish women of the shtetl, serve such an indispensable function.

NOTES

¹I discuss this in S. Daniel Breslauer, "Women, Religious Rejuvenation, and Judaism," *Judaism* 32:4 (1983): 466-75.

²See David Biale, *Eros and the Jews: From Biblical Israel to Contemporary America* (New York: Basic Books, 1992), 162-68, especially 166.

³*Ibid.*

⁴*Ibid.*, 168-169.

⁵See Esther Fuchs, *Israeli Mythogynies: Women in Contemporary Hebrew Fiction* (Albany, NY: SUNY Press, 1987), 24-25.

⁶This encompassed the immigration of Jews from Eastern Europe to the land of Israel from 1904-1913.

⁷Y. L. Peretz, "The Reader," in *Kitvei Y.L. Peretz* (Jerusalem: Dvir, 1960), 185.

⁸An argument for Peretz's view of women and its modern relevance can be seen in Ruth Adler, *Women of the Shtetl: Through the Eyes of Y. L. Peretz* (Rutherford: Fairleigh Dickinson University Press, 1980), 34, and throughout the book.

⁹See Esther Hauftzig, *The Seven Good Years and Other Stories of I. L. Peretz* (Philadelphia: Jewish Publication Society of America, 1984), 8. Her translation of the tale that she titles "Peace at Home" is found on pages 17-22. Another useful translation, "Happiness in Marriage," is found in Eli Katz, *Yitshkok Leybush Peretz: Selected Stories, Bilingual Edition* (New York: Zhitlowsky Foundation for Jewish Culture, 1991), 2-11.

¹⁰See Adler, *Women of the Shtetl*, 23 and 67.

¹¹*Ibid.*, 28.

¹²Y. L. Peretz, "Sholom Bayis," in *Kitvei*, 184-85; the story appears in Yiddish in *DI Verk Fun Yitshak Laybush Peretz* (ed. D. Pinski; vol. 3; New York: Farlag "Idish," 1920), 7-11.

¹³See also the chapter in this volume, Susan A. Brayford, "The Domestication of Sarah: From Jewish Matriarch to Hellenistic Matron."

¹⁴*Ibid.*, 64.

¹⁵*Ibid.*, 64-65; see the comparison in the two stories about wealth found on the Sabbath.

¹⁶See Shmuel Yosef Agnon, "The Tale of Azriel Moshe, the Keeper of the Books," in *Kol Kitvei S. Y. Agnon* [Heb] (vol. 2; Jerusalem: Schocken, 1968), 388-94.

¹⁷See Adler, *Women of the Shtetl*, 41-60.

¹⁸Martin Buber, *For the Sake of Heaven: A Chronicle* (ed. L. Lewisohn; New York: Harper and Row, 1966).

¹⁹*Ibid.*, xii.

²⁰*Ibid.*, 25-26.

²¹*Ibid.*, 64-69.

²²*Ibid.*, 30-32.

²³*Ibid.*, 31.

²⁴*Ibid.*, 32.

²⁵*Ibid.*, 35.

[26]Adler, *Women of the Shtetl*, 44.
[27]*Ibid.*, 84-89.
[28]*Ibid.*, 158-61.
[29]Buber, *For the Sake of Heaven*, 314.
[30]*Ibid.*, 387.
[31]*Ibid.*, xiii.

A Derivative Hatred:
Images of Jewish Women in Modern
Anti-Semitic Caricature

Henry Abramson

The depiction of Jewish women in anti-Semitic art and caricature is one of the oldest themes in anti-Judaic representations.[1] In fact, it is the female rather than the male Jew who is most prominent in medieval church art, from approximately the ninth to the fifteenth centuries, as the twin sisters representing Church and Synagogue [*ecclesia et synagoga*].[2] In this set piece, two women stand on either side of a divider (often Jesus on the cross), the woman symbolizing the church on the viewer's left and the woman symbolizing the synagogue on the viewer's right. This orientation symbolizes the greater favor shown to the church by Jesus, as she stands next to his right hand; often there is a definite act of affirmation accompanying the hand, as in Giovanni da Modena's fifteenth century "Living Cross," where the cross extends an appendage down to place a crown on the head of the church [fig. 1]. Other features of the image, typical of the hundreds of similar depictions scattered throughout Europe, emphasize the greater status of the woman representing the church: her hair is neatly arranged, she rides with an upright, proud posture, her mount is a majestic winged lion with a woman's face, and she holds the chalice (the Holy Grail) that receives Jesus' blood. The Jewish woman representing the synagogue, on the left [Latin: *sinister*] side, is the very picture of degradation: the cross brandishes a sword and brutally drives it through her skull, she is blindfolded, symbolically blind to the tenets of Christianity, her hair is unbound, her posture is bent, and her mount is the lowly goat.[3]

There are hundreds of variations on this theme of *ecclesia et synagoga*, perhaps the most famous being the so-called "Strasbourg sisters," a pair of thirteenth century statues at the cathedral in Strasbourg [fig. 2].

fig. 1 *The Living Cross*

fig. 2 *The Strasbourg Sisters*

Although lacking the more violent imagery common in the "Living Cross" motif, the woman representing the church looks on with disdain at the bareheaded synagogue, portrayed in an attitude of decline, her staff broken and the tablets representing her connection with the divine falling from her hand. The *ecclesia et synagoga* images, it must be remembered, were "official" art, commissioned by the church for the purpose of edifying the illiterate masses and instructing them in the finer points of Christian thought, in this case the Pauline doctrine of replacement theology, wherein the Jews lose divine favor and the new, Christian nation inherits it.[4]

Other medieval depictions emphasize a sexual metaphor: the synagogue as an unfaithful wife. Perhaps the starkest example is the thirteenth century ceiling painting outside of Oslo, Norway, in which she is portrayed

fig. 3 *Untitled*

semi-nude (wearing a transparent shift), her eyes only partially covered (indicating that she is willingly blinded to Jesus), and with a wry smile on her face [fig. 3]. At the level of her genitalia she holds a decapitated ram's head, symbolic of "carnal Israel," in contrast to the docile lamb of

Christianity.[5] Often the Jewish woman is portrayed as actively abandoning the church, as in the stained glass window of the Elizabeth Church of Marburg.[6] Perhaps the most concrete examples of the unfaithful church are the twin medallions at either end of the eleventh century Gunhild Cross [fig. 4]. The synagogue is portrayed with bared breast, unbound hair, and holding a sheaf of barley; these are all markers of the *sotah* [the woman ritually humiliated on suspicion of adultery

fig. 4 *Gunhild Cross*

(see Num 5)]. Jewish woman are also portrayed as emasculators, particularly in connection with circumcision: medieval artists charged with portraying the circumcision of Jesus, evidently disgusted with this act that was perceived as both a "Judaizing" and a "feminizing" of Jesus, often placed the circumcision blade in the hands of a woman rather than a man [fig. 5].[7]

An unusual shift in the representation of Jews in medieval art seems to occur in the fifteenth century, the era of both Gutenberg's invention of the printing press and the Protestant Reformation. The sudden availability of mass-produced secular imagery, combined with the diminishing control that the church had over such information, is

fig. 5 *Circumcision*

reflected by the increasing violence of anti-Semitic caricature—it is difficult to use the term "art" in this context—and its masculinization. This is perhaps most evident in the hundreds of depictions of the so-called "ritual murder" or "blood libel" charges, in which Jews were accused of murdering Christian children, often using their blood for ritual or magical purposes.[8] Consider, for example, the typical late-fifteenth century engraving depicting the martyrdom of Simon of Trent: the child is strangled by his Christian betrayer (note the bulging bag of money at his belt, most likely his payment from the Jews) as three Jewish men torture the child in various ways [fig. 6]. At the extreme right, far from the center of activity, is a Jewish woman (so identified by the *rouelle* [Jewish badge] on her head covering). Whereas she was central to the *ecclesia et synagoga* theme, she is now marginalized in a secondary, helping role: bringing torture instruments to the men who are busy with their work.

    This trend of shunting the women to the side in anti-Semitic caricature is also quite evident in the *Judensau* [Jewish pig] genre of anti-Semitica. Originally a judicial tool of the fifteenth century, images

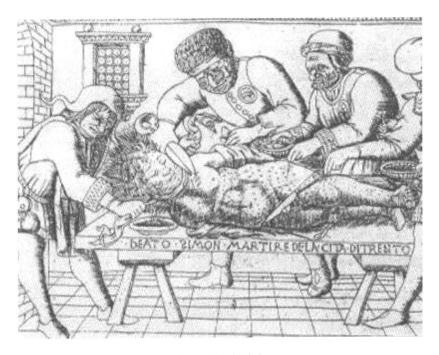

fig. 6 *Blood Libel*

commissioned by the court to defame petty criminals, the *Judensau* eventually lost its original connotations while remaining a popular anti-Semitic theme to the twentieth century.[9] The repulsive central images—the devil assisting a Jew eating a pig's excrement while another rides it, a third suckling underneath—are the main focus of attention. The Jewish woman, on the other hand, has been shifted to the background, where she fondles herself and holds a decapitated ram's head aloft [fig. 7]. In other examples, she rides a live ram, often holding a horn in one hand while lifting its tail with the other, exposing it for sexual access.[10]

I have suggested two possible reasons for this evident shift of focus away from the female representation: the diminishing control of the church over the production of imagery and the increasing demand (and availability) of imagery for secular purposes. To expand on this slightly, it is important to note that however violent some of the *ecclesia et synagoga* images may have been, they were still intended for the churchgoing public, and as such there were limitations on the graphic content of the images. The primary purpose of church art was, after all, to educate rather than to titillate, whereas secular caricature was shaped by a more

fig. 7 *Judensau*

basic economic motive, catering to a lower common denominator. Moreover, the very nature of depicting Jews as women might have had a moderating effect on church art, as violence against women (or the depiction of women committing extreme acts of violence) may have been contrary to the developing feudal code of chivalry, once again offending not only the sensibilities of the medieval churchgoing public but even the masses who consumed this early form of anti-Semitic pornography that circulated from the fifteenth century on. The location of anti-Semitic hatred in men was therefore a more tenable focus point for this subterranean animosity; as such, Jewish women, when they appear in post-fifteenth century medieval anti-Semitica, tend to be marginalized.

This is generally true of anti-Semitic caricature to the present day—women, if they appear at all, are usually secondary to the negative representations of men. A typical example is "Little Israel Swallowed a Ducat" (1820). The caption describes the "true story": Israel, seeing how much his father, Baruch, loves gold, concludes that it must be a wonderful delicacy; testing this theory, he swallows a golden ducat. The family is horribly alarmed at the loss of the coin, and all of them (the typically Jewish names are listed, as if their strange Semitic sounds were funny in themselves) gather around the dining room table as the father administers oil to the boy, with the family waiting expectantly for Israel to produce the ducat in the chamber pot [fig. 8]. The women here are secondary to the central events.

fig. 8 *Israel Swallows a Ducat*

Looking more closely at this image, however, another element of modern anti-Semitic depictions of Jewish women is evident: one of the presumably comic elements present is the physical resemblance of Jewish women and their men. The portrayals of the women often have little ideological content in themselves; rather, they are imitation men. This is likely a consequence of the influence of nineteenth century *Völkism*, an inchoate, pre-racist body of theories that posited the existence of distinct groups of people, constituted by their common ancestral heritage and possessed of characteristic physiognomies. Women are portrayed as imitation men, the humor found in the supposed uncanny resemblance between the Jewish genders [fig. 9]. Features classically associated with late-nineteenth century anti-Semitic caricature are ascribed to both men and women: the bulbous nose, fat lips, and receding chin are noted in particular. Beyond the relative absence of Jewish women from modern anti-Semitic caricature, they are portrayed as virtual ciphers, their gender subsumed within their nationality.[11] This phenomenon is so pronounced that it is repeated even when the stylistic representation of Jews is different, as, for example, when Jews are portrayed as emaciated and angular [fig. 10].[12] Indeed, the very looseness of Jewish gender representations seems to betray an underlying fear of Jewish domination, as a Jewish family promenading on a boardwalk appears as an invasion of Semites [fig. 11]; conversely, Jews driven from Germany appear as a great cleansing, celebrated by a happy Aryan child in Elvira Bauer's disturbing Nazi propaganda [fig. 12].

Certain body features occasionally appear in a distinctive manner, not always associated with men. Although the exaggerated nose is associated with them, this feature is even more prominent in women, perhaps in an attempt to provoke a greater sense of irony [fig. 13]. Massive breasts are occasionally evident, perhaps an allusion to the stereotypical Jewish mother who smothers her child with excessive concern.[13]

Finally, certain Jewish women appear in contemporary anti-Semitic caricature because of their political or social importance. Perhaps the most commonly depicted woman, especially in the Arab world, is former Israeli Prime Minister Golda Meir. Another extremely offensive image— striking because it is an example of the contemporary Arab borrowing of the medieval Christian "blood libel"—is the portrayal of Yitzhak Shamir's wife in a 1990 Bahrain newspaper. Holding a bucket, she chides some Israeli soldiers who are brutally murdering a Palestinian

fig. 9 *Ces Bons Juifs!*

fig. 10 *David and Batsheba*

fig. 11 *Kurgaeste*

fig. 12 *Nazi Children's Book*

fig. 13 *The Nose*

fig. 14 *Golda Meir*

child, asking them to save the blood for ritual purposes [fig. 14]. The "domesticity" of the Jewish woman is made horrific in this image; beyond that, there is nothing to label it specifically as misogynist.

In summary, over the course of the last eighteen centuries, Jewish women have virtually disappeared from anti-Semitic caricature. Once prominent in the polemic *adversus iudaeos* imagery of official church art, they are shunted to the side with the popularization of mass-produced imagery and the diminishing control of the church over the production and dissemination of these images. By modern times they lose most of their distinctive features and are typically portrayed as imitation men, occasionally with unusual features such as overly large breasts. By the twenty-first century, the negative portrayals of Jewish women are a derivative hatred—Jewish men have become the lightning rod for anti-Semitic caricature.

IMAGES

Figure One: *The Living Cross*. Giovanni da Modena. Painting, 1421, Basilica S. Petronia, Bologna, Italy. Source: Heinz Schreckenberg, *The Jews in Christian Art: An Illustrated History* New York: Continuum, 1996, p. 65.

Figure Two: "The Strasbourg Sisters." Artist unknown. Stone sculptures, c. 1230, Strasbourg cathedral, Strasbourg, France. Source: Heinz Schreckenberg, *The Jews in Christian Art: An Illustrated History* New York: Continuum, 1996, p. 47.

Figure Three: Untitled ceiling painting on wood, latter half of 13th century. Ål Stave Church (C no 11707), Oslo, Museum of National Antiquities, Norway. Source: Heinz Schreckenberg, *The Jews in Christian Art: An Illustrated History* New York: Continuum, 1996, p. 53.

Figure Four: Artist unknown. Detail from Gunhild Cross, Walrus tusk relief, 11th century. Copenhagen Nationalmuseet, Denmark. Source: Heinz Schreckenberg, *The Jews in Christian Art: An Illustrated History* New York: Continuum, 1996, p. 34.

Figure Five: Artist unknown. Miniature c. 1400 in Guillaume de Digulleville, *The Pilgrimage of the Soul the Pilgrimage of Jesus Christ* (France). Brussels BR MS 10176-8. Source: Heinz Schreckenberg, *The Jews in Christian Art: An Illustrated History* New York: Continuum, 1996, p. 145.

Figure Six: Caricaturist unknown. Engraving c. 1475-1485, probably Florence, Italy. Source: Heinz Schreckenberg, *The Jews in Christian Art: An Illustrated History* New York: Continuum, 1996, p. 280.

Figure Seven: Caricaturist: "Johann" (uncertain if this is the creator of the original work of which this is a copy, or the caricaturist who adapted it here). Engraving, early 18th century, Frankfurt am Main, Germany. Source: Eduard Fuchs, *Die Juden in der Karikatur: Ein Beitrag zur Kulturgeschichte* Munich: Albert Langen, 1921, p. 31.

Figure Eight: Caricaturist unknown. Colored engraving, 1820. "Israelchen hat einen Ducaten verschluckt." Germany. Source: Eduard Fuchs, *Die Juden in der Karikatur: Ein Beitrag zur Kulturgeschichte* Munich: Albert Langen, 1921, p. 105.

Figure Nine: Caricaturist unknown. Pamphlet cover, late 19th century, Raphaël Viau, "Ces Bons Juifs!" France. Source: Eduard Fuchs, *Die Juden in der Karikatur: Ein Beitrag zur Kulturgeschichte* Munich: Albert Langen, 1921, p. 307.

Figure Ten: Caricaturist unknown. "David and Batsheba," 1820. Apparently published in magazine or journal. England. Source: Eduard Fuchs, *Die Juden in der Karikatur: Ein Beitrag zur Kulturgeschichte* Munich: Albert Langen, 1921, p. 63.

Figure Eleven: W.J. Konijneuburg, "Kurgäste," 1895. Originally published in *De Kroniek*, Amsterdam. Source: Eduard Fuchs, *Die Juden in der Karikatur: Ein Beitrag zur Kulturgeschichte* Munich: Albert Langen, 1921, p. 191.

Figure Twelve: Book illustration, 1935. Originally published in Elvira Bauer, *Trau keinem Fuchs auf grüner Heid und keinem Jud bei seinem Eid* Nuremburg: Der Stürmer, 1935.

Figure Thirteen: "Stauber," untitled, 1851. Originally published in *Fliegende Blätter*. Source: Eduard Fuchs, *Die Juden in der Karikatur: Ein Beitrag zur Kulturgeschichte* Munich: Albert Langen, 1921, p. VII.

Figure Fourteen: Reproduced in Arieh Stav, *Peace: The Arabian Caricature: A Study of Anti-Semitic Imagery* New York: Gefen, 1999.

NOTES

[1] This research was sponsored by the National Endowment for the Humanities and the Division of Sponsored Research of Florida Atlantic University. I am also grateful to the students in my seminar on Medieval Jewish History who provided useful comments and criticisms on an earlier draft of this paper.

[2]The classic work on this topic is Wolfgang Seiferth, *Synagogue and Church in the Middle Ages: Two Symbols in Art and Literature* (New York: Fredrick Ungar, 1970). See also Bernhard Blumenkranz, *Le juif médiéval au miroir de l'art chrétien* (Paris: Etudes Augustiniennes, 1966), and *Juden und Judenthum in der mitteralterlichen Kunst* (Stuttgart: Kohlhammer, 1965). See also two groundbreaking studies of *Bible moralisée* imagery by Sara Lipton, "The Temple is my Body: Gender, Carnality, and Synagoga in the *Bible moralisée,*" in *Imagining the Other: Visual Representations and Jewish-Christian Dynamics in the Middle Ages and Early Modern Period* (ed. Eva Fromjovic; Boston: Leiden, 2002), 129-154, and *Images of Intolerance: The Representation of Jews and Judaism in the Bible moralisée* (Berkeley: University of California Press, 1999).

[3]I discuss these images in greater detail in "A Ready Hatred: Depictions of the Jewish Woman in Medieval Anti-Semitic Art and Caricature," *Proceedings of the American Academy for Jewish Research* 62 (1996): 1-18.

[4]Replacement theology, and its implications for later anti-Semitic thought, is widely discussed in post-Holocaust research. For an analysis of the medieval evolution of Christian doctrine toward the Jews, see Jeremy Cohen, *Living Letters of the Law: Ideas of the Jew in Medieval Christianity* (Berkeley: University of California Press, 1999). See also Rosemary Ruether, *Faith and Fratricide: The Theological Roots of Anti-Semitism* (Minneapolis: Seabury, 1974); Alan Davies, ed., *Antisemitism and the Foundations of Christianity* (New York: Paulist, 1979). See also John Gager, *The Origins of Anti-Semitism: Attitudes toward Judaism and Pagan and Christian Antiquity* (New York: Oxford, 1985); Peter Schäfer, *Judeophobia: Attitudes toward the Jews in the Ancient World* (Cambridge: Harvard University Press, 1997).

[5]On the significance of the Ram's head, see Richard Hamann, "The Girl and the Ram," *The Burlington Magazine for Connoisseurs* 60 (London, 1932): 91-97; on carnality in general in the pivotal thought of Pope Gregory the Great (590-604), see Cohen, *Living Letters*, 90-92.

[6]See Konrad Schilling, ed., *Monumenta Judaica: 2000 Jahre Geschichte und Kultur der Juden am Rhein* (Köln: Kölnisches Statdmuseum, 1965), plate 68. Also noted in this image is the transparent blindfold.

[7]Carrie Hannon and I have discussed this aspect in "Depicting the Ambiguous Wound: Circumcision in Medieval Art," in *Circumcision: New Perspectives on an Ancient Rite* (ed. E. W. Mark; Hanover: University Press of New England/Brandeis University Press, 2003), 98-113.

[8]For more information on ritual murder and blood libel, see the work of R. Po-Chia Hsia, *The Myth of Ritual Murder: Jews and Magic in Reformation Germany* (New Haven: Yale University Press, 1992), and *Trent 1475: Stories of a Ritual Murder Trial* (New Haven: Yale University Press, 1988).

[9]The most detailed study of the *Judensau* is found in Isaiah Shachar, *Judensau: A Medieval Motif and its History* (London: The Warburg Institute, 1974).

[10]See examples in Heinz Schreckenberg, *The Jews in Christian Art: An Illustrated History* (New York: Continuum, 1996), 335-37.

[11]For other examples, see Judith Vogt, *Historien om et Image: Antisemitisme og antizionisme i karikaturer* (Copenhagen: Samlerens, 1978), 66-67, 82; Eduard Fuchs, *Die Juden in der Karikatur: Ein Beitrag zur Kulturgeschichte* (Munich: Albert Langen, 1921), 100, 142, 153, 159.
[12]See Fuchs, *Die Juden in der Karikatur*, 172.
[13]See Vogt, *Historien om et Image*, 77.

Judy in Disguise:
D. W. Griffith's *Judith of Bethulia*

Dan W. Clanton, Jr.

The apocryphal story of Judith has been one of the most reinterpreted and retold tales in all of biblical literature. Some works have appeared that analyze many of these interpretations, yet strangely almost no work has been done on one of the most notable retellings of this narrative: D. W. Griffith's 1913 film, *Judith of Bethulia*.[1] This film, partially based on Thomas Aldrich's play, is significant not only for the unique place it occupies in Griffith's cinematic output, but also for its transformation of the story of Judith. Before addressing the film, I summarize the story of Judith. I then discuss the interpretation of this story in the play and the film, as well as comment on how the film, like all significant artistic interpretations, allows us to reencounter the original narrative with new questions and perceptions.

The first seven chapters of the story of Judith recount the military buildup of the Assyrians; Judith is introduced in chapter eight. The narrative tells of the increasing presence of the Assyrian army in Palestine and of the rising tensions between the Assyrians and the citizens of Bethulia, a small town in Judea. Things begin to get serious when the Assyrians cut off the water supply to the town, after which the Bethulians urge their leaders to surrender. Beginning in chapter 8, we hear of the response to this situation by Judith, a wealthy widow living in Bethulia. She convinces the elders to allow her to resolve the conflict. After praying to God, Judith gives herself a makeover and emerges as a startling beauty. She leaves Bethulia and crosses over to the Assyrian camp with her maid, where she gains the trust of the Assyrian general Holofernes. She tells Holofernes that she will give Bethulia and all of Judea into his hands. Judith returns to his tent later, where he attempts to seduce her. After he passes out from too much liquor, she beheads him and then slips away with her maid back to Bethulia. Upon her return, she instructs the army to attack the Assyrians, who promptly flee in fear once they discover the headless body of their leader. Judith is praised for her actions not only by the townspeople, who throw a festival in her honor, but also by a visiting delegation of elders from Jerusalem. After her "fifteen minutes of fame," Judith returns to her estate and lives out the rest of her life as a widow. The last word we hear about Judith is that, "No one ever again spread terror among the Israelites during the lifetime of Judith, or for a long time after her death" (Jdt 16:25).

From this brief summary, it is easy to see why so many artists, writers, and librettists have been, and continue to be, drawn to the story of Judith.[2] The story contains religious piety, a brave and sexually appealing heroine, an underdog story line, and a gruesome beheading. Thomas Bailey Aldrich found it fertile ground for an artistic retelling; when he tried his hand at interpreting Judith, first in poetic form in 1896, and then as a stage play in 1904, the subject would have been well known.[3] As J. B. Kaufman notes, when Aldrich's play opened in Boston on 13 October 1904, it undoubtedly would have been guaranteed success not only by the subject matter, but by Aldrich's reputation: "Today Aldrich may be a forgotten literary figure, but in his own time he was considered the equal of such contemporaries as Mark Twain and Henry Wadsworth Longfellow."[4]

Aldrich's play alters the story of Judith—and Judith herself—in an attempt to add emotional and psychological depth to the biblical account. His earlier poem even includes a prefatory note:

> In the following narrative the author has taken such liberties with the myth as suited his dramatic purpose. He has widely departed from precedent in his delineation of Judith, who moves through the Apocrypha a beautiful and cold-blooded abstraction, with scarcely any feminine attribute excepting her religious fervor....Judith's character throughout the ancient legend lacks that note of tenderness with which the writer has here attempted to accent her heroism.[5]

In Aldrich's work, Judith observes the suffering of her fellow townspeople from her tower, a common symbol of seclusion and chastity. Once Judith descends from her tower in Bethulia to travel to the Assyrian camp, she is thrust into an unknown and anxious environment. Renate Peters notes:

> Metaphorically speaking, the descent from the tower indicates a descent from saintliness and moral superiority into moral confusion, from angelic neutrality into a flesh and blood

existence, and from the light of faith into the darkness of doubt and death. Unlike the biblical Judith, Aldrich's hero is plagued by doubts as soon as she enters Holofernes' camp.[6]

The main source of Judith's doubt is her growing love and desire for Holofernes, who now no longer appears to be an anonymous tyrant, but rather a "gentle prince, with gracious words and ways."[7] By contrast, the apocryphal Judith is quite matter-of-fact about her relationship with Holofernes and even seems to relish making ironic puns about his eventual fate and her disdain for him (Jdt 11:5-6, 16; 12:4, 14, 18).[8] By investing his Judith with doubt brought on by her desire for Holofernes, Aldrich is evidently trying to enhance the suspense and eroticism of the narrative. However, because Aldrich offers no internal motivation for Judith's temptation and her hesitation to kill Holofernes, his attempt fails. Judith pities Holofernes, yet she decapitates him; she is sure what she does is approved by God and therefore good, yet is not happy at the survival of her home.

At the end of the play, she refuses the honors her fellow Bethulians offer her and vows to:

dwell apart, alone / In mine own house, where laughter may not come / Nor any light, vain voices of the world / Only the sorrowful shall find the door / Unbarred and open / In thy memory / Keep me as some beloved wife or child / Or sister that dies long and long ago![9]

The final words Aldrich attributes to Judith in the tragedy evince a state of near hysteria: "Let no one born of woman follow me!"[10] Margarita Stocker comments on this ending: "This curiously redundant phraseology of childbirth provides the closing image because of Aldrich's subtext, which is intended to recuperate the independent virago for a lesson in woman's true destiny, marriage and motherhood, as her only route to fulfillment."[11] As we shall see, this lesson is also implied in Griffith's film. In sum, as Peters notes, Judith "remains an eminently incomprehensible and ambiguous figure in Aldrich's play," one who "remains the other for the others [in the play] and for herself," a woman who has "put herself outside humanity."[12]

D. W. Griffith began filming *Judith of Bethulia* in June 1913, while still employed by Biograph Pictures. Ever the shrewd businessman, Griffith avoided possible copyright infringement issues by purchasing a treatment of the subject from a writer named Grace A. Pierce in Santa Monica, even though he carried a copy of the Aldrich play on the set with him at all times.[13] During the month of June, Griffith and his Biograph troupe—Blanche Sweet as Judith, Henry B. Walthall as Holofernes, and other minor players including Lillian and Dorothy Gish and Lionel Barrymore—shot the exterior scenes for the film in Chatsworth Park near Los Angeles. At the beginning of July, the company returned to New York, where the interior scenes were shot at Biograph's studio in the Bronx. It was during this shooting that Nance O'Neil, the first actress to play Aldrich's Judith, visited the set; she gave some tips to Blanche Sweet, who was only seventeen years old. While shooting in New York, Griffith's already strained relationship with Biograph took a turn for the worse. Biograph was in the habit of releasing only one-reel films, and Griffith's conscious defiance of this policy—he shot six unedited reels for *Judith* at the outrageous cost of $36,000—was causing quite a stir. In response to Griffith's actions, Biograph informed him that henceforth he would supervise other directors, but that after *Judith* was completed, he was not to direct any more films himself.[14] This proved to be too much for Griffith; at the end of September 1913, he left Biograph and took many of its best and brightest with him, thus sealing the fate of the company.[15] Nevertheless, Biograph finally released *Judith of Bethulia* in London in November 1913, to both commercial and critical acclaim. The picture was a hit again in March 1914, when it opened in New York; the various editions of the film to appear later only testify to its popularity over time.[16]

In *Judith*, Griffith weaves together four interrelated story lines: the situation of the Bethulians, the relationship between the two young lovers Naomi and Nathan, the story of Judith, and the attack of the Assyrians led by Holofernes.[17] Of these plots, the story concerning Naomi and Nathan is the most abbreviated, and rightly so: it is completely absent from the apocryphal account and has only marginal status in the Aldrich play. Even so, Naomi is important in the film, for she provides a counter example to Judith's character. Naomi is invested in her people; she is in love with Nathan, who loves her as well, and who eventually saves her after the Assyrians capture her. Griffith takes pains to present Naomi's status after her capture: she is chained to a post and turned into a chaste spectacle. As Peters writes, Naomi "is the Victorian ideal, the normal woman, virtuous virgin, an object on display, to be gazed at, passive, helpless, bound and the object of sadistic men's desires."[18] In other words, for Griffith and his audience, Naomi is the woman to be admired, the paradigmatic repository of appropriate womanly behavior and values. This characterization of Naomi is at odds with Griffith's use of dancing girls to entertain Holofernes, but, as noted, Naomi's character is provided as contrast to Judith.

Judith in Griffith's film is similar to the character in Aldrich's play. In both, Judith is somewhat isolated from her community in spite of (or perhaps because of) the Bethulians' reverence for her status as a widow. In addition, Griffith's Judith is physically separated as well; she gazes on the Bethulians through a window in a large wall that marks off her space from theirs. Interestingly, Griffith also includes scenes of Holofernes looking out from his tent in an almost solitary visage, thus juxtaposing the two characters from the start. The Assyrians invade and cut off the town's water supply, demonstrating a military frenzy Griffith would master one year later in his *The Birth of a Nation*.[19] In the aftermath, Judith receives a vision from God instructing her as to her mission. This vision serves to downplay Judith's own initiative and creativity; in the apocryphal account it is Judith herself who devises the plan to kill Holofernes. Thus, Judith is not only separated from her townspeople, but Griffith, following Aldrich, has also diminished her as a moving force in the story. She becomes passive in her Bethulian context, unable even to offer any sympathy to a young mother who holds out her sick child for Judith to see.

However, once Judith and her maid reach the Assyrian camp, the first of a number of reversals takes place, similar to the apocryphal narrative. Holofernes becomes passive, shown reclining on an enormous couch that serves as his substitute throne. After Judith enters the Assyrian camp, Holofernes gets off this couch only once, to inquire about her. Indeed, most of the physical action after Judith arrives in the camp is performed by Holofernes' dancing girls and his head eunuch Bagoas, who seems constantly delighted and amused by Judith's presence. The only time Holofernes engages in any leadership is when a dissenter is brought in for punishment (interestingly, the punishment is crucifixion). By including the troupe of dancing girls, symbolizing an almost bacchanalian fury, as well as the allusion to the Roman crucifixion of Jesus, Griffith here seems to be foreshadowing his 1916 film, *Intolerance* (one most critics would consider more successful).

Like Aldrich, Griffith tries to invest Judith with more emotion by having her fall in love with Holofernes. Even before the decapitation scene, Judith is twice shown smiling as she thinks of Holofernes, but is then racked with guilt as she recalls her fellow townspeople. The titles for these scenes indicate her inner struggle: "Then did Judith wrestle with her heart, for Holofernes now seemed noble in her eyes.... Again Judith faltered for the love of Holofernes—yet struggles to cast away the sinful passion." In effect, the gulf between Judith and her townspeople now widens to separate Judith from her own feelings. That is, even though Judith does not feel at one with the other Bethulians, their suffering and God's plan for her conspire to alienate Judith from the first pangs of love she has felt since the death of her husband. This plot device finds its fullest expression in the penultimate scene, when Judith is invited to drink and feast with Holofernes.

The decapitation scene itself is actually quite brief. Judith enters Holofernes' tent and asks him to send Bagoas away so that she may serve him alone. She continues to force more and more drink on him and cozies up to him; he eventually passes out. Judith then picks up Holofernes' own sword. It is obvious that Griffith departs from the apocryphal narrative here, for Judith seems quite reluctant to grasp the sword, and one senses that she is perhaps too dainty to do so, a weakness completely at odds with the apocryphal Judith. She holds the sword aloft and then hesitates when Holofernes stirs, obviously racked with conflicting emotions. She loves Holofernes, but she is an instrument of God chosen to deliver her town from certain death. To emphasize her inner conflict, Griffith shows us brief views of dead Bethulians at the town's well and inside the town starving people, including Nathan, who seems to be taking his last drink of water. Karl Brown, assistant to Griffith's cameraman Billy Bitzer, later recalled the importance of this sequence:

> His [Griffith's] highest objective, as nearly as I could grasp it, was to photograph thought. He could do it, too. I'd seen it. In *Judith of Bethulia* there was a scene in which Judith stands over the sleeping figure of Holofernes, sword in hand. She raises the sword, and then falters. Pity and mercy have weakened her to a point of helpless irresolution. Her face softens to something that is almost love. Then she thinks, and as she thinks the screen is filled with the mangled bodies of those, her own people, slain by this same Holofernes. Then her face becomes filled with hate as she summons all her strength to bring that sword whistling down upon the neck of what is no longer a man but a blood-reeking monster.[20]

Judith finally accepts her fate and cuts off Holofernes' head. She seems immediately sickened by the act and drops the sword in disgust— again, in contrast to the apocryphal story, where she is almost businesslike in her execution of Holofernes. After she and her maid retrieve Holofernes' decapitated head, they return to Bethulia. Miraculously, the Bethulian soldiers still have enough energy to rout the Assyrians, who retreat in a panic after discovering Holofernes' headless body. For her part, Judith immediately returns to her secluded space, and as she observes the soldiers rush out of the city gates, she looks on in horror. Nathan rescues Naomi, bringing closure to that story line as well. At the end of the film, Judith leaves her secluded house and revels in the adoration and praise of the Bethulians. If she has any regrets or is forlorn over killing Holofernes, she does not show it. Thus, Griffith embraces the apocryphal narrative's ending for Judith, in which she is lauded by all and shows no remorse; he abandons Aldrich's ending, where Judith is racked with psychological and emotional distress over killing the man she loves. Interestingly (and perhaps not accidentally), one of the final gestures Judith makes in the film is to caress her own neck; perhaps she is still thinking of her love for Holofernes.

In his work on Griffith's film, William Rothman singles out Judith's ambiguous sexuality for special discussion.[21] In his other films, Griffith tends to idealize women; here he seems to focus on Judith as an embodied or natural woman. He also presents Judith as being aware of her sexuality, even having sexual desire for Holofernes. Rothman claims: "The presentation of the good Judith drawn to the splendid yet brutal Holofernes is perhaps unique in all of Griffith's films in its acknowledgment, and acceptance, of the dark side of a woman's sexual desire."[22] However, the fact that Judith assumes a "man's role" in saving her town complicates her already ambiguous presentation in the film. In this respect, Griffith's Judith is similar to the apocryphal character, as Amy-Jill Levine notes: "Present in the public sphere, sexually active and socially involved, she endangers hierarchical oppositions of gender, race, and class, muddles conventional gender characteristics and dismantles their claims to universality, and so threatens the status quo."[23] Thus, in both the apocryphal story and Griffith's film, Judith questions assumptions of gender and appropriate behavior.

Based on the provocative nature of Judith's character, Rothman addresses the intersection between Judith's "masculine" nature and

Griffith's more conventional perception(s) and subsequent presentations of women like Naomi:

> *Judith of Bethulia* centers on the dramatic struggle within Judith—spiritual, yet imaged in sexual terms and mirrored by the armed struggle between the Bethulians and the Assyrians—to perform an act that appears to deny her womanly nature. How can this struggle, and specifically its triumphant and liberating resolution, be reconciled with the affirmation, fundamental to Griffith's work, of an order in which sexuality can be fulfilled naturally only through love within a marriage?[24]

Rothman posits that Griffith, in a complicated and mainly symbolic fashion, allows Judith to be fulfilled as a woman (in his view), yet still perform her violent, "manly" act. Briefly, since Judith is a widow, her womanhood has already been achieved, but, in Griffith's view, she would still need a man to provide a child in order to fulfill her role as a woman. Because of her affection for Holofernes, the viewer may suspect that he is the one who will "fulfill" her. However, because of his failure to capture Bethulia, as well as his willingness to become intoxicated, Judith realizes that she actually has power over him and is thus free to carry out, in a proper "womanly" role, the vision presented to her by God. Rothman comments on this process:

> When she displays the severed head in the marketplace, she acts as Bethulia's triumphant leader, revealing—to her people and to us—that she has assumed her dead husband's place....The moment at which she unmasks Holofernes, the moment at which she gives herself completely to this higher power, is the moment of her fulfillment as a woman. Yet, paradoxically, this is also the moment at which she performs a man's act, is transformed into a man. This paradox is fundamental to Griffith's understanding of what it is to be a woman. When her trust is threatened, a true woman reveals that she possesses a man within her.[25]

Finally, in terms of fulfilling her role as mother, Rothman claims that since Judith restores life to Bethulia, she can be seen as the mother of the city. Thus, according to Rothman's analysis, Griffith's gender ideology is still present in the film, albeit muted. However, the presence of these assumptions does not diminish the power and impact of Judith's character: even though Griffith's ideas about gender and appropriately "womanly" roles may still be present, Judith's story can still affect the way viewers and readers imagine gender relationships, as Levine writes: "Each time her story is told, this woman who represented the community as well as exceeded that representation will both reinforce and challenge Bethulia's—and the reader's—gender-determined ideology."[26]

As noted above, the portrait of Judith in Griffith's film has received little scholarly attention, perhaps because of the perceived status of the film in the context of Griffith's work. For instance, at the end of the film, Griffith seems to give up his attempt to psychologize Judith, as Aldrich does, and simply allows the character to relish the praise of her townspeople without trying to delve more deeply into her emotional state. This reticence on his part is not in keeping with his attempt to flesh out Judith's character earlier in the film, and as such it represents a significant weakness.[27] Many critics have commented on the film's shortcomings over the years. Richard Schickel, one of Griffith's most important biographers, remarks:

> The film is, on the whole, unsuccessful....What one applauds here is a noble ambition, not a fully realized one....Compared with the spectacles from abroad, *Judith* was perhaps superior. But compared with the standards Griffith had set in his shorter films and would shortly establish in his longer works, it cannot be judged as more than a most interesting transitional film.[28]

Edward Wagenknecht and Anthony Slide disagree with Schickel's overall disapproval of the film, yet still criticize Griffith's work: "The battle scenes in *Judith* are, perhaps, the biggest disappointment. The staging is quite frankly a mess, and there is every sign of a small group of people desperately pretending to be a crowd."[29]

On the other hand, I agree with Robert M. Henderson and Rothman in their positive appraisal of the film. Henderson describes the film as "the crowning achievement of Griffith's career at Biograph, not for its length alone. *Judith* makes use of almost all the cinematic advances that Griffith had perfected in his shorter films."[30] In turn, Rothman notes, "Everything points to the conclusion that *Judith of Bethulia* is a key film in Griffith's career. Indeed, it is a film of considerable compositional complexity, thematic directness, and cinematic artistry."[31]

In sum, *Judith of Bethulia* is more than just a transition piece in Griffith's early output. It shows Griffith pushing the boundaries of early cinema, perhaps in response to new, longer films from Europe like *Quo Vadis?*, released in April 1913. It also foreshadows some of Griffith's most important work, such as his controversial masterpiece, *The Birth of a Nation*, and his cinematic response to his critics, *Intolerance*. Placing the film in its historical and literary context, as well as understanding what Aldrich and Griffith are trying to accomplish, allows us as viewers and readers to understand the story of Judith in a more profound way than before. The importance of this understanding lies in the recognition that the biblical text is not static, and that artistic interpretations, like Aldrich and Griffith's, deserve to be taken seriously. Once we accept the validity of artistic interpretations, we are able to use them to elucidate unwritten undercurrents in the biblical text, so that the story world of the text becomes more alive to us. We can then approach the text with fresh eyes, fresh ears, and even fresh minds.

NOTES

[1] Interestingly, one of the most recent treatments of Judith and its artistic and cultural recycling mentions Griffith's film only in passing. See Margarita Stocker, *Judith, Sexual Warrior: Women and Power in Western Culture* (New Haven & London: Yale University Press, 1998), 146, 184, and 200.

[2] For example, see Edna Purdie, *The Story of Judith in German and English Literature* (Paris: Librarie Ancienne Honoré Champien, 1927); Patricia Montley, "Judith in the Fine Arts: The Appeal of the Archetypal Androgyne," *Anima* 4 (1978): 37-42; Diane Apostolos-Cappadona, "'The Lord Struck Him Down by the Hand of a Woman': Images of Judith," in *Art as Religious Meaning* (eds. Diane Apostolos-Cappadona and Doug Adams; New York: Crossroad, 1987), 81-97; David A. Radavich, "A Catalogue of Works Based on the Apocryphal Book of Judith, from the Mediaeval Period to the Present," *Bulletin of Bibliography* 44 (1987): 189-92; Raymond J. Frontain, "The Price of Rubies: The Weight of Old Testament Women in Western Literature," in *Old Testament Women in Western Literature* (eds. R. Frontain and J. Wojcik; Conway: University of Central Arkansas Press, 1991), 2-19; Elizabeth Philpot, "Judith and Holofernes: Changing Images in the History of Art," in *Translating Religious Texts: Translation, Transgression, and Interpretation* (ed. D. Jasper; Studies in Literature and Religion; New York: St. Martin, 1993), 80-97; and, most recently, Stocker, *Judith, Sexual Warrior*.

[3] See Thomas Bailey Aldrich, *Judith and Holofernes: A Poem*, (Boston & New York: Houghton, Mifflin and Company, 1896); and *Judith of Bethulia: A Tragedy* (Boston & New York: Houghton, Mifflin and Company, 1904).

[4] J. B. Kaufman, "*Judith of Bethulia*: Un 'Piccolo' Film Epico / *Judith of Bethulia*: Producing the 'Little' Epic," *Griffithiana* 50 (1994): 179.

[5] Aldrich, *Judith and Holofernes: A Poem*, v-vi.

⁶Renate Peters, "D. W. Griffith's Transformation of the Legend of Judith" (paper presented at the Canadian Comparative Literature Arts Conference, 1998), 5. I would like to thank Peters for her graciousness in allowing me to use her unpublished work for this paper.

⁷Aldrich, *Judith of Bethulia: A Tragedy*, 50.

⁸See Carey A. Moore, *Judith* (Anchor Bible 40; Garden City: Doubleday, 1985), 78-85 and *passim*. Moore views irony as the key to interpreting Judith.

⁹Aldrich, *Judith of Bethulia: A Tragedy*, 97.

¹⁰Aldrich, *Judith of Bethulia: A Tragedy*, 98.

¹¹Stocker, *Judith, Sexual Warrior*, 185.

¹²Peters, "D. W. Griffith's Transformation of the Legend of Judith," 6.

¹³Evidently, Biograph purchased the treatment from Pierce in April 1913. Kaufman, "*Judith of Bethulia*," 179, raises the possibility that Pierce may have been a fictitious character, but quickly disproves the theory. See also Robert M. Henderson, *D. W. Griffith: The Years at Biograph* (New York, Farrar, Straus and Giroux, 1970), 151-52, and Richard Schickel, *D. W. Griffith: An American Life* (New York: Simon and Schuster, 1984), 191. Kaufman, 189, n. 2, is also intrigued by the fact that there was a film version of Judith prior to Griffith's: in 1907, Cines Roma released a one-reel picture titled *Giuditta e Oloferne*, which was first shown in the United States in 1908. Griffith may have been influenced by it as well.

¹⁴See Henderson, *D. W. Griffith: The Years at Biograph*, 154-55.

¹⁵For a complete list, see *ibid.*, 155-56.

¹⁶Kaufman, "*Judith of Bethulia*," 185, discusses the different versions of the film produced over the years. The version used for this paper is the Kino International version, drawn mainly from Biograph's 1917 elaboration of Griffith's film titled *Her Condoned Sin*.

¹⁷This juxtaposition of plots foreshadows his more successful attempt in *Intolerance* in 1916. For an excellent overview of *Intolerance*, see Scott Simmon, *The Films of D. W. Griffith* (Cambridge Film Classics; Cambridge & New York: Cambridge University Press, 1993), 137-60. For a discussion of the portrayal of Jesus in *Intolerance*, see W. Barnes Tatum, *Jesus at the Movies: A Guide to the First Hundred Years* (Santa Rosa: Polebridge Press, 1997), 33-43.

¹⁸Peters, "D. W. Griffith's Transformation of the Legend of Judith," 8.

¹⁹For an analysis of *The Birth of a Nation*, see Simmon, *The Films of D. W. Griffith*, 104-36.

²⁰Karl Brown, *Adventures with D. W. Griffith* (New York: Farrar, Straus and Giroux, 1973), 21.

²¹William Rothman, "D. W. Griffith's Judith of Bethulia," *Twentieth-Century Literary Criticism* 68 (1997): 216.

²²Rothman, "D. W. Griffith's Judith of Bethulia," 217.

²³Amy-Jill Levine, "Sacrifice and Salvation: Otherness and Domestication in the Book of Judith," in *A Feminist Companion to Esther, Judith, and Susanna* (ed. Athalya Brenner; FCB 7; Sheffield: Sheffield Academic Press, 1995), 209.

[24]Rothman, "D. W. Griffith's Judith of Bethulia," 218.

[25]Rothman, "D. W. Griffith's Judith of Bethulia," 219.

[26]Levine, "Sacrifice and Salvation," 222-23.

[27]For this position, see Robert M. Henderson, *D. W. Griffith: His Life and Work* (New York: Oxford University Press, 1972), 129-30.

[28]Schickel, *D. W. Griffith: An American Life*, 192.

[29]Edward Wagenknecht and Anthony Slide, *The Films of D. W. Griffith* (New York: Crown, 1975), 29.

[30]Henderson, *D. W. Griffith: His Life and Work*, 127.

[31]Rothman, "D. W. Griffith's Judith of Bethulia," 215.

Creative Expressions of Resistance: Original Theater of Orthodox Israeli Women

Reina Rutlinger-Reiner

Until recently, theatrical activity was regarded amongst traditional Jews as idolatrous, or at least *bitul Torah* [a waste of time that should be dedicated to Torah]. The concept of women's theater, even when presented to an all-women audience, has been seen as completely contrary to the ideal of the modest Jewish woman as she is described in Psalms 45:14: "The king's daughter (the royal princess) is all glorious within." Nonetheless, in the past few years, Orthodox women have initiated all-women theater productions. Within this non-traditional artistic activity, constraints of propriety, halacha, and tradition are respected, often at the expense of artistic freedom. The fact that most women's theater troupes perform exclusively before all-women audiences limits their ability to influence their communities, since men, who constitute "important and culturally esteemed spiritual venues," cannot witness their performance; yet it also means that "women have some level of autonomy in developing their own perspectives, constructing their own value system, managing their own resources and forging their own rituals."[1] The result is sometimes called by anthropologists an "alternative reality," "women's subculture," or "women's second world."[2]

CHANGES AMONG ISRAELI ORTHODOX WOMEN

This newly-accepted artistic activity is, in my opinion, yet another example of the changes taking place in the status of Orthodox women in Israel over the past decade. Orthodox women have become involved in politics (especially after the Oslo agreements in 1994), in the study of Torah and Talmud (yeshivas for women have opened all over the country), and specially trained Orthodox women appear in litigation in rabbinical courts after intensively studying halachic regulations in

connection with *toanot rabaniot* [divorce laws]. In addition, the voice of
Orthodox women has surfaced for the public to see, read, and hear in
the fields of art, literature, film, journalism, and visual arts. What is
most interesting about Orthodox women's theater in Israel is it has
forced male rabbinic authority to deal with the relationship between
art and religion generally. As a result, it has transformed the traditional,
negative attitude towards theater into its acceptance as a legitimate
form of artistic and religious expression. Another result of Orthodox
women's initiatives is the formation of all-male theater groups, whose
members are yeshiva graduates. These men have followed in the women's
footsteps and in some ways are now even more active and successful
than them.

THE INVOLVEMENT OF RABBIS IN ORTHODOX WOMEN'S THEATER

Many of the women involved in theater do not separate themselves
from male authority in questions of halacha relating to their theater
work. They consult with rabbis when any doubts or questions arise
about writing or directing, even though most rabbis are not familiar
with this art form (some have only rarely attended the theater, much
less studied it). For example, a group working in Bat Ayen, headed by
Dina Shohat, was told by the rabbi they consulted to create a visible
distinction between themselves and the biblical figures of the mothers,
Rachel and Leah, they were portraying onstage. The artistic solution
they found in order to comply with the demands of the rabbi was to
use Greek masks.

Some rabbis wish to limit Orthodox women's theater in content
and form when they are consulted, but they are not always consulted.
Other rabbis are willing to take what they call the "risk" of allowing
Orthodox women to explore their deep religious feelings through theater
without intervening in the process; they will accept the consequences if
the theatrical productions become subversive. These rabbis are in the
minority in Israel, belonging to the "modern Orthodox" element.

ORTHODOX WOMEN'S THEATER AS ACTIVISM

The nature of Orthodox actresses' art and discourse resembles activist
cultural practices that have existed in the West since the 1960s. Common
to both is their democratic impulse to give voice and visibility to the
disenfranchised and to connect art to a wider audience: they are process-

rather than object- or product-oriented, and both are collaborative art forms that challenge art-world notions of individual authorship and the cult of the artist.[3] Yet, as younger and more professional women form new theater groups or join existing ones, I believe the field will change rapidly from a community-activist type of art to a much more professional one.

One woman who has been very active in the field for the past few years, Dina Shohat, initiated the theater group, "The Jewish Point." She lives in the small settlement of Bat Ayen in Gush Etzion between Bethlehem and Jerusalem. Most of the inhabitants of this settlement are artists who are *chozrim betshuva*, that is, Jews not raised in Orthodox homes who have become observant and affiliated with contemporary Hassidic tendencies. Shohat, for example, is closely connected to Chabad Hassidism. She has directed and produced three plays in the past six years for all-women audiences, comprising ultra-Orthodox and Orthodox alike. When she hears that her children are opposed to her putting on a new play she says:

> I hear what they are saying and I understand them. I know it is not easy for them when I go out in the evening, so I try to compensate for my absence at other times. Yet I think the importance of the matter justifies the effort. Especially women with large families—most of their attention is directed to the children and the home. They should have the opportunity to express their creativity and apply their talents elsewhere, too.[4]

THE TEXTS

Most theater groups are not interested in dealing with existing texts from the Western repertoire. Searching archives to discover suitable texts is not favored by troupe members. They demonstrate their ability to create innovative and unique Jewish theater by writing original texts based on the Jewish canon—biblical passages describing dilemmas and choices of biblical figures (usually female, such as Rachel and Leah), passages from the Talmud, Hassidic tales, and stories of righteous Jews— as well as personal monologues narrating life histories of themselves or members of their families. These original plays demonstrate the relevance of the religious canon and religious belief to everyday life.

EXAMPLES

The following are examples of what I would term avant-garde type theater, which by its nature is more subversive and critical of Orthodox norms and Israeli society than other forms or genres. Like mainstream Israeli theater, its themes are predominantly secular and leftist, and may seem bewildering or off-putting to those who have close ties to Israel, since they tend "to de-romanticize certain traditional elements of Jewry."[5] But not all theater performances by Orthodox women are subversive. Those theater groups or individual performers who are considered mainstream ("kosher" in the eyes of the Orthodox authorities) tend to use story-telling techniques and are therefore more static and conservative in style. Thus, it follows that the works I have chosen to describe constitute only a small selection of a wide range of theatrical activity, ranging from conventional to subversive, among Orthodox women in Israel.

"CAN THIS BE NAOMI?"

This student production took place in the late 1990s; its title comes from a verse in *Megillat Ruth*. The only sentence heard at the end of the scene is this rhetorical question: "Can this be Naomi?" an exclamation uttered by the women of Bethlehem when Naomi, formerly a rich, respected woman, returned to the city, transformed into a poor widow after her sons die in Moav.

The scene describes a young married woman calmly and sweetly setting the Shabbat table while humming the traditional "Eshet Hayil" [Woman of Valor], a tune sung before Kiddush, the blessing of the wine on Friday evening. The lyrics, taken from the last chapter of Proverbs, praise the Jewish woman, perfect in every way: in the household, in her righteousness, in her wisdom, and in her love of God. It is a song that is used repeatedly as background music in scenes of Orthodox women, usually to highlight the contrast between the expectations for Jewish women and reality. Throughout the scene, the actress hums the tune and acknowledges the presence of the audience as witnesses, by smiling at them and gesturing to them, as she places ritual objects—such as a white table cloth, candles, and challahs [special braided loaves of bread eaten on Shabbat]—on the table as if she were sharing a common experience with the all-woman audience; they know, as does she, exactly what objects should placed, how, and where. As the actress incorporates the audience into her scene, they share with her this timeless weekly ritual of setting the table and preparing Shabbat.

What takes the audience by surprise is that her calm smile, gestures, and nods, together with the sweet humming, persist even after she turns upside down all the exactly positioned ritual objects. For example, she lays the bottle of wine face down, she shakes salt all over the table, takes the candles out of their candlesticks, and throws flowers from the vase onto the floor. She even bares her body by taking off her white head covering and white shirt—she is now seen wearing a tight fitted black dress with a daring neckline, exposing the contours of her pregnant body. These actions are performed in the same calm tempo and with the same deliberation as the first. She continues to perform them in this way as she ties the four corners of the tablecloth over the disarrayed objects, as if to wrap them up and get them out of sight. Not only her modesty but also the sincerity of her actions are questioned in the preparation of the Shabbat table, the symbol of Jewish unity and family life.

At the end of the scene, this actress, who has dared to defy what is expected from her and chosen to rebel by causing chaos, turns her back on the audience, the witnesses to this transformation, and looks at her reflection in a mirror placed at the rear of the stage. The reflection is unfamiliar and frightening; when she turns back to the audience, she echoes the exclamation of the women of Bethlehem: "Can this be Naomi?" As she asks this rhetorical question, her calm, smiling face is transformed into one contorted by anger and urgency, suggesting that underneath the surface of the ideal Jewish woman—sweet, perfect, and conforming to Orthodox norms—there lurks the a frightening potential to rebel. The scene, which begins as a charming affirmation of the customary Orthodox way of life for a young, married woman, ends with the destruction of the Shabbat table. Public exposure of anger and frustration thus question her desire or ability to be the woman of valor she is expected to be.

It is not surprising that this scene met with resistance, especially from older women who were policy-makers at the institution from which the actress was about to graduate. They were shocked that a student was questioning the validity of the basic tenets of Orthodox life; the fact that this was done in a public arena, the stage, by a "product" of their education shocked them even more. The deliberate actions so familiar to all made this theatrical scene:

an intrusion that sees through for the eye that otherwise cannot look. It is theater returning to its root sense as a way of seeing the world while we are conscious of our partial removal from its flow. What we are allowed to see in theater is the mystery of the ordinary: real, but always in its paradox this removal is accompanied by a shift in emotional grounding.[6]
The actress's subjective experience—challenging as it did official, monolithic, dominant formulations of the ideal Jewish woman—encountered aggressive resistance from the older members of the audience immediately after the performance and at many staff meetings that followed. The outcome of this resistance was a complete change in the policy of the college with regards to theatrical productions (which would henceforth be monitored far more closely), the resignation of one of the secular directors involved in this production, and the hospitalization of the actress, who was pregnant. due to the intensive stress she experienced.

"HERITAGE"
In the explanation I received from the performer of this piece, she indicated that she wished to show her ambivalence towards her heritage as a Yemenite Jewess, especially in connection with women's prayers. She recorded her father and brother reciting one of the central prayers of Yom Kippur, in Yemenite dialect, as background music. This is the only prayer in the liturgy that she can relate to and recite in Yemenite dialect since, unlike her brother, girls are not sent to the *Mori* [Yemenite religious tutor] to learn how to recite prayers or read the Torah. She dances according to the traditional Yeminite style, but the movements she uses are typical of Yemenite men; a Yemenite woman would never dance in this manner. Throughout her performance, she changes the distance between an upright empty seat wrapped in prayer shawls (symbolizing the prayers and associated rituals exclusively performed by men) and herself, the female dancing in male style. This unconscious "play" with gender through movement and dance is concluded when the actress adopts a typically feminine position, her hands folded over her chest with eyes tilted upwards, as if to minimize the space she is taking for herself. In this way she returns to her traditional place, posture, and voice as she softly joins in the prayer, as observant Jewish Yemenite women do in the women's section of the synagogue. Yet identification with her heritage is not complete: she joins in the prayer, but not in the Yemenite dialect heard in the background. She retains her Israeli accent

while reciting the prayer. This is intentional and serves to demonstrate how ambivalent she is about her heritage. On the one hand, she embraces and celebrates its active, masculine liturgy and hegemony; on the other, even after assuming this typically feminine position, she joins in the prayer using the accent of a modern Orthodox Israeli-born woman, thereby showing that she also cannot fully identify with her Jewish Yemenite heritage.

ORTHODOX WOMEN AND THE ACRE ALTERNATIVE THEATER

In 2001, the Alternative Theater of Acre accepted a group of young religious women to work weekly with two male directors on its staff. After a few months, a performance comprised of personal monologues was presented to a small audience of friends and family members. These women, some married and one of them already a mother, are university graduates who have studied theater, but wish to perform as a group because they feel their common background allows them more freedom to explore their lives as religious women They leave their homes every Thursday afternoon and travel to Acre to work together throughout the night until the early hours of Friday morning. They sleep for a few hours in the Haifa area, as guests of some of the members' parents, and later travel home so that they arrive before Shabbat. The two scenes I describe below deal directly with social and political problems in Israel today.

In Honor Of...And In Honor Of The State Of Israel
This scene is a parody of the "sacred" secular ceremony that takes place on Mt. Herzl in Jerusalem on the evening between Memorial Day and the Day of Independence, when twelve torches (representing the tribes of Israel) are lit by people who have been specifically chosen for their contributions to Israeli society or their family connections. The language used by this group of actresses is formulated in accordance with the official national rhetoric heard on this occasion. However, instead of a formal and dignified scene, they reduce the ceremony to something sloppy and infantile. For example, the torches, some of which are not even lit, are swayed to and fro by actresses who have lined themselves against the walls of the ancient fortress of Acre singing about "Women of Valor." They use parody, as when each torch-lighter mentions figures of popular culture not considered very respectable or de-legitimizes the

importance of others. The target of the parody is the Israeli secular
lifestyle and its values. "The availability of cross reading between cultures
and theater performances allows the hegemonic to be interrogated,
exposed or even subverted."[7] This ironic presentation of popular heroes
of secular Israeli culture in the context of the most revered secular
ceremony of the Israeli calendar aims to strip both the ceremony and
the objects of adoration of their significance.

After each actress recites her piece, she runs up the ramp of one of
the fortress walls from the grassy area where she has been standing with
the audience. She holds the torch high, standing erect in a frozen position,
awaiting the end of the ceremony. Then "Woman of Valor" is sung in
unison, the performers swaying with the torches high above their heads.
The text is translated as follows:[8]

> I, Rachel, the daughter of Yona, am honored to light this torch
> in honor of the women who support (stick up for) their husbands
> and manipulate state affairs: Yaffa Derei, Sara Netanyahu, and
> Lili Sharon [the wives of Israeli politicians and former politicians
> who are known to be active in their husbands' careers and on
> their behalf].

> I, Nirit, the daughter of Ella, am honored to light this torch in
> honor of the heroines of our culture: Sandy Bar, Dana
> International, and Judy Nir-Moses [a model, a transvestite who
> is a singer and won first prize in the Eurovision Song contest
> two years ago, and a rich, populist journalist, who is also the
> wife of a Minister of Finance].

> I, Nehama the daughter of Ella, am honored to light this torch
> in honor of a woman, a mother and a brave business woman:
> Pnina Rosenblum [a self-made, very successful, attractive
> businesswoman who also has political aspirations].

> I, Rachel, daughter of Yona, am honored to light this torch in
> honor and memory of Leah Rabin, who even in times of feud
> and crisis did not prevent the spirit of national unity from
> pulsating from within her. [She is insinuating the opposite:
> Lea Rabin insisted that the inscription at the memorial for her
> husband in Tel Aviv state that the assassin was a Jew who wore
> a *kippa* (head-covering worn by Orthodox men). In the traumatic
> months following Rabin's assassination, this insistence stirred
> up a wave of antagonism by secular Israelis against the Orthodox
> and of ill feelings by the Orthodox against the secular].

I, Orly, daughter of Aviva, am honored to light this torch in honor of all the women here who reinforce the spirit of the Jewish woman—in honor of my mother, yours, theirs; it is only thanks to their righteousness that we are present today.

Theater as a Holy Activity
In addition to being a space for self-expression and social criticism, some actresses feel their theatrical activity is holy [*avodat kodesh*], an extension of their worship of God; it is a space for religious self-exploration denied them by their traditional "second class status in the Orthodox synagogue," as Blu Greenberg defines it.[9]

One of the scenes by the Acre group deals with the experience of ecstasy in prayer. The actress in this scene, dressed in a white robe and white head covering, receives instruction from an Arab director on how to achieve religious ecstasy according to the Sufi tradition. She twirls around on the first floor, while the director stands with the audience and her fellow actresses high above her on a wooden platform that serves as the second floor. She keeps asking him for practical instructions about how to use her hands and how to spin, but his answers to her practical questions are instead philosophical: "Let God come to you rather than you try coming to God" or "Make yourself invisible." In the background, the other actresses are singing a Hassidic chant taken from the famous prayer, "Aveenu Malkenu [Our Father, Our King]," which affirms the Lord as the one and only God. This scene fits Jerzy Grotowsky's definition of the actor as "a person drawn from theater for purposes trans-theatrical, spiritual."[10] The technique she uses resembles the ones he used in his theater work; namely, encouraging the search for truth through the mobilization of all the actor's physical and spiritual forces, as speech becomes incantation and the actor totally beyond the reach of the spectators, performing a "sacred act."[11]

THE APPROPRIATION OF THEATER BY ORTHODOX WOMEN
Theater "is the most secular of all Israel's cultural achievements,"[12] and its adoption by Orthodox circles may bring about what Gershon Shaked calls "a neo-Jewish theater" and possibly lead to a fusion of Western, secular, artistic values with religious, Judaic values and materials. In addition to its influence on cultural practices within Orthodox society, this new trend takes place at the same time the secular Israeli population has begun to take an interest in learning about "the Jewish bookcase"

(Jewish literature). Orthodox women's theater may thus contribute towards a new cultural dialogue between the two main factions of Israeli society, secular and religious.

I would like to close with this translation of a prayer written and recited by Yael Shechter several years ago, before she and her fellow actresses went onstage in a production called "Time Out—Woman," directed by Amalia Shachal and performed in front of an all-woman audience in Haifa:

A pure heart the Lord has created me
Allow me, God, to create out of purity
Make it possible to create from the holy.
You, who create worlds
And I, that have been created in your image
and draw my creativity from you .
Each one of us was given tools with which he can
Discover Godliness in the universe
And to me, you have given the "imaginary powers,"
The need to act and the possibility to "meet" characters.
My soul is beckoning me to create, to discover, to express and transfer
In my words and
My body—the holy.
Please give me the privilege to activate this holiness.
Make me a tool for your calling
May it be your will that I will not stumble or fail and not become proud
Because everything is yours—and it is all from you.
Amen.

NOTES

[1] Susan Sered, "She Perceives Her Work to Be Rewarding," in *Feminist Perspectives on Jewish Studies* (ed. L. Davidman and S. Tenenbaum; New Haven: Yale University, 1994), 169-86.
[2] *Ibid.*, 174.
[3] Nina Felshim: *But is it Art? The Spirit of Art as Activism* (Seattle: Bay, 1995).
[4] In an interview with the author, 1999.
[5] Linda Ben Zvi, ed., *Theater in Israel.* (Ann Arbor: University of Michigan, 1996), ix.

[6]Geoff Pywell, *Staging Real Things: The Performance of Ordinary Events* (Lewisburg: Bucknell University Press, 1994), 31. See also Norman K. Denzin, *Interpretive Ethnography: Ethnographic Practices for the 21ˢᵗ Century* (Thousand Oaks: Sage, 1997), 267.

[7]Janelle Reinelt, *Crucibles of Crisis: Performing Social Change* (Ann Arbor: University of Michigan, 1996), 8 .

[8]Translated by the author.

[9]Blu Greenberg, *On Women and Judaism: A View from Tradition* (Philadelphia: The Jewish Publication Society of America, 1981), 88.

[10]Richard Schechner, "Exoduction: Shape-shifter, Shaman, Trickster, Artist, Adept Director, Leader Grotowski," in *The Grotowski Sourcebook* (eds. L. Wolford and R. Schechner; London: Routledge, 1998), 456-92.

[11]*Ibid.*

[12] Gershon Shaked, "Actors as Reflections of Their Generation: Cultural Interactions between Israeli Actors, Playwrights, Directors and Theaters" in *Theater in Israel* (ed. L. Ben-Zvi; Ann Arbor: University of Michigan Press, 1996), 85-101.

Fixing It and Fitting In: Contemporary Jewish American Women Artists

Ori Z. Soltes

PROLOGUE: ISSUES AND IDEAS

There is a natural question that many modern Jewish artists have asked themselves: "Where do I, as a Jewish artist in the West, fit within the history of Western art, a history that has for much of the past sixteen centuries been essentially Christian?" For American Jewish artists in particular, the growing participation of immigrant artists wrapped itself around a second question: "How do I fit in as an American, and how do I visually articulate my American identity as one of the array of issues, ideas, and elements that suffuse my art?"

During the last quarter of the twentieth century, perhaps the most noteworthy group of contributors to American art, in particular among American Jewish artists, has been women. Like their male counterparts, Jewish women artists have been drawn to a range of subjects. Some give no obvious evidence of confronting issues beyond the aesthetic challenges of the media in which they work, but this propensity seems rarer than that of interweaving aesthetic with other concerns. If Jewish artists address questions of identity that pertain to the connection between their Jewishness, their work, and the world, Jewish women artists often address an additional question pertaining to the connection between their Jewishness and their selves as women. Thus, "How do I fit into Western (largely Christian) art as a Jew?" becomes interwoven with "How do I fit into Judaism and Jewish art as a woman?" The range of work by American Jewish women artists is both broader and more complex than these formulae might suggest, as even a small sampling can show.[1]

AESTHETICS WITHIN AND BEYOND JEWISH QUESTIONS

The *Alluvial Paintings* (1995-2000) of Elaine Kurtz, contrived of paint mixed with sand, minerals, and pebbles poured and dispersed over the canvas, create crusty ridges and mounds [fig. 1]. Abstract, they also suggest formations in nature, their mysterious and misty quality recalling nineteenth century Romanticism. Pouring onto the floor-bound canvas and rotating it to assert some control over the shapes formed upon it recall Helen Frankenthaler's work, but there are sharp contrasts. Frankenthaler offered pigment thinned to the delicacy of watercolor in contrast to the thick, dense, slow-moving compound offered by Kurz. Her canvasses are river deltas, glacial flows, and interior landscapes, visual metaphors for the very process of creating them as they redefine the parameters of painting. Redefinition is certainly not only a Jewish prerogative, but many Jews have engaged in that type of creative act.[2]

fig. 1 *Alluvial Painting*

Susan Schwalb's work is similar to Kurtz's in being abstract, different in being non-gestural. It is finely-textured, nearly smooth, where Kurtz's is rough-textured. It is also opposite in the way it addresses the ongoing question of Jewish art within in a non-Jewish world. This is most apparent in Schwalb's series of triptychs titled *Creation.* Where Kurtz' paintings imply the very magma of geological creation of the earth, Schwalb addresses the biblical account. Schwalb's triptychs offer completely abstract compositions, inspired by the opening images of the famous *Sarajevo Haggadah.* "Creation XX" (1990) [fig. 2] presents six circles swirling in silverpoint against an earth-brown background in its lower register, separated from the sky blue background above by a white gold leaf frame. Embedded in the upper register is a circle identical to those below, but much larger. Creation has been re-visioned in the abstract and endless geometry of the circle. The artist has thus redefined this Christian form of visual self-expression, with its triune symbolism, in the general terms of non-figuration and the specific historical terms of her own source of inspiration. She writes:

When I first came across the *Sarajevo Haggadah* I was powerfully stirred to find images of arc and circle....Unlike familiar Christian portrayals of the creation, the image of God is not represented. But sun, moon and earth are clearly rendered by circular forms.[3]

fig. 2 *Creation XX*

Certain of Schwalb's works, such as "Beginnings" (1988), add a downward-pointing triangle with vertical line from mid-base to apex to this arc/circle configuration, a symbol of the female traceable to Neolithic art. The role of artistic creator so long suppressed for women is restored in the very textures of the silverpoint surface she works. Thousands of fine lines engender an active energy—flesh-like, water-like, sky-like— within the static confines of the framing forms. It suggests both the watery depths over which God swoops in Genesis 1:2 and the amniotic fluid of the womb, connecting the birth of humans to the birth of the universe.

If Kurtz in part evokes Romanticism, and Schwalb turns back to the medieval and Renaissance periods for inspiration, significant portions of Ruth Mordecai's work connect to Western antiquity. They are visually Greek and spiritually Jewish. Mordecai's early turn to the human torso in sculpture and drawing as a meeting point between varied contrapuntal rhythms connects to architecture, particularly Greek. The ultimate curve is an arched form, defined by the surging right side of the body as it turns toward the left from leg to shoulder, as if the casements and arches of doorways have been turned sideways and at angles. Her drawings, collages, and sculptures of 1985-87 vary in scale from the small to the gigantic as they shift from the twisting torso to the swooping arch [fig. 3].

fig. 3 *from Sacred Arch series*

But Mordecai instinctively sensed a connection between the arched form and a specifically Jewish sacred context. She became aware in the mid-eighties of the important role of the arch in the architecture of the early synagogue: the Syrian gable over central doorways of synagogues like Kfar Nahum and Kfar Bar'Am. Expressed, for example, in her *Arch Series: Sacred Place*, this sensibility would carry into the 1990s to her *Altar* series of monoprints and sculptures that, together with her *Seven Series*, offer the sort of large-scale abstract Chromaticism that charts a deliberate course of connection with the work of Barnett Newman, Mark Rothko, Adolph Gottlieb, and Philip Guston.[4]

Rose-Lynn Fisher is both a photographer and a painter. As a painter, she works in a manner that often combines different media as well as figurative and abstract elements. Again and again her landscapes are topsy-turvy exercises in rectilinear perspectival geometries that play with the Albertian issue of transforming a flat surface into the illusion of volumetric space.[5] Her "Doorway" (1995), for example, offers a hilly realm of Rubix Cube-like patterns across which a figure moves, carrying a pair of doors to resemble a St. Andrew's cross. The figure struggles at the horizon with his burden as he crosses a Golgothean landscape. He is what he bears: a doorway. He is the meeting of spiritual and aesthetic realms, and struggles with the weight of transition [fig. 4].

fig. 4 *Doorway*

The only color used in this landscape is a burnt orange shade, copper leaf almost sepia in tone, as if to underscore the allusion to an earlier era of Western art history. The title of the work and its underlying concepts address subtly much of what Fisher's photography, focused on shared elements of Jewish, Christian and Muslim spirituality, addresses overtly: the blurring of edges that separate us from each other in our own minds. As she has written:

> The metaphor of threshold is the thread of constancy in my work. As a point of entry and departure between the known and the unknown, a threshold is the internal structure of spatial, temporal and spiritual transition. Here the sacred meets the mundane, the absurd joins the poignant...a vanishing point becomes visible....Patterns in perspective create distance; patterns in time create tradition.[6]

Fisher's fascination with otherness in time, space, experience, and being places her constantly at the boundaries between the selves that define her: artist, woman, Jew, American, Los Angelina.

Shirley Klinghoffer's work in part comments broadly on the position of women in the American world. The combination of her father's experiences as a Jewish refugee and her mother's battling a long illness helped generate her sensibilities. Her "Doormat" offers a black cast rubber rectangle shaped from fifteen Barbie dolls: paragons of soulless body-perfection in a white American suburban realm, where physical flaws are expected to be as scarce as mud in an entry hall [fig. 5]. If this work carries us over a threshold of humor, Klinghoffer's "Untitled" slumped glass installation, molded from the torsos of women who have survived breast cancer, pushes us toward the boundary between life and death. It is an eighteen-part series (eighteen being the number that in the Jewish tradition symbolizes life). Transparent, glowing figures and quotes from survivors that accompany them suggest both vulnerability and strength.[7]

Artists like Fisher and Klinghoffer wrap their Jewish concerns around larger social issues. They recall the sort of Social Realist sensibilities that defined earlier American Jewish male painters like Raphael Soyer, Ben Shahn, and Jack Levine. The concept of *tikkun olam* [repairing the world] has continued to carry Jewish artists through a range of themes, extending from the oppression of the poor to the threat of nuclear war. Joyce Ellen Weinstein's focus on the difficulties in our world that require repair is close to home. One of the most compelling of these is the predominantly African American high school where she taught for six years, where any of her students might not make it through school alive.

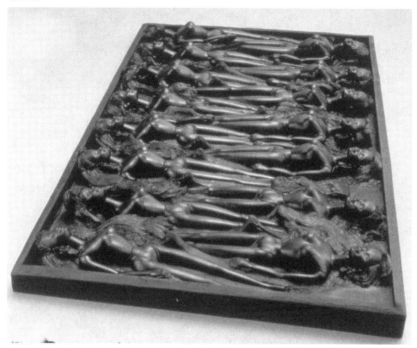

fig. 5 *Doormat*

Weinstein began a series that memorialized *The Bold Dead Boys* [fig. 6] in 1988, continuing to work on it through the mid-1990s:
As I watched the community of youngsters disintegrate around me—twelve of my students were murdered during my six-year tenure—I became more aware of the need for community and of how this community acts like a glue to hold its members together....[This] brought me to a deeper understanding...of my own community as a Jew.[8]
Sixteen portraits and eight smaller details were done in charcoal on paper and dripping red oil paint. These colors of purgatory offer the names "Malcolm," "Kevin," "Robert," "Dean," and the others. Their names and the dates of their births and deaths (none older than twenty-one years old) tell a story that requires no elaboration: their blood cries out to be heard by society.

fig. 6 *The Bold Dead Boys*

fig. 7 *Odalisque*

Similar exercises in societal commentary emanate from Weinstein's portraits of friends, as well as from her play on a recurrent theme in Western art, the "Odalisque" [fig. 7]. This motif, an alluring nude female stretched out along a settee, has been explored variously by artists from Titian to Philip Pearlstein. Weinstein uses the expressionist-distortionist technique found in her portraits to turn a woman into an alien, an almost amphibious being who stares back at us with enormous eyes. The women ogled by generations of male artists and their patrons have suddenly converged and been twisted into a being of tormented calm who ogles men; the distortion is an act of defiance.

Distortionist defiance against stereotypes imposed from within and without can take various forms. Weinstein's "Odalisque" focuses on the issue of women; Deborah Kass is focused on Jews in the repeated images of "Four Barbras (The *Jewish Jackie* Series)" or "Double Red Yentl, Split (My Elvis)" and her enormous "Sandy Koufax." These are overt acts of homage to Andy Warhol and to mass media. But homage is subsumed within the issue of Jewish identity, for Koufax contradicts the non-physical image of the Jew. Further, equating Streisand with Jackie Kennedy suggests a Jewish equivalent to the virtual royalty that defined her in American pop consciousness.[9]

The matter of absorbing and repeating stereotypes about one's self and one's group is also part of what Cynthia Madansky's work is also about. "On the Jewish Question," its title recalling the famous essay written by Karl Marx in 1843-44, asks who and what Jews are in terms that non-Jews have used for centuries. Acquiescencing to stereotype, Marx refers in his essay to money as the Jewish god.[10] Madansky takes Marx's text and literally beats it into panels that are illegible, scarred, and distorted. The panels look remarkably like the metallic plates used to print paper money; they shimmer like giant square coins [fig. 8]. They cut us concisely not only with their commentary on Marx, but with their blurred edges between his Judaism and his Christianity and between text (that preeminent Jewish preoccupation) and visual art (which Jews are said to eschew).

If Madansky grapples with Marx's struggle to fit in as Jew or Christian, Cary Herz's 1994 photographs of a particular group of New Mexican gravestones are part of the record of a different context for this issue [fig. 9]. Her series, *Crypto-Jewish Burial Sites*, is a visual parable of the struggle for and against self-assertion that has so often marked Judaism and is present even among American Jews. Thus, a gravestone bearing

fig. 8 *On the Jewish Question*

the first five commandments of the Decalogue, probably removed from a synagogue and re-used as a gravestone, raises the question of whether the new use was intentionally both Christian and Jewish. Whether such images represent true Crypto-Jews, descended from refugees from Spain, or reflect a more recent form of false Crypto-Judaism—crypto-Crypto-Judaism—they signify the boundary between individual and group and the edge between true and false knowledge of one's roots, as well as between memory and forgetting.[11] For Herz, "this photographic essay

fig. 9 *The Five Commandments*

has redirected me back to my own spiritual center and my Judaism. It has connected me with my own past," even if the question of identity posed by her images finds no definitive scholarly answer, like so many of the other questions defining the Jewish relationship to reality.[12]

One aspect of Jewish American identity that has recently received due attention is the Sephardim, from whom the New Mexico "Crypto-Jews" claim they are descended. Sephardim once accounted for virtually the entire American Jewish population, but the waves of Ashkenazi Jews who washed onto these shores in the last one hundred and fifty years have led to the frequent identification of Ashkenazi as Jewish in terms of customs, traditions, and language. A growing focus on Sephardic Jewish history and culture by American women artists is evident during the past decade.

Sandi Knell Tamny's "The Chosen" is a startling and stunning array of twenty-seven stylized black-painted wooden figures, measuring six and a half feet tall and resembling coffins. Twenty-six of them are individually enhanced with found objects to represent the individual Sephardic Jews they commemorate, from Benedict (Baruch) Spinoza and Menasseh Ben Israel to Camille Pissarro and Annie Nathan Meyer. The twenty-seventh figure represents the thousands whose names and lives remain unknown to us: "Those who were killed; those who converted and killed their Judaism; and the death of Spanish Jewish civilization as a whole."[13]

Very different is Deborah Davidson's enormous "Trace," a hanging that extends from ceiling to floor and then continues along the floor. It is actually an artist's book: each of its ninety-five pieces is a sheet of handmade paper; all are connected by knots that function as hinges and form an unravelling scroll, offering a gigantic text along which a series of narrative lines are traced in five vertical "chapters." Against a variously pigmented background, large black letters trace key words that then trace the edges of a poem, an epitaph found in the Jewish cemetery in Turin, Italy, part of a memorial to its Holocaust victims. Two of those named are Davidson's great-grandmother and great-great-grandmother. On the wall near the hanging she constructs a family tree that leads back to the Spain in 1350 and then forward through a history that ended in part with the Holocaust, but continues in other branches of the family to America and the artist herself. A second text is a Job-like dialogue with God, her identity, and creative/destructive humanity.[14]

QUESTIONS OF THE HOLOCAUST

Gravestones are among the most important dialogue markers between life and death, for they visually connect both the living and the dead and the present and the past. Not surprisingly, among the most interesting places where Jewish visual self-expression has been exercised are the old Jewish cemeteries of Eastern Europe, many of them decimated during or since the Holocaust. As the long reach of the Holocaust extends from generation to generation, one Jewish artist after another feels compelled to address this subject; among contemporary Jewish artists, the number of women artists stirred to respond continues to grow.

The paintings of Geraldine Fiskus include details from single gravestones or from groups of stones. As she wrote several years ago: "Through metaphor they reveal family and religious values which were the locus of community life. As reinventions, they continue the Yiddish culture which ended with the Holocaust."[15] Fiskus' series, *Reinventing the Visual Language of Jewish Stelae of Eastern Europe*, is first of interest due to its intrinsic aesthetic merit and her unusual method of underpainting with black rather than white gesso [fig. 10]. These works also turn her and her viewers to the discussion that dominated her

fig. 10 *detail from Eastern European Grave Markers*

childhood, the Holocaust, and to some of the ways in which Jewish American women artists have addressed that subject: "My life view was formed in this context; punctuated by a profound sense of losing a world which I actually never had."[16] This sense of Holocaust-related loss is most obvious in her larger works in the series, such as "Stele IV: Birds and Fallen Branches" or "Stele VI: Fallen Limbs," where "The cut limbs resonate with the forced separation of Jewish families, the transports of young children taken from their mothers to the death camps."[17] The tree of Jewish life is not uprooted, but it is truncated. It can continue to grow, but in which directions?

Elyse Klaidman's works offer a particular intensity of response. Born in New York City in 1960, she grew up in Washington, D.C., in an environment where she felt little connection to Judaism or the Holocaust. But in 1989, together with her mother, brother, and American-born father, she visited Slovakia and the farmhouse where as small children her mother and uncle had been hidden with their grandparents in the last years of the war. As a result of that visit, Klaidman found herself charged with a new focus. Among the paintings completed after that year were portraits of relatives, *Distant Relations*, who were destroyed by, or survived despite, the Nazis. Based on family photographs that had little meaning for her before, these haunting faces from the past include "The Sisters," Elyse's mother's two cousins, taken to Auschwitz at age twelve and fifteen respectively [fig. 11]. The younger died there; the older survived because she was close enough to womanhood for an SS officer to pull her from the line to the gas chamber, saying, "You're too beautiful to die." The eyes of both sisters are deep, dark, and intense. There is irony in the spring-green color of their dresses; it militates against the dark blood-like red that the artist has allowed to drip freely down the canvas.[18]

We also recognize in Klaidman's *Crucifixion* series continuity with the interest in Jesus' death as explored by earlier Jewish artists and paintings (Chagall's 1938 "White Crucifixion" is perhaps the best known). We repeatedly find colors we recognize: the purgatorial combination of dripping red and black, punctuated by patches of spring-green. Sometimes a lurid yellow appears, which has in Western Christian art been associated over the centuries with Judas; the same yellow was precisely adopted by that failed artist, Hitler, in imposing the yellow star on his Jewish victims. Conversely, Klaidman often weaves the

fig. 11 *The Sisters*

suggestion of a Star of David into the cruciform elements of her compositions.

Elyse Klaidman's mother, Kitty Klaidman, is a respected artist who in 1989 also turned toward the Holocaust after that journey home to Slovakia. For the five years following that excursion into and confrontation with a long-buried part of her past, painting became an exploration and perhaps an exorcism of what had been buried for forty-four years. But Kitty's is a calmer exorcism than might be expected. Works like those in her 1991 *Hidden Memories* series are golden-brown, monochromatic fields, crossed by diagonal and horizontal lines. The re-vision of the attic crawl-space where her family was concealed becomes filled with a pale blue light; as the series develops, it becomes more and more a study of contrastive geometries and colors, rather than of the literal memories of the beams and joists that defined her early childhood. Indeed, it is only by the subtitles—"The Attic," "The Ladder," "The Trapdoor," "Crawlspace"—and our knowledge of Kitty's life story that we understand their hidden meaning [fig. 12].

fig. 12 *Trapdoor*

These works fall between the representational and the abstract as they sit between pain and healing. By 1992, both processes had shifted further. Kitty's series, *The Past Purged: Abstracting Memory*, completes the restructuring of buried memories into ordered geometries, in which color has deepened and line has sharpened [fig. 13]. Most interestingly, her paintings offer a striking contrast to the work of her daughter, revealing a pattern that seems to repeat itself in distinguishing survivor artists from second generation artists. The softer work of the mother serves as an instrument of resolution and healing, whereas that of the daughter expresses her anger at horrors she could not actively witness, much less prevent.[19]

A different calm speaks from Sherry Zvares Sanabria's large, still images, which depict empty buildings and rooms at sites like Dachau and Matthausen, Edward Hopper-like in their silences, but screaming in their implications [fig. 14].[20] Silences are symbols. So too are towers of a particular sort, and chimneys and their oven counterparts. And, of course, railroad tracks. In the works of Alice Lok Cahana, a teenaged survivor who eventually came to live in Houston, the tracks lead, ladder-like, upward, ending nowhere but in the emptiness beyond the canvas. There their smoky passage plays on the sardonic reference of Rudolph Hoess to the Auschwitz train tracks as *himmelweg* [path to heaven] [fig. 15].[21]

Railroad tracks converge in a vanishing point deep within the picture plane or simply repeat themselves in abstract patterns, in works by Sherry Karver, child of survivors, and Judith Liberman. Karver's work is ceramic, painted, smashed with her father's hammer, and restored; it offers a literal act of destruction and reconstruction. The title, "Souvenir," portrays her uncle viewed through the window of memory. Karver plays on the relationship between the French meaning of the title, memory, and its English meaning, memento. The tattooed numbers on his arm are the latter; the striped shirt in his hands provokes the former. The abstract pattern of the background confirms this; on closer examination, it is seen to be a series of repeated railroad tracks [fig. 16].[22]

Liberman's work is textile. There is irony merely in her use of soft materials for the hardest of narratives. Against the patterns of cattle cars and train tracks she often portrays Anne Frank, thus synthesizing the anonymity of Nazi-yielded numbers with the most unforgettable of innocent child faces to have emerged from the ashes. Occasionally she

fig. 13 *The Past Expunged*

fig. 14 *Prison Door (Dachau)*

fig. 15 *Jacob's Ladder*

fig. 16 *Souvenirs*

portrays herself as Anne Frank, as if to transcend the impossibility of grasping the terrifying experience she did not have herself.[23]

Another symbol is the suitcase. Suitcases piled up or in spaceless isolation connote the Jewish experience of being alone: one thinks of suitcases on the concentration camp platform. This intense solitude is present in the paintings of Janis Goodman, whose suitcases speak with an eloquent silence. They take on a quality of subject, not just object, a reverse reflection of the condition of those who packed their suitcases for their final journey, but who were reduced to objects by their killers, even as their outward contexts are simply those of the loneliness of travelers [fig. 17]. [24]

fig. 17 *Suitcase*

Dorit Cypis' photographs expand in a different way some of the specific details of Auschwitz. Her "Aesthetic Lessons" may be seen as a series of abstract plays with line and form, curved shape and contrasts of dark and light. We slowly realize that these are in fact piles of hair and eyeglasses. "Hybrid Eyes," a further play on pop art re-visioning and its various offshoots, is an eerie vision of familiar elements—what more so than our eyes?—within unfamiliar combinations. We look and look again, questioning whether our first vision was a true one [fig. 18]. Knowing the context of the experiments in the Nazi camps with eyes and eye color, as well as with other body parts, these enormous "off-eyes" deeply disturb as they refuse to leave us when we move away from them.

Science and medicine emphatically abandoned their historical responsibility to improve the condition of humankind during the Holocaust. Yet there were those who stood up. This issue stands at the center of Gay Block's series, *Rescuers*. We see one face after another of non-Jews who, in the course of the Catastrophe and at dire risk to themselves, rescued Jews from the Nazis. "Reverend Mediema" is particularly compelling as he stares at us with such severity, cigarette in hand; without Block's title, we might think him a killer of Jews rather than their savior, superbly demonstrating how appearance can be deception [fig. 19].[25]

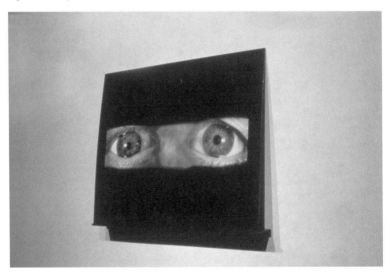

fig. 18 *Hybrid Eyes*

fig. 19 *Rev Miedema*

EXPANDING JEWISH EXPLORATION
AND INTERNAL JEWISH QUESTIONS

Many Jewish artists have used the Holocaust as a starting place for a broader visual discussion of human violence, brutality, and the need for *tikkun*. For example, Selma Waldman's grim, masterfully executed drawings connect the hungers and horrors of the Terezin concentration camp to ongoing acts of human inhumanity in our own time. The intensity of her social concerns is matched by the ferocity of her gestural imagery. Figures billow up like pillars of smoke from the fires of human cruelty and suffering. Emaciated figures from her *Terezin* series (1980s) connect to those in her *Killing Fields* series (1992) by the raw pathos of her line and the eloquence of her chiaroscuro [fig. 20]. No line separates yesterday's Czechoslovakia from today's Bosnia. A starving figure clutches a brick of bread, alone; another shares it. Gaunt figures with hollow, questioning eyes stare out at us. A soldier raises his rifle toward a fleeing mother and child. In *Rubber Bullet*, the concentration camp world of blacks in South Africa and the struggle of the Palestinians to assert their independence speak through the mother and child Waldman depicts: a bruised and battered Madonna, one whose sacrifice will yield no redemption save that of persistent courage and pride.

Clearly, the Holocaust has served as a major, if varied, point of departure for Jewish American women artists over the past twenty-five years. Andra Ellis's (Avigayil Elsner) colorfully painted ceramic reliefs reflect a rebirth of spiritual awareness from quite another source.[26] Her work emulates Paul Gauguin's ruling principle of how the artist can express, by means of color, the internal rather than the external world. To color, line, form, and volume, Elsner adds the fifth dimension of

fig. 20 *Invitation to the Dance: The Masked Ball*

texture: a burning, blistering, sandy, grainy, gouged texture that recalls Kurtz's assault on the canvas. Elsner's work, however, is ceramic relief, consistently defying its frame. Portrait-like works, such as "The Echo and Visions: A Loss of Faith and Reason," address the Holocaust and its ramifications for our own times. As Elsner wrote in 1992:

> Many of my pieces probe and document the pain and anguish in the late twentieth century; its sexism, violence, its rampant social inequities. These pieces speak of my fears for my child— for all our children—as we approach the year 2000.[27]

At that time, her *Joyous Journey* series, with its frameless shape and its recurrent boat-like image, derived from a radical shift in her life [fig. 21]: "In moving from New York to Charlotte, North Carolina, I felt as if I were leaving (not to but from) Egypt."[28] For there, in Charlotte, away from the million Jews who inhabit New York City, her own Jewish identity began finally to take shape. Never before having participated in an evening-long Passover Seder, she did so in Charlotte, until 3 a.m. Exiled in North Carolina, she found herself for the first time a part of the House of Israel.

The Passover Seder is for many the most emphatic Jewish festival with regard to transforming past into present. One particularly noteworthy aspect of the Seder in the last decade has been the development of a new ritual object, the Miriam Goblet, which reintroduces the sister of Moses and Aaron to the Seder table, side-by-side with Elijah and his Cup. The list of those who have contributed to this development in the past few years is by now lengthy indeed.[29]

Other aspects of Jewish custom and ritual are engaged elsewhere, as in one of Devorah Neumark's installations, which focuses with wit and irony on the double edge of Jewish married life, wedding and divorce. The installation is titled "*Harrei At Mutteret...*" [Behold you are released], words spoken when a man divorces his wife. The phrase echoes words spoken by the groom to the bride as he places a ring on her finger: "*Harrei At Mikoodeshet (lee)*" [Behold you are sanctified (unto me)]. Neumark's installation follows the cycle of Jewish marriage in documents and images. Historical illustrations by unknown and well-known artists depict the joy of the Jewish wedding, with its culminating moment of historically-impelled sorrow: the breaking of the wineglass [fig. 22]. Neumark adds scores of goblets to her installation; the shattered forms of some of them simultaneously recall the relative ease of divorce in

fig. 21 *Joyous Journey*

fig. 22 *Harrei At Mutteret...*

Judaism and the virtual impossibility of divorce if the husband should not desire it.

The coexistence of positive and negative in general and in particular where the place of women falls is stunningly addressed in Shari Rothfarb's video installation, "Water Rites." The artist projects twenty-seven comments regarding the significance of the mikvah [the pool of ritual purification into which Jewish women have traditionally immersed themselves, most often before the Sabbath and after menses] into a tiled, mikvah-like pool of water. These quotations are not simply commentaries, but narratives; one speaks of a group of women who insisted to their Nazi executioners that they be allowed to immerse themselves properly before being shot to death. Landscapes of lush and provocative imagery form a backdrop for these speakers, including footage of ancient and modern mikvahs from Massada, Jerusalem, and the Galilee. In a unique combination of word and image, stasis and motion, stillness and power, Rothfarb's work suggests a wide range of understandings for this aspect of Jewish tradition.[30]

Such commentaries are rich with paradox, as narrow as Judaism at its narrowest and as broad as humanity at its broadest. Helene Aylon's "Epilogue: Alone with my Mother" and "The Book That Would Not Close" are installations that carry the viewer back to the beginning of Jewish self-conception by way of the most fundamental Jewish texts, which women have traditionally not been allowed to study directly or read publicly in the synagogue. Aylon offers a series of five books in "The Book That Would Not Close," paralleling the five books that comprise the Torah [fig. 23]. In her texts she singles out, deletes, or highlights passages that reflect traditional negativity toward women, thus highlighting her own struggles to reconcile religious and gender identities. One might argue that she frees God Itself from the male-oriented bonds that traditional terms have imposed on the Deity.

With Aylon we are returned to our original point of departure; namely, issues pertaining to women within questions pertaining to Judaism, the Torah, and ultimately the entire Hebrew Bible. New Englander Janet Shafner has been engaged for a number of years on a series of thirty-six paintings focused on biblical themes.[31] Her readings are both modern and cognizant of centuries of Jewish interpretation. They are simultaneously filled with the Jewish mystical tradition and informed by everything that might be called compelling in the world of today. Thus, for example, her first work, "Adam and Eve: The Sparks,"

fig. 23 *The Book that Would Not Close*

leads from the upper lunette, where the aboriginal pair approach the fateful and fatal tree, to a large bottom section in which a quasi-pointillist style offers a scattering of colorful sparks. These are the sparks that, in the kabbalistic tradition, were scattered when the vessel containing the primordial light of creation was smashed. This occurred after Adam and Eve abrogated God's command. The divine sparks do not wholly disconnect humans from their source, thereby offering hope even as their scattering represents a dark descent from the garden of perfection [fig. 24].

Not surprisingly, many of the biblical figures upon whom Shafner focuses are women, ranging from the well known, like Eve and Sarah, to those such as Timna and Hagar about whom we typically hear much less. Biblical women are also a focus in the work of New York artist Ruth Dunkell, both the well known and those less so. By means of a

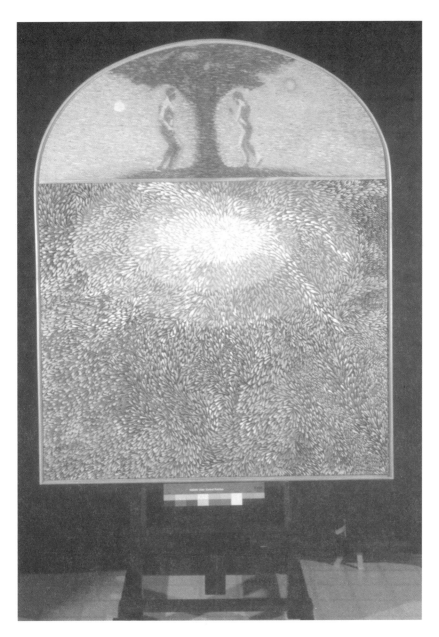

fig. 24 *Adam and Eve: The Sparks*

fig. 25 *He Took to Wife Jezebel*

completely different style, she portrays them in a large series of black and white drawings, densely cross-hatched with pen and India ink on Arches paper. They are part of what she refers to as *Night Drawings* (for the time of their creation and perhaps also the shadowy elements of style) [fig. 25].

Dunkell's drawings shift between more abstract and more figurative sensibilities. They are "not literal interpretations, but rather spiritual evocations," she comments, of phrases from Genesis, Isaiah, Esther, and above all the Song of Songs. Different queens are invoked, like Esther, Vashti, and Jezebel. The first (semi-abstractly straight, tall, and unadorned before a curtain-like element; an actress before the critical audience who is the king) is the ultimate heroine; the last is the ultimate spiritual villainess (overwhelmed with decorative elements that may also be construed as the dogs that ultimately tear her apart); between is the one whose feminist refusal to accede to a drunken husband's lusty demands led not only to loss of position and perhaps life, but also to obscurity within the mytho-historical record of Judaism.

So, too, sweet-smelling substances are offered, which, like the lovely eyes of doves in the Song of Songs, evoke the eternal bride: myrrh and frankincense, spikenard and saffron. Eve, the mother of humankind, is represented from the birth of her being as "woman" to the act of leading Adam out of the garden by means of the forbidden fruit; so too is the mother of Judaism and Christianity, Sara, who "shall give rise to nations." Also present is the female who is even more eclipsed by Eve than Vashti is by Esther, for her very name, Lilith, is lost in the text of Genesis. We know her primarily through rabbinic literature, where her proud refusal to be dominated by Adam led to exile and gained for her the reputation as a stealer of babies and a danger to mothers. Dunkell's is a restorative vision of Isaiah's restorative vision, wherein, as Israel is returned to Zion after its exile, even "the Lilith shall repose [there]."

Dunkell began as a student of Raphel Soyer and as a vivid colorist; mid-life she shifted dramatically to large paintings that could be considered "Jewish pop art." She gained access to the storage rooms at the Jewish Museum in New York, creating a series of mostly large, flat paintings of Jewish ritual objects. If Kass' repeating Jewish celebrities mirror Warhol's celebrities, Dunkell's ritual objects in silver and gold mirror Warhol's soup cans [fig. 26]. Her *Night Drawings* represent the most recent phase of her work.[32]

fig. 26 *Silver Tuvah Breastplate*

As both Dunkell's *Night Drawings* and her pop ritual objects deliberately flatten the spatial and the conceptual reality of the images, Suzanne Benton's *Masks of Biblical Women* explode them outward, invading the physical and psychological space of the viewer. Sara and Hagar, Rachel and Leah, Miriam and Job's Wife, the Queen of Sheba and Potiphar's wife, Esther and Vashti, Jael and Jephtha's daughter speak to us from behind the stirring faces prepared for us, their public. The cast and welded steel and the bronze and copper material connect the faces behind these faces to the world in which they moved, the Bronze and Iron Ages. They also connect to the text that presents these figures as fighting battles for and against the Covenant—paradoxically, with strengths other than and beyond those offered by metals.

Benton has interspersed well-known biblical characters with those less well known. In some cases, these figures are anonymous, not necessarily even Jewish. Indeed, these masks play in different directions. They suggest, in being masks, the notion of subterfuge as necessary not only for biblical and other women, but for all minorities. The artist's masks are a reflection of the false face presented to the outside world while the true face remains hidden, shielded, and inaccessible except through the eye slits.[33]

The ultimate hidden face is God's, which remains behind the veils—or masks—of our answerless questions. These masks are mirrors of those we humans wear across our patterns of culture and history. It is the goal of the mystical tradition to seek God beyond the veils and masks. Since one of these veils is words, both extending and limiting us, we must sometimes resort to other than verbal means to find God. Not surprisingly, a growing number of artists have addressed aspects of mysticism among the other areas within the Jewish tradition. This reflects in part the intensified spirituality that drew both Jews and non-Jews in increasing numbers at the approach of the Christian millennium. It also reflects a deepened, specifically focused search for identity. Among a number of interesting artists whose work intersects the concerns of Jewish mysticism by means of letters and words are Marilyn Banner, and Jane Logemann.[34]

Words and letters play colorlessly in work like that of Diane Samuels. Her "Letter Liturgy (for Leon)" (1993-99) reflects an old Hassidic story regarding what God accepts as piety: not book-learned knowledge of the prayers or the Torah, but purity of *kavanah* [spiritual intention], symbolized by the illiterate Jewish peasant who cannot read the prayers but keeps reciting the Hebrew alphabet, allowing God to combine the letters into words.[35] Samuels plays on the abstract symbolism of letters that in combination represent words and ideas. Are the "letters" in her "book" letters? If not, is this a book? Can non-letters form the words that comprise prayers? Do prayers require well-wrought words or, for a textual people like the Jews, well-shaped letters? With what instruments—words? melodies? gestures? images?—does one effectively address God?

Surely it is not coincidence that so many contemporary Jewish American artist-word-purveyors and art-book artists are women. Is this in part another creative response to centuries of exclusion from direct access to the Book that underlies Judaism? We have seen a small sampling of the scores of American women artists who since the early 1980s have wrestled with the question of where and how they fit as women into the Jewish tradition. Often Torah scrolls, prayer books, and *tallitot* [prayer shawls] are used and transformed in their work, underscoring the difficult issue of the patriarchal history of Judaism. Artists like Helene

Aylon or Carol Hamoy, using the very *elementa* of Jewish ritual as media, offer a tactile form of the question regarding the many levels at which women remain excluded from ritual and celebration within traditional Judaism.[36] They and their colleagues ask without hesitation: "Where do I as a female artist fit into Judaism and the images that are part of Judaism's history?" rather than merely the question of where they as Jewish artists fit into Western art.

EIGHTEEN NEW YORK ARTISTS
The range of issues that we have been exploring may be seen in summary form in the work of a group of Jewish American women artists who have been meeting together periodically for more than fifteen years. In March 1987, the group (hereafter referred to as "The Eighteen"—my designation) began consistent but informal meetings to consider the issues that connect and separate them as women, as Jews, and as artists whose diverse stylistic and subject tendencies take shape in diverse media. It has remained a varied group.[37]

The work of any one among the group might serve as a symbolic statement of the whole.[38] Marilyn Cohen's enormous triptych, "Tea Party," is certainly one. Cohen's technique—tour de force collages—always functions in part as a metaphor for her subject. At first glance, the works appear to be delicately rendered watercolor paintings. It is only upon closer study that one realizes that they in fact comprise fragments of torn pieces of paper that have been subtly drenched in color; the care in their crafting belies the notion of arbitrary lines that torn paper suggests.

The small slabs of paper are layered within the artist's carefully organized compositions, reflecting the kind of subject matter she depicts. "Tea Party" invites the viewer to a sweeping presentation of female accomplishment, both Jewish and non-Jewish, across American history [fig. 27]. Twenty-three figures sit or stand, gesture or smile, across a colorful trio of collages. They are all heroines from American history and imagination, from poet Emma Lazarus to pioneering pilot Amelia Earhart, from Eleanor Roosevelt to modern dance pioneer Isadora Duncan, from athletic superstar Babe Didriksen Zaharias to singer Marian Anderson, from sculptor Louise Nevelson to social and political activist Susan B. Anthony. Their number also includes fictional mystery-solver Nancy Drew, over-the-rainbow heroine Dorothy and her dog Toto, and Wonder Woman. Symbols of America, its flag and the torch

fig. 27 *Tea Party*

of the Statue of Liberty, complete the backdrop for this magnificent array. The triptych-formed question of placement in the Christian art world is merged with that of how many women's accomplishments are placed in the back rather than foreground in a male-dominated world.

In a conceptually related series completed in 1997 titled *Teach Me the Songs My Mothers Sang to Me*, the artist depicts a range of women who have defined the American past. Eighteen of them, each in her own frame, have had a major impact on aspects of twentieth century life not often associated with women, for example, aviation and baseball, but have remained obscured in the shadows of male counterparts.

The first and most extensive of works to which Cohen applied her technique focused specifically on the history of Jews in America. In an extensive series of collage-paintings, *Where Did They Go When They Came to America?* (1989-94), she presented the story of one Jewish family from each of the fifty states. The series summarizes the extraordinary immigration history of Jewish America within the extraordinary immigration history of the United States.[39]

Famous females of sorts as the subjects and objects of art rather than as people are part of Elyse Taylor's canvasses. "Assimilate/ Assimulate" presents the stunning Botticellian Venus on the half shell, not swept up on the shore of Cyprus, but translated into the colored geometries of contemporary art. Her "Radioactive Odalisque," playing on the classic "Odalisque" by Ingres, adds a peacock-feathered duster to assert the subject's identity: sexual object to be stared at, but without abandoning her role as housekeeper [fig. 28].[40]

Leonora Arye's amusing sculpture, "Breaking Through the Glass Ceiling," underscores the not-yet-completed struggle for acceptance of women at upper political, social, and commercial levels. The solid, large-limbed, spherically-shaped figure that holds up (rather than presses against) a glass rectangle also reflects the artist's years of upbringing. in Mexico, as it challenges the Barbie Doll proportions that have for decades been an American (male) ideal of women [fig. 29].

Arye's solid figurative sensibilities carry through a range of stone media and subjects. She turns to biblical characters, but not as we have customarily seen them. Her Zuni-red alabaster "Eve" offers us the mother of humankind stepping fearlessly forth with her arms protectively wrapped around her baby: this is both the Eve who took the lead in tasting the fruit of knowledge and the Eve who strides out of the protected garden into the unknown world. Her tiger eye "First Born

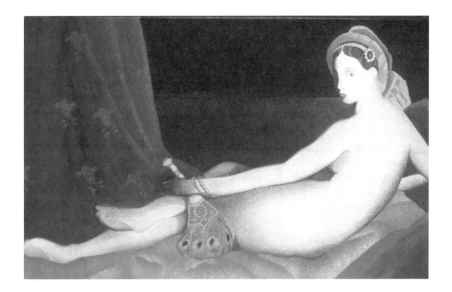

fig. 28 *Odalisque*

(Cain)" once again offers us the mother of mothers, lovingly cradling her first-born son. The man we are used to seeing as the first murderer is here re-visioned as the innocent babe he once was, the paradigm of all babies whose future lives are the consequence of the many factors that contribute to their development. His mother, massive and eternal as the earth itself, kneels to shelter the tiny infant whose fate she cannot control or even, at this moment, guess at; she, ignorant of the future, is where she is for having eaten of the Tree of Knowledge, which both doomed and exalted all the generations to come.

Much of Rachel Giladi's work parodies the limitations to which women have been traditionally confined as mothers. Giladi's "Sterile I" is a grimly humorous installation, offering four babies' bottles painted matte black, a reminder that our world considers the woman who fails to become a mother to have failed. Her "Triplet" is a triptych of sorts: three diapers symbolize the triple load of work that successful maternal creativity engenders [fig. 30].

Giladi also plays on other centuries-old prejudices and traditions. "*Mamzer* [bastard]" is a plastic toy store baby, with a hospital identification tag around its wrist. The choice of this Hebrew term inevitably associates the work with the long technical discussion in the

fig. 29 *Breaking Through the Glass Ceiling*

fig. 30 *Triplet*

Talmud regarding the unfavorable status of a bastard in traditional Jewish society. On the other hand, the term, in both modern Hebrew and Yiddish, has also come to be slang for someone who is terrific, wonderful, and successful, or at least lucky, which all babies are anticipated to be (even Cain, Arye's "First Born") by doting parents.

Carol Hamoy often focuses on aspects of the heroic history of women. Her series of *Seven Prophetesses*, for example, draws from the Hebrew Bible not only obvious figures such as Deborah, but also Bathsheba, the pawn of King David's passion, whose righteous Hittite husband was destroyed by the Israelite king he served so that David might have his wife [fig. 31].[41]

Hamoy includes another of David's wives, Abigail, who impressed the king with her wisdom. Also included are Queen Esther, wife of Ahasuerus and heroine of the Purim story, and Huldah, the unique prophetess consulted by King Josiah concerning the Book of the Law discovered during repairs on the Temple area. In each of the artist's altar-like wall constructions, gold paint completely covers objects that are traditionally associated with women and their societal roles, from necklaces and beads to lace and high-heeled shoes, and an array of flotsam

fig. 31 *Prophet 3/Deborah*

and jetsam drawn from the textile trade. The latter elements recall Hamoy's own childhood, as her mother brought home piecework from the sweatshop to help supply the family larder.

Louise Kramer also focuses on heroines, inspired by the image of her own mother as "an activist, a suffragette who spent time in prison for that." Her subjects include the anonymous heroines who maintained their families under difficult conditions on the immigrant-filled Lower East Side of New York City in the early twentieth century. Her startlingly massed portraits depict figures who actively sought more reasonable rights for women and children soaking in the sweatshops; they include tributes to those who perished in the great sweatshop fires.

Kramer also focuses on the Holocaust. "Six Heads" symbolizes the six million Jews who perished in the ovens. They hover on the wall as disembodied spirits. Their sizes, expressions, shapes, and angles of disposition are each unique, like the myriad victims they symbolize. Drawings and a life-sized plaster installation memorialize "Four Hanged Women," saboteurs who attempted to destroy the machinery of death at Auschwitz. The machinery devoured them, four anonymous numbers among endless numbers of deaths, whose courageous act would no doubt remain forgotten were it not for this work [fig. 32].

Not all of Kramer's work has a deliberate or overt political or social context. Her "Untitled" monoprint series, at least at first glance, is simply an exploration of depths of color and texture. We might imagine that this turn to an apparently pure aesthetic direction reflects in part the artist's need to turn away from the haunting issues that define so much of her other subject matter. But we then realize that this visual direction follows a continuum that flows from the New York-based Jewish Chromaticists of fifty years ago. Kramer, whether for her own need or for her audience, has put the world back together in these richly unified works, the very name for which, monoprints, suggests the consoling unity of reality that they offer the viewer, even as they may also be understood as simple experiments in color within space.

Abstract Realities

Several other artists in this group of eighteen also focus on the apparent simplicities of color within space. Marilyn Megabow explores the relationship between two dimensions and three; in this sense, her "Not This. Not That" turns back to the Renaissance (albeit abstractly), with its concern to create the illusion of volumetric space on flat surface.

fig. 32 *Four Hanged Women*

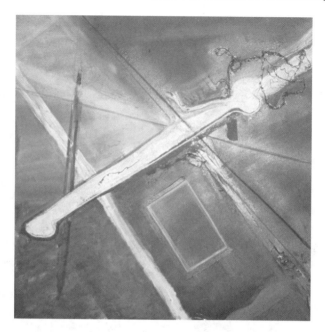

fig. 33 *Black Beard and Dry Bones*

fig. 34 *Hommage to Bonnard*

This is also true in her "Black Beard and Dry Bones" [fig. 33], which functions as a kind of diptych that hurtles us through the galaxy of her layered, textured canvasses. The titles force the viewer to consider the narrative possibilities of these mixed media works, while the eye and brain are engaged in a dialogue of pure spatial possibilities.

A sense of depth suffuses the canvasses of Marilyn Perlman as well. The cosmic sense that Megabow's microcosms offer is echoed in both the form and the title of Perlman's "My Apollo 13, 1997." The vast emptiness of space and its colors are subtly present within a Chromaticist simplicity of black and white. The human presence is perhaps suggested by the intrusion of a mottled, multi-hued spherical figure. The trademark diagonal that one perceives as a backdrop to the spatial depths of this work (the presence of the creator behind the creation) is also found in Perlman's "Homage to Bonnard." The foreground is a continuously layered vertical flow of thick, lighter colors and spiked, narrow, darker ones. The palette of the French Neo-Impressionist has been recast in the abstract terms of pure pigment [fig. 34].

Johanna Gillman's gentle pigments surge in textured acrylic and paper combinations across and away from the canvas. "Hide and Seek" combines the unifying sensibility of the New York School Chromaticists with an Actionist foreground explosion of reds, pinks, yellows, and blues. These two aspects of her composition offer a forest-like depth through which the eye moves lyrically back and forth, over and under, in and out.

Gillman's "Many Paths" tears away the canvas frame altogether; the empty space of the wall beyond it offers the visual setting for dynamic contrasts between greens and pinks, sharp and blurred lines, full and empty portions of the composition, and positive and negative space. "Crosscurrent" does the same, combining the abstract with the apparently figurative. The work is a study in contrasts of color and texture. At the same time, the irregular shaping of the work suggests a female figure, leaning at a diagonal angle, seemingly dancing with head to the side, arm on hip. A series of non-narrative abstractions are rife with representational possibility, limited only by the imagination of the viewer, whose viewing may be said to complete the work [fig. 35].

Muriel Taub Glantzman's work reflects a riotous coloristic sensibility. Her tiny (8 x 9 inches) watercolor collage, "Landscape," is an explosive, rhythmic ode to the chaotic order of nature, sifted through a powerfully hued prism that weds the disciplined geometries of Mondrian to Dadaist

fig. 35 *Crosscurrent*

wildness. Even as her canvas expands and her palette shrinks to more subdued blues, reds, and blacks, in "Life" her sense of harmony overwhelms the viewer with delight. The landscape of Glantzman's life, location, and times unfolds with her triptych "My City, My World." Again a circus of pigment dances before our eyes, as we sense New York's constant motion and commotion cavorting before us [fig. 36]. The triptych form reminds the viewer that the question of what it means to be a Jewish artist has not been fully answered even in New York, where the Jewish presence in culture is strong.

That such an issue is not lost even on highly secularized Jewish artists is suggested by Glantzman's "Ode to Russian Icons," which demonstrates how distinctly Christian visual ideas are part of the wide range of interests and influences that have enveloped her. This small watercolor and collage is punctuated by abstract allusions to forms characteristic of icons: scintillating circles recall halos, half moons suggest cradling arms, and attenuated shadows imply ethereal limbs.

Francine Perlman also often works in pure color. Unlike Glantzman, but like others within this group, her Chromaticism presents itself as a drenching of the canvas with a confined spectrum of intense hues. Her "Red Wall" is soaked in the color of blood, of sacrifice, but of birth as well: it is the color most emblematic of the continuous cycle of life and death.

Perlman's water, glass, wood, oil, and pastel installations carry her perspective into three dimensions. "The Immigrant" is a study of perspective; each viewer, approaching a large cube half-filled with liquid, experiences the visual wrestling match between the image that rests within the water and its appearance through layers of glass and water, between what is and what seems to be—in this case, between stereotypes of the newly-adopted country and its reality. Substances ordinarily thought of as clear are distorted before our limited vision. Her "Interlude" fills an eight-foot cube of space in which yellow spheres are suspended at various levels above the ground and below the ceiling. A sea of motes, of gigantic atoms, patterns the space in chaotically ordered rhythms. This work intermediates between the chaotic order (or ordered chaos) of microscopic and macrocosmic realities [fig. 37].

fig. 36 *My City, My World*

fig. 37 *Interlude*

Image and Text

The incorporation of texts into images and the imposing of images onto texts are also broadly found among the artists of "The Eighteen." Evelyn Eller's work is one example of this. She has produced a series of artist books with self-referential titles such as "Milestones" and "Defining Woman." The first of these imposes old family photographs and documents, such as a Jewish marriage certificate, on a softly contoured maroon and white ground. The second overruns the repeating black and white sketch of a woman's face with an array of dictionary definitions: daughter, wife, goddess, heroine, mother-in-law, witch, widow, womb, barren, care—terms traditionally associated with "images" of what women are and do.

While such pieces by Eller focus on particular (female, Jewish) aspects of humanity, others focus on the whole and its most significant part, language. Her texts in the *Language* Series are exercises in the juxtaposition of visual fragments for aesthetic purposes; these fragments are also part of the endlessly fragmented Babel of human communication

fig. 38 *Defining Woman #IV*

and miscommunication. Eller's wonderful paper collages layer Cyrillic and Arabic and Hebrew letters and Mayan hieroglyphs not only with Braille, but also with undulating staffs of music and mathematical formulae. One in this series offers another version of "Defining Woman," reorganized in a colorful circular configuration [fig. 38].

Jenny Tango offers work that defines women within the context of Jewish folklore. Her *Women of Chelm* series reflects on the not-often-mentioned female folk in that quasi-fictional Polish Jewish *shtetl* [village], about which so many tales are told. Brightly dark humor overruns the artist's encounter with the possibilities conjured by the lives of fictionally real, imagined actual Jewish women. The issue of madness and normalcy reflects the layers of insider-outsider that contour that condition. Each of her characters has character and is a character: "Fraydl," for example, in love with a non-Jew, converts out of the faith; to the hermetic understanding of her community, she ceases to exist. She will actually cease to exist, in spite of no longer being a Jew, when she is taken by the Nazis; however, when they exterminate her, she will have the chance to rise to immortality by way of Christian sainthood.[42] That is, Fraydl's condition changed as it did not change; it did not change as it changed.

Image and text combine in a comic book-like exploration of the seriousness of being in the world and wondering where and how we fit into it if we don't fit in. The style itself is a witticism; after all, its ostensive subjects, the Chelmites, are notorious for their lack of witty intellect. All kinds of characters populate this world: saintly and not-so-saintly figures: the expected and accepted ones, like the *rebbetzin* [rabbi's wife] and the rich man's daughter; and the denied or ignored ones, like the whore and the rich man's lesbian daughter. Tango places her Chelmite women in the front seat instead of the usual back seat of the vehicle representing this extraordinary village [fig. 39].

One might say the opposite direction is taken by Marilyn Rosenberg's artist book. "Istoria Leonardo: What Happened to Leonardo?" is an exploration of the ultimate exemplum of pure intellect. The artist has overrun her sheets of handmade paper with quotations from the artist-scientist's notebooks, along with imagery and sketches and notations and observations. She is the notator and observer of the ultimate observer and notator [fig. 40]. He was the ultimate hybrid— artist and scientist—whom she contains within the pages of a book that is not a book but a work of art (it's visual) and a work of art that is not a work of art but a book (it's textual).

fig. 39 *Mindele, The Mesuganeh*

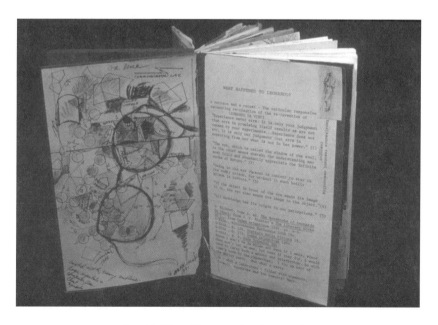

fig. 40 *What Happened to Leonardo*

fig. 41 *Beaded Snake*

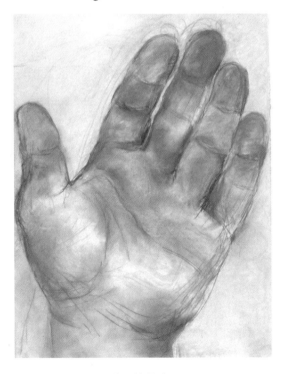

fig. 42 *Palm*

It is a book about a dyslexic, whose words and images are experienced as upside down and backwards. It is about what it means to be different or to do things differently, whether one is a woman, a Jew, a dyslexic, or a Leonardo. By contrast, Rosenberg's "She/Her" is pure imagery, pure sweeps of lyrical color. The text defining "Her" requires no words; its statement of beauty and joy as feminine attributes is expressed by offering self-evident visual beauty and identifying it with a double female pronoun.

Even less textually rooted are the *Books* of Miriam Rachel Milgram. The question of definition—What is Jewish? art? woman?—is turned not only toward the question of art, but toward the question of bookness. Does "book" imply text? Words? Does it imply paper? What about a book made of felt that offers only a handful of sheets overrun with color and form? Is it both book and art, although not what one imagined art and books to be? Is it a visual Mendelssohnian "song without words?" Is the work less art because it is made of fabric rather than shaped by a brush or palette knife?

Milgram's chosen medium, textile material, falls within the parameters of both female-focused media and that aspect of ceremonial art in which Jewish women have been particularly prominent over the centuries. She turns "book" into textile object and "belt" into a surface on which she inscribes concise poetry. Belts yield to *Beaded Snakes*, inspired by Macedonian beaded snakes symbolizing fertility and luck, that are sometimes signed in Hebrew (are they thereby more Jewish?) [fig. 41]. Are snakes an allusion to that first relationship in the Garden of Eden that led to knowledge, woman in the lead, when the serpent offered the fruit to Eve first, or are they no more than Balkan-inspired objects of luck-bringing art?

Language and Unanswered Questions
What are the parameters within which the language of art may properly speak to conform to our preconception of its place in the world? What are the languages that connect and separate us, as individuals, as families, as communities, as tribes, as genders, as humans? The human hand creates in an endless array of directions. The destructive/creative impulse has suppressed many aspects of female accomplishment. That same impulse has sought to destroy Jewish accomplishment across national and ethnic and linguistic boundaries. We bind each other and ourselves with limitations. Myrna Minter-Foster meditates on the hand that

creates and destroys. The language spoken in pastel and in oil is the language of the human "Palm." Its colors, its size, the details of its wrinkles change, but all hands are hands [fig. 42].

"I remember my mother's hands as 'magic hands,'" the artist comments.[43] All hands partake of the magically creative hands of her mother. All humans are uniquely equipped with the kind of hands that have been essential to human creativity, with opposable thumbs allowing us to grasp the instruments that produce images and eternalize language through writing. In an ongoing series, Minter-Foster reflects, as Monet does by way of haystacks and cathedrals, on the changing immutability of this instrument and its five components that grasp tools to build cathedrals, gather hay, and engender painted reflection.

Fingers spread out to grasp and to encompass. They gesture to bless and to curse, to greet and to send away, to embrace and reject. A silvery-yellow hand turns its two interior fingers downward; thumb and the two exterior fingers push upward: it spells in concise gesture, "I Love You." No words, no text, just image. The gesture is the text is the image. The image is the words; the painting has become as briefly complete a book as Milgram's fabric sheets of felt.

As with every artist, Ann R. Shapiro's paintings are a means of reading through the book of her life, only more so. The text sweeps from black and white to color and from playfully representational to darkly abstract. Interwoven are the elements that reflect a New England childhood—as in "Spheres of Remembrance," where a white picket fence and enormous leaves from an enormous tree sprout from the autumnal canvas. As is often the case, their leaves acquire the shape of a Star of David. They rise up from the Jewish part of her childhood, the desire for a Bat Mitzvah that was crushed by her father's death when she was thirteen years old. They rise from a tree that, thus crowned, is a "Tree of Life" [fig. 43].

This, then, is a study in memory and identity from past to present. It remains unchanged even as it changes, as in "Town and Country: West 28th Street," which reflects the unchanged change of moving into the big city. Small figures are dwarfed by trees, leaves, and the amorphous shapes of buildings that are simple blocks of pigment. In "New York Underground," the urban landscape is pigmented black and gray, except for the brilliant blue moon-like sphere dropped at our feet. That blue moon drops at the feet of the artist, who finds herself an alien in this world: rural in the city, a Jew in the gentile world, a woman in a world dominated by men, a cancer victim in a world of healthy people.

fig. 43 *Tree of Life*

Shirley Samberg reflects on the opposite condition: when the moon and the sun alike are swallowed in darkness. With burlap, wood, and dark paint, she creates simple, stylized *Figures* that huddle in inward-directed defense against the cold that defines the world, or whose arms are thrown outward and up in a silent cry against injustice that comes in various forms and flavors, at no time more richly represented than in the twentieth century and never more layered than in its representation as the Holocaust. Samberg's figures are timeless and spaceless, but they cannot be separated from her Jewish awareness of the Holocaust as the ultimate exemplum of horror [fig. 44].

They are like the howling *Wolves* that she creates of the same materials. There is irony here: the same burlap, wood, and paint and the same upward-crying body language, but the wolves, following their intuitive nature, howl because the moon is there and they must howl. Human figures howl in anguish at the suffering inflicted on each other out of anger and blind hatred, or for entertainment. Is this part of our intuitive, unthinking human nature?

The artist cries out for humanity, which like wolves cries out for us to recognize the personhood of each individual around us and beyond us. Categories like race, religion, and gender may subdivide us, but they melt before the encompassing category, humanity. When this category disappears from the vocabulary of our everyday lives, we are all doomed. And we are self-denying when we ascribe to animals the horrific behavior that only humans exhibit toward each other. Cataclysms like the Holocaust may produce inhumane behavior, but not behavior that is inhuman.

CONCLUSION

Samberg restores death to life by using junk; detritus is the material that becomes her figures. In the dehumanizing context of holocausts and human atrocities, she reverses destruction with a boldly creative building up. She and her seventeen colleagues set before the viewer life and death, the blessing and the curse. Their work implores us to remember life and to engage in its constant restoration, *tikkun olam*. It is fair to say that using art as an instrument to improve the world, and not merely to express one's aesthetic ambitions, is a prevailing aspect of the work of Jewish American artists in the twentieth century and certainly of contemporary Jewish American women artists. They present a continuum with their male, New York, Chromaticist colleagues of half

fig. 44 *Figure*

a century ago, who wondered how one might put back together in visual terms what the Holocaust had torn apart and whether Judaism had anything to do with this process of restoration. The artists discussed in this narrative, and a wide array of others left outside this discussion in the interests of space, add to that wonder other questions and other issues as they and we plunge more deeply into a new millennium.

ACKNOWLEDGMENTS

I gratefully acknowledge all the artists whose work appears throughout this article for their permission to use their images. The work of a number of additional Jewish American women artists will also be found in many of the texts to which reference is made in the preceding footnotes, particularly in *Edge* and *Fixing the World*, but also in other exhibition catalogues from the B'nai B'rith Klutznick National Jewish Museum, dating from late 1991 through late 1998, and in my essay on "The Bible and Art at the End of the Millennium: Words, Ideas and Images," in *Sacred Text, Secular Times: The Hebrew Bible in the Modern World* (vol. 10, Studies in Jewish Civilization; eds. Leonard J. Greenspoon and Bryan F. Le Beau; Omaha: Creighton University Press, 2000), 163-97.

NOTES

[1] There are a number of already internationally known Jewish women artists whose work I am deliberately ignoring (including, for example, Ruth Gikow, Elaine de Kooning, Helen Frankenthaler, Judy Chicago, Mimi Gross, and Susan Rothenberg) because their important place in shaping American art in the twentieth century is already so familiar and accepted. My focus is mostly on those not yet as well known (although some of these have also, of course, begun to achieve wider recognition). Where no image appears for a given work, none was available for publication.

[2] For further discussion of Kurtz's work, see Ori Z. Soltes, *Fixing the World: American Jewish Painters in the Twentieth Century* (Hanover: University Press of New England, 2002), 125-26.

[3] For more on Schwalb's work, see Soltes, *Fixing the World*, 111-15, and Ori Z. Soltes, *Everyman a Hero: The Saving of Bulgarian Jewry/Susan Schwalb: The Creation Series* (exhibition catalogue; B'nai B'rith Klutznick National Jewish Museum, Washington, DC, 1993).

[4] For more on Mordecai's work, see Soltes, *Fixing the World*, 117-18, and also Ori Z. Soltes, *Journeys of the Spirit: Works by Ruth Mordecai Slavet and Deborah Davidson* (exhibition catalogue; B'nai B'rith Klutznick National Jewish Museum, Washington, DC, 1996).

[5] The Florentine humanist and architect, Leon Battista Alberti (1404-72) articulated, among other things, the theory that by subtle use of orthogonal lines in a composition that converge at a "vanishing point" on the horizon line, one could create the sense of looking through a window into three-dimensional space.

[6] Quoted in the artist's statement from the exhibition *Jewish Artists: On the Edge* (O. Z. Soltes, curator; J. B. Zeiger, project director; Marian Art Center and the Gallery of the College of Santa Fe, Santa Fe, NM, 2000, and Yeshiva University Museum, New York, 2001-2002). More will be found on 66-67 of the exhibit catalogue of the same name (ed. O. Z. Soltes) and in Soltes, *Fixing the World*, 121-22.

[7] For more on Klinghoffer's work, see Soltes, *Edge*, 75.

[8] Artist's statement from the exhibition *A World of Family: The Work of Joyce Ellen Weinstein* (exhibition catalogue by O. Z. Soltes; B'nai B'rith Klutznick National Jewish Museum, Washington, DC, 1996), Soltes, *Fixing the World*, 107-10, and Soltes, *Edge*, 74-75.

[9] For more on Kass's work, see Soltes, *Fixing the World*, 128-29, and Norman Kleeblatt, ed., *Too Jewish? Challenging Traditional Identities* (exhibition catalogue; The Jewish Museum, New York, 1996), 9-10, 129-30, 139 and 159-60.

[10] Marx, although born Jewish, was baptized at the wishes of his father when Karl was six years old. Marx spent summers in the country with his Orthodox Jewish grandparents, but spent the school year in the city with his nominally Christian parents. Therefore, the question much discussed in post-Emancipation Prussia cannot help but have had a strong personal resonance for the young scholar, and it was the first subject on which he wrote after receiving his doctoral degree, in response to Bruno Bauer's anti-Jewish coverage of the subject. Ironically, given its ostensive intention, Marx's essay has most often been interpreted less as a defense of Jews than as virulently anti-Semitic. For a summary discussion of this, see among others, Julius Carlebach, *Karl Marx and the Radical Critique of Judaism* (London: Littman Library of Jewish Civilization, 1978).

[11] Judith Neulander has recently argued that apparent Marrano (crypto-Judaic) customs may be traceable to other than originally Jewish sources. See Judith Neulander, "The Ecumenical Esther: Queen and Saint in Three Western Belief Systems," in *Esther through the Ages* (eds. S. W. Crawford and L. J. Greenspoon; Sheffield: Sheffield University Press; forthcoming).

[12] Soltes, *Edge*, 73.

[13] For more on Tamny, see Ori Z. Soltes, *The Circles of History and Jewish History* (exhibition catalogue; B'nai B'rith Klutznick National Jewish Museum, Washington, DC, 1997), 4-9, from which the quotation is taken. There was also a beautiful catalogue of "The Chosen" authored by Tamny that traveled with the exhibit; it may still be available from the artist.

[14] For more on Davidson's "Trace," see Soltes, *Journeys of the Spirit*. Among other important artistic efforts with regard to Sephardic culture and history, mention should also be made of Michaela Amato's very strong recent installations.

[15] Quoted from the artist's statement in Soltes, *Edge*, 84.

[16] *Ibid.*

[17] *Ibid.*

[18] For more on Elyse Klaidman's work, see Soltes, *Fixing the World*, 99-103, and Ori Z. Soltes, *Intimations of Immortality: the Paintings of Kitty Klaidman and Elyse Klaidman* (exhibition catalogue; B'nai B'rith Klutznick National Jewish Museum, Washington DC, 1993), 15-26.

[19] For more on Kitty Klaidman's work, see Soltes, *Fixing the World*, 103-4, and Soltes, *Intimations*, 2-14.

[20] Sanabria applies the same technique, silent architectural portraiture, to other subjects with and without Jewish content (for example, Mexican houses or African American slave quarters). For more on her work, see Ori Z. Soltes, *Spirit and Vision in Holocaust Art* (exhibition catalogue; B'nai B'rith Klutznick National Jewish Museum, Washington, DC, 1994), and Soltes, *Fixing the World*, 104-5.

[21] For more on Cahana's work, see *From Ashes to the Rainbow: A Tribute to Raoul Wallenberg, Works by Alice Lok Cahana*, (exhibition catalogue; Hebrew Union College Skirball Museum, Los Angeles, 1986), and Soltes, *Fixing the World*, 80-82.

[22] For more on Karver's work, see Soltes, *Spirit*.

[23] For more information, see Judith Liberman, *The Holocaust Wall Hangings* (South Deerfield: Schoen Books, 2002.)

[24] For more on the work of Janis Goodman, see Ori Z. Soltes, *The Content of History: Works by Janis Goodman and Michael Katz*, (exhibition catalogue; B'nai B'rith Klutznick National Jewish Museum, Washington, DC, 1995), and Soltes, *Fixing the World*, 104-06.

[25] For more on the work of Gay Block and Dorit Cypis, see Soltes, *Edge*, 80-81, 88, and Gay Block and Malka Drucker, *Rescuers: Portraits of Moral Courage in the Holocaust* (New York: Holmes & Meier, 1992).

[26] The change in the artist's second name was due to marriage; the change in her first name was a result of her decision to pursue a more intensely Jewish life style, as marked by the turn to a Hebrew name.

[27] The quoted passages are found in Ori Z. Soltes, *Textures of Identity* (exhibition catalogue; B'nai B'rith Klutznick National Jewish Museum, Washington, DC, 1995).

[28] *Ibid.*

[29] For more information on Miriam's Goblet, see the brochure from the major exhibition focused on that object at Hebrew Union College Joseph Gallery, New York City, 1996, and Ori Z. Soltes, *Realm Between Realms* (exhibition catalogue; B'nai B'rith Klutznick National Jewish Museum, Washington DC, 1997), 7, 23, and supplement.

[30] For more information on the work of Devorah Neumark and Shari Rothfarb, see Soltes, *Edge*, 76-77. No still photograph can do justice to the kinetic delicacy of Rothfarb's video installation.

[31] For more on this body of Shafner's work see *Women of Mystery, Men of Prophecy: Biblical Paintings by Janet Shafner*, published by the Jewish Heritage Project, Inc in conjunction with the exhibition of that name at the Lyman Allen Art Museum, New London, January-June, 2003.

[32]The quotations from the artist are found in Ori Z. Soltes, *Jews, Women and Art* (exhibition catalogue; B'nai B'rith Klutznick National Jewish Museum, Washington, DC, 1998), 49-50. More on her pop icons will be found in Soltes, *Realm*, 28-29. There is a poignant biographical aspect to all this. Ruth Dunkell and her husband, Dr. Sam Dunkell, lost their first child to Tay-Sachs Syndrome; in consequence, they helped pioneer methods that have led to the virtual eradication of this disease, which particularly affects Jews from certain areas of Eastern Europe. Each of her changes in style and subject parallels developments in that battle. See the Yeshiva University Museum exhibit *Reaching for the Moon* (curated by Ori Z. Soltes, New York, Spring, 2000), which tells this story in greater detail. A catalogue of the same name, discussing Ruth's work and written by Ori Z. Soltes, was published by the Dunkells in New York in January, 2003.

[33]For more on Suzanne Benton's masks, see Soltes, *Jews, Women and Art*, 50-52.

[34]For a discussion of the work of Banner and Logemann in relationship to Jewish mysticism, see Ori Z. Soltes, *Seven Artists: Mysticism in Jewish Art* (exhibition catalogue; B'nai B'rith Klutznick National Jewish Museum, Washington DC, 1996), and Soltes, "Spirituality into a New Millennium: Mysticism in Jewish Art" in *Studies in Jewish Civilization 13: Spiritual Dimensions of Judaism* (eds. L. J. Greenspoon, et. al.; Omaha: Creighton University Press, 2003). Logemann is also discussed further in Soltes, *Fixing the World*, 133-35.

[35]Samuels' piece is discussed at greater length in Soltes, *Fixing the World*, 138-40, and in Ori Z. Soltes, "Contexts: Jews and Art at the End of the Millennium," in *Faith: The Impact of Judeo-Christian Religion on Art at the Millennium* (exhibition catalogue; Aldrich Museum of Contemporary Art, Ridgefield, 2000).

[36]For Carol Hamoy's work, see Soltes, *Textures*, 19-27, and below.

[37]The number eighteen is felicitous in symbolizing "life" in Hebrew numerology. The group's membership has had occasional changes. For example, Ruth Dunkell was briefly a member of the group in the late 1990s. Several others have come and gone, but the number of members has tended to remain constant; in any case, that is the number as of this writing. At present, Naomi Schechter, and Sheila Granda, whose work I do not discuss for lack of current information, have joined; Jenny Tango has left, and Leonora Arye, sadly, passed away recently.

[38]Each of the eighteen artists discussed in the balance of this essay is discussed at somewhat greater length in Soltes, *Jews, Women and Art*, 3-42. Several of them are also discussed in Soltes, *Textures* (Hamoy); Soltes, *Edge* (Cohen, Giladi), and Soltes, *Fixing the World*, part 3 (Cohen, Eller, Rosenberg, Taylor).

[39]For information on this particular series, see Marilyn Cohen and Ori Z. Soltes, *Where Did They Go When They Came to America?: Over a Century of Jewish Life in America* (exhibition catalogue; B'nai B'rith Klutznick National Jewish Museum, Washington, DC, 1994).

[40]In commenting on the tradition according to which male artists depict naked females for ogling male audiences, she also calls to mind the "Odalisqe/Self-Portrait" by Joyce Ellen Weinstein discussed above.

[41]The first-born son of David and Bathsheba died shortly after birth as the Lord's punishment for David's lust. His second son by Bethsheba was Solomon. Nowhere in the biblical narrative are Bathsheba, her thoughts, her feelings, or her ultimate fate discussed.

[42]Apparently, this character alludes to the recent debate regarding the validity of the canonization of Edith Stein, a Jewish-born convert to Catholicism who became a nun and perished at Auschwitz.

[43]To the author during the preparation of the exhibit *Jews, Women and Art* (see above, fn. 32).

Women on the Wall

Gail Twersky Reimer

The Jewish Women's Archive (JWA) was founded in 1995 to uncover, chronicle, and transmit the diverse and rich history of Jewish women in North America. In partnership with scholars, archivists, individual researchers, educators, and dedicated women in communities across the country, the Jewish Women's Archive furthers its mission through a variety of programs and products that afford access and meaning to the cultural and historical experience of Jews, specifically of Jewish women in North America.

One of JWA's signature products is its *Women of Valor* posters, a series featuring notable Jewish women that JWA began producing and disseminating in 1997. The *Women of Valor* project has since expanded to include virtual exhibits, lesson plans, curricula, and public programs that feature contemporary women carrying on the legacy of the *Women of Valor*. In numerous venues, most notably in classrooms in Jewish day and afternoon schools, these posters are the only visual representation of Jewish women in evidence.

The *Women of Valor* posters were not the first mass-produced series to focus on American Jewish women's history. In 1974, under the direction of Dr. Jacob Rader Marcus, the American Jewish Archives (AJA) began producing posters featuring Jewish women as part of its series on American Jewish heroes. A comparative analysis of the AJA posters, produced over two decades ago, and JWA's *Women of Valor* posters, created in the final years of the twentieth century, offers us a unique opportunity to examine the impact of feminist scholarship on the public presentation of Jewish women's history. Differences in the language of representation in the two series, both textual and visual, point to significant changes in the determination of what is historically significant, who is considered historically significant, and how we construct historical narratives.

AJA, founded by Marcus in 1947, began producing and circulating posters in 1961. Current AJA promotional literature describes the posters as presenting "a bona fide group of American Jewish heroes" to a nation longing for heroes. Intended primarily for educational use within the Reform community, the posters came out in several historical series. The first, produced in 1961, treated the Civil War. An eastern European/ Lower East Side immigrant series followed in 1966, and an eighteenth century Colonial Revolutionary War series appeared in 1967.

In 1971, the emphasis shifted from historical periods to professions, with the production of a series of posters on Jews in medicine and another on American Jewish philanthropists. Neither the historical series nor the professional series featured any women. For more than a decade, all the "bona fide heroes" in the AJA pantheon were male.

It was not until 1974 that the AJA came out with posters portraying women. That year, AJA produced three posters featuring women; two years later AJA produced another five posters of women. In 1981, seven years after AJA produced its first posters with women, Marcus published *The American Jewish Woman, 1654-1980.*[1] In his preface to this important volume he wrote: "Why did I write this book? Actually, I was pressured into it by colleagues and associates."

Can we speculate that seven years earlier, when the first posters on women were produced, they too were the result of pressure from colleagues?[2] A brief look at the historical context in which the posters were produced, a decade that Marcus has referred to as the decade of "Jewish feminist revolt," sheds some light on what motivated their production.[3] Just one year before AJA came out with its first group of posters profiling women, *Response* magazine published a special issue dedicated to the concerns of Jewish feminists. That same year the first National Jewish Women's Conference took place in New York City. In 1972, two years before the posters appeared, Sally Priesand was ordained rabbi by Hebrew Union College-Jewish Institute of Religion (HUC-JIR), the first woman in history to be ordained by a rabbinical seminary. Priesand's thesis for her rabbinical degree was the design for a course titled, "The Historic and Changing Role of the Jewish Woman." In one of her final chapters, Priesand attempted to redress the neglect of historical research on Jewish women who had long been denied due recognition for their accomplishments. Included in this chapter were short profiles of four women: Ernestine Rose, Bertha Pappenheim, Hannah Senesh, and Golda Meir.

Whether Priesand's presence at HUC or her thesis played a role in Marcus's decision to produce posters featuring women cannot be determined. It is, nonetheless, worth noting that a final poster, now included in the AJA series on Jewish women, marks the tenth anniversary of Rabbi Priesand's ordination [fig. 1]. Unlike the other posters in this series, this one celebrates an occasion, the ordination of women, rather than a person. Although this occasion was precipitated by the courage and determination of a particular woman, her name does not appear in bold letters, nor is her image at the center of the poster. The ordained (Rabbi Priesand), with head bowed, shares the space with the ordainer (HUC Chancellor Alfred Gottschalk), who towers above her. Neither the design nor the content of this poster emphasizes Priesand's heroism and importance. Its puzzling inclusion in a poster series on American Jewish women heroes might be an implicit acknowledgement of her responsibility for the series as a whole. Wherever the impetus originated, Marcus's decision to produce a women's series was groundbreaking and far-sighted. As with his founding of AJA, Jacob Rader Marcus once again demonstrated an understanding of how the interaction between American Jews (in this instance, Jewish women) and the American world (in this instance, the feminist movement) would soon give birth to a new Jewish reality.

When JWA embarked on the production of its poster series in late 1996, the shift that Marcus had anticipated was well underway. Jewish women were being ordained in ever-growing numbers, not only in Reform seminaries, but in Conservative and Reconstructionist ones as well. The Jewish women's caucus of the Association for Jewish Studies had been meeting for over ten years and had recently sponsored the publication of a collection of course syllabi titled, *Gender and Jewish Studies: A Curriculum Guide*.[4] The syllabi in this collection represented a quantum leap forward from the course Priesand had designed for her thesis, with the focus no longer on "women worthies," but on "the neglected perspectives and experiences of the female half of the Jewish people."[5] And, perhaps of most significance, in 1996 the groundbreaking two-volume encyclopedia, *Jewish Women in America: A Historical Encyclopedia*, was nearing completion.[6]

The *Women of Valor* poster series was the inaugural project of the JWA, developed in partnership with Ma'yan: The Jewish Women's Project of the Jewish Community Center of the Upper West Side of New York.[7] This collaboration grew out of a shared interest in Jewish

fig. 1 *10th Anniversary of the Ordination of Women in the Rabbinate*

women's history. Ma'yan's historical inclinations were evidenced in one of the new rituals the organization had developed for its increasingly popular community feminist seders held in New York City. Linking each of the Seder's traditional four cups of wine to the story of an exemplary Jewish woman, Ma'yan hoped to provide Seder participants with the opportunity to hear the names and learn the stories of historic Jewish women—women many participants had never heard of or knew little about.[8] The collaboration was also necessitated by the fact that the JWA, launched just a few months earlier, had only one staff person and no infrastructure to support the research, design, and production of posters. Finally, the collaboration was facilitated by a lead donor the two organizations shared in common. Barbara Dobkin, the founder of Ma'yan, was also the founding board chair of JWA.

JWA conceived of this project as a way to market an idea that was the backbone of its mission: the value of Jewish women's history. JWA hoped that by stimulating interest in the lives and achievements of Jewish women, it could promote widespread understanding (beyond the halls of the academy) of the importance and usefulness of uncovering, chronicling, and studying the record of Jewish women's lives and experiences. In a grant proposal submitted to the Ms. Foundation for Education and Communication, the first foundation to fund the project,[9] this effort was described as follows:

> Designed as a six year project, *Women of Valor* will bring recognition to, and increase knowledge about, eighteen outstanding Jewish women, while heightening awareness within the Jewish community of the importance of women's history generally, and both within and outside the Jewish community of the contributions of Jewish women to Western civilization.

JWA titled the series *Women of Valor*, drawing on the biblical phrase used in Proverbs and in the book of Ruth. The title was also meant to position the posters in relation to several poster sets issued earlier in the decade, titled *Women of Hope*.[10] Developed by the Bread and Roses Project in New York, their aim was "to demonstrate the diversity of American life." The *Women of Hope* poster sets showcased accomplished African-American women, Asian-American women, Latina women and Native American women. As with so many other multicultural projects, programs, and curricula, *Women of Hope* did not consider Jewish women or their significant contributions to the diversity of American life as worthy of a poster series of their own.[11]

Jewish meaning was also implicit in the decision to develop a set of eighteen posters rather than follow the twelve poster model developed by the Bread and Roses Project. Seizing on the symbolic value of the number 18 in Hebrew (the numerical value of the letters in the Hebrew word *chai* [life] is eighteen), JWA staff saw the poster series as giving new life to Jewish history by recovering women's part in shaping it.

As a first step, JWA assembled an advisory board of thirteen distinguished Jewish women historians and educators to guide the selection of the individuals to be featured in the posters. Though a few of the scholars expressed concern that the project, with its focus on "women worthies," was a step backward, most recognized the significance of a women's panel making the selections and were eager to play a role in determining which historic Jewish women would become central to the collective imagination of this generation.

They were also eager to see the posters distributed to as broad an audience as funding would allow. As a result, they were particularly sensitive to aspects of women's lives that might offend one or another population. Emma Goldman, for example, was on nearly everyone's list for inclusion. There was general agreement, however, that beginning the series with a figure as controversial as Emma Goldman might doom it from the start. Knowing that the series was designed to produce eighteen posters over the course of six years, the advisory board was able to take a long view. Not creating a poster of Emma Goldman at the outset did not mean that she would be ignored. Rather, by starting with women who were relatively recognizable and relatively uncontroversial, *Women of Valor* could gain entrée into the full range of Jewish educational and communal institutions and pave the way for eventual acceptance of controversial heroes like Emma Goldman.

When the advisory committee first met, JWA had not yet made the decision to limit its focus to Jewish women in the United States and Canada. The initial list of approximately sixty women presented to the board included Israeli and European women. Nearly everyone had her personal favorites and strong arguments against featuring other women. Some added names to the list, but eventually a consensus emerged to include six women, four of whom were Americans. The recommendation was that three be profiled in the first year and three in the second. After that the group was to reconvene to evaluate use of the posters and to select the next three women to profile. The first set of *Women of Valor* posters featured Gluckl of Hameln, Henrietta Szold, and Rose

Schneiderman. By the second year of the project, JWA had refined its focus; from then on, the series would include only North American women.

Four women appear in both the AJA series and the JWA series: Henrietta Szold, Rebecca Gratz, Lillian Wald, and Emma Lazarus, though how they appear is strikingly different. The other four women featured in the AJA series are Abigail Minis, Abigail Levi Frank, Sophie Irene Loeb, and Ernestine Rose. In the aggregate, the AJA posters reflect Marcus's interest in the early American experience, his preference for liberal, socially active women, his recognition of both suffrage and Zionism as two of the central movements in the modern era, and his privileging of married women with children. Every woman in the AJA series, with the possible exception of Abigail Franks, bears witness to Marcus's preference for liberal, socially active women. The JWA series also includes a fair number of liberal, socially active women. But it includes more radical women like Rose Schneiderman and Emma Goldman as well.

Marcus's interest in the early American experience is evident in the choice of Gratz, as well as the two Abigails: Abigail Levi Franks, wife of the country's wealthiest Jewish merchant in the colonial period, whose extensive correspondence with her sons "offers a vivid picture of life among the elite, Jewish and non-Jewish, of eighteenth century New York"; and Abigail Minis, a Southern businesswoman and landowner known for her support of the Revolutionary cause. Like Gratz, both of these women belonged to the elite of their society. Unlike Gratz, both were married women with children. The text on the Minis poster mentions her husband (quite literally) only in passing. It reads:

Abigail Minis (1701-1794), the Colonial matriarch, arrived in Georgia in 1733, one of the first white women to settle in that colony. After her husband's death, she took over the management of his ranch, store and tavern.

In contrast, the text on the Abigail Franks poster (nearly three times the length of the text on the Minis poster) emphasizes this Abigail's role as daughter, wife, and mother—and little else. It begins:

London-born Abigail Levy (1696-1756), the daughter of a successful business man, was only sixteen when she married another Londoner, Jacob Franks (1687/88-1769), who subsequently became one of Colonial New York's most important merchant-shippers. Abigail bore her husband seven children, four boys and three girls.

Of the children who survived, two sons were sent off in their teens to England, where they were trained for mercantile careers and married relatives, members of well-known Anglo-Jewish families. A son and daughter who remained in America married non-Jews of aristocratic background—though this last clearly was small solace to their Orthodox Jewish parents.

Even her husband's dates of birth and death are included in this introductory text to Abigail's life.

Half of the women in the AJA series were married (though one of these divorced) and half were not. The four who were not married also appear in the JWA series. But as we saw earlier in the text from the Abigail Franks poster, the privileging of family is not simply a matter of who was chosen, but how these women's lives were represented on the posters. So, for example, the text on Ernestine Rose's poster begins apologetically: "Though married to an English non-Jew, Polish born Ernestine Louise Rose (1810-1892) was the daughter of an Orthodox rabbi." Apologia runs all the way through this narrative, which concludes with the puzzling summation: "Neither fool nor fanatic, Mrs. Rose was possessed of a keen mind and the power to speak with logic as well as eloquence."

Rose, it seems, was a problematic figure for Marcus. This is evident in the poster text just cited as well as in his comments on Rose several years after the poster was produced. In his book on American Jewish women, Marcus asks, "Does Ernestine Rose deserve a place in the story of the American Jewess?" Rather than answering the question directly, Marcus offers an explanation as to why he posed the question:

> She seems to have had no interest in Jews except as fellow human beings; she defended them ably when they were attacked by a prejudiced commentator. At best her relationship to the American Jewess is a tangential one. By furthering the status of all women—and she did—she furthered the status of the American of Jewish descent. She was not a women's liberationist; she was preeminently an egalitarian. She did not set out to separate or to "liberate" women from men; her hope was that women would enjoy the same rights as men, and work closely with them on a common plane.[12]

Given Rose's leadership in the struggle for women's rights and Marcus's awareness of suffrage as a central movement in the modern era, his inclusion of Rose in the pantheon of Jewish women heroes was almost an imperative. But in order to include her, he needed to be convinced that Ernestine Rose was no fanatic.

Were the AJA series more extensive, it is easy to imagine that there would have been additional overlap. Surely Hannah Grenebaum Solomon would have figured in the group. After all, Marcus refers to the founding of the National Council of Jewish Women as a "watershed, inaugurating a new era for American Jewesses."[13] Justine Wise Polier might also have qualified as a "bona-fide American Jewish hero." Liberal, socially active women both were also wives and mothers.[14]

On the other hand, as suggested above, Marcus would have rejected some of the women featured in the JWA series for their radical politics. Others, I believe, would have been rejected for not being sufficiently active in the public arena. While JWA's poster series seems predisposed to women who are politically active, the series is inclusive of Jewish women whose achievements span a range of fields, including the arts (Molly Picon, Anna Sokolow), sports (Bobby Rosenfeld), business (Beatrice Alexander), science (Gertrude Elion), and scholarship (Barbara Myerhoff).

Women from the East Coast predominate in both the JWA series and the AJA series. Each series has a single poster on a southern Jewish woman. The AJA southerner is Abigail Minis of Georgia, and the JWA's is Gertrude Weil of North Carolina. JWA opted for the liberal, socially active woman, whereas AJA chose a colonial pioneer. The first white woman to settle in the colony of Georgia, Abigail Minis made her mark as a successful businesswoman. Gertrude Weil, on the other hand, is notable for her tireless efforts to challenge the racism and sexism that characterized much of Southern culture and to extend political, economic, and social opportunities to those long denied them.

Weil is unique among the women in the JWA series. Her prominence was at the local rather than the national level. A lifelong resident of Goldsboro, NC, Weil focused the greatest part of her activism in her home town and state. As member, advisor, leader, or benefactor of numerous organizations, she took an active role in every aspect of life in Goldsboro. Like many other women across the South and the nation, Weil shaped the political and social culture of her community, helping to make it into a vital and meaningful home for all its residents.

The JWA series also includes a woman from Chicago (Hannah Grenebaum Solomon), a Californian (Barbara Myerhoff), and a Canadian

(Bobbie Rosenfeld). Symbolically, at least, the series recognizes the achievements of North American Jewish women from coast to coast, as well as beyond the borders of the USA. Both series celebrate women of achievement, but the JWA series casts a wider net. It follows the lead of AJA in recognizing suffrage and Zionism as two central movements in which American Jewish women played a prominent role. But JWA expands this list to include the labor movement (Rose Schneiderman), civil rights (Gertrude Weil), the settlement house movement (Lilian Wald), and feminism and environmentalism (Bella Abzug). The stories of these women as recounted on JWA posters have the potential to inspire civic engagement. Other posters in the JWA series suggest a less didactic use of role models to heighten awareness of possibilities rather than to channel viewers in a particular direction. It could be argued that these other posters, at least implicitly, pay homage to the centrality of the feminist movement.

The influence of feminism is also evident in the visual language of the JWA series, a language that differentiates the two sets of posters even more than their textual content. AJA's posters follow the conventional wisdom regarding posters—that less is more—as, for example, in the poster of Rebecca Gratz [fig. 2]. The text here is unusually short, but our interest is less in the length of text than in the general design of the poster. The assumption that less is more is also the operative design principle in the *Women of Hope* posters produced by the Bread and Roses Project. But this is where the similarity between these series begins and ends. Even in its minimal content, each of the posters produced by Bread and Roses gives women both a voice and a material presence. The elements of composition are photographic portrait, name, identifying tag line, and a quotation [fig. 3].

In the posters produced by AJA, the women remain voiceless, with only one exception. In the poster of Emma Lazarus, where a women's own words do appear, the immortal lines from her poem, "The New Colossus," are featured prominently, while Lazarus herself nearly disappears—a disembodied head floating in space [fig. 4]. Similarly, the pen that is responsible for Abigail Levy Frank's significance as a chronicler of eighteenth century life is not in her hand but floats at the side of her head, a kind of ornamental feather in her hair [fig. 5]. And although Sophie Loeb is represented writing, it is unclear what she is writing. A letter? A newspaper article? Legislation? Her text is rendered illegible by design [fig. 6]. The only legible text in the AJA posters is

fig. 2 *Rebecca Gratz*

fig. 3 *Rebecca Gratz*

fig. 4 *Emma Lazarus*

fig. 5 *Abigail Franks*

fig. 6 *Sophie Irene Loeb*

the paragraph produced by their creator, Dr. Marcus. Like the image that dominates the poster, the master narrative distills each woman's life to its essence.

It would be disingenuous to claim that master narratives are absent from the JWA posters. However, in these posters the summary paragraphs are but one of several textual and design elements—and rarely the dominant element in a complex composition. Rich compendia of information, JWA's *Women of Valor* posters challenge the rule that less is more. Their design is based in part on the conviction that when it comes to women, less is not enough. Rather than reducing a woman to "her essence," the *Women of Valor* posters present an expansive view of each woman's life.

The production of the JWA posters relies on a considerable amount of research in primary and secondary sources. After visual material is collected and several pages of evocative and representative quotations compiled, the researchers meet with the designer, Cynthia Madansky, to present their emerging understanding of the texture of each woman's life. Following this meeting, Madansky conducts her own research on the period. She then selects colors, typeface, and other design elements that represent for her the featured woman, the historical period in which she lived, and the arena of her major achievements.

Color, which in the AJA posters seems to be rather arbitrarily chosen, is used in the JWA posters to convey something about the subject. The bold red used in the Rose Schneiderman poster, for example, suggests her feisty spirit and fiery activism. The more muted reds mixed with blues in the Gratz poster recall her patriotism, while the deeper reds and blues of the Lazarus poster point to the iconic status of the Statue of Liberty, which bears her poem, "The New Colossus," on its pedestal.

Midway through the design phase, when the final text for each poster is decided upon, scholars of the period review all written material. This includes the summary paragraph, the timeline, and the selected quotations. The summary paragraphs in the AJA series included birth and death dates and generally provided some information about historical context. What they did not do was show the lived life in relation to historical time. By incorporating both the public and private, the timelines in the *Women of Valor* posters resist the dichotomization that renders only one's public life noteworthy. In addition, the timelines offer a significantly different perspective from that of the AJA summary paragraph referred to earlier as the "master narrative."

The quotations incorporated in the JWA posters serve more than one function. They give women their own voice, allowing them to speak for themselves. At the same time, they transform the viewer of the poster from passive recipient of information into an active interpreter. Coupled with the photographs and images of primary documents incorporated into many of the posters, the quotations accomplish in miniature what Marcus hoped to accomplish with his thousand-page *American Jewish Woman: A Documentary History*.[15] Published as a supplement to his narrative history of the same title, this collection of primary sources was intended to serve as a "control" for the "opinions, the conclusions, and the divagations of the writer of history." Documents, Marcus writes in the introduction, "speak for themselves and permit every reader to be his or her own historian."[16]

Quotations, timelines, and summary paragraphs, taken together, offer a range of perspectives on each woman. These various informational elements are organized so as to allow the viewer to receive them in any order she or he chooses. The JWA poster not only resists any single, fixed interpretation, but actually encourages multiple readings.

Through a complex layering of words, images, and design, the JWA posters convey the texture of women's lives; in documenting that there was much that women said and did that is worth recording, they send the message that women are not simply objects to be gazed at. Full of surprises and challenges, they coax viewers to come closer. While the posters can be noted quickly in passing, their design invites people to engage with the posters, to read the text, and to linger over the images. Unlike the viewers of the AJA posters, whose stance is primarily passive and distanced, viewers of the *Women of Valor* posters are encouraged to become historians themselves, bringing their own sensibilities to bear on the construction of meaning in these women's lives.

The production of the AJA posters of women coincided with the beginning of a new chapter in American Jewish life, one in which women would increasingly assert their right to full participation in religious and communal life and to authentic representation in the texts that tell the American Jewish story. AJA's expansion of a visual narrative of male heroes to include female heroes was an important step towards the development of American Jewish women's history. But, as our analysis has demonstrated, it was a conflicted step, marked by anxiety about the demands of "women liberationists" and refusal to relinquish male control of the narrative.

Superficially, JWA's *Women of Valor* series continues to tell the story of notable women begun by AJA [figs. 7-9]. On closer examination, however, it becomes clear that embedded in the design of the *Women of Valor* posters is a substantially different attitude towards both subjects and viewers. Though they still feature "women worthies" and thus stay within the bounds of what theorists of women's history call compensatory history,[17] they reflect the maturation of the field of women's history and the imprint of a generation of feminist scholars who have examined women's past through the eyes of women. Filtered through the prism of gender, the lives of notable Jewish women, as represented in the JWA posters, bear witness to the relatively unknown richness and complexity of the cultural and historical experience of Jewish women in America.

NOTES

[1] Jacob Rader Marcus, *The American Jewish Woman, 1654-1980* (American Jewish Archives; New York, Cincinnati: Ktav, 1981).
[2] In the absence of any documentation regarding the production of the AJA posters, all we can do is speculate.
[3] Marcus, *The American Jewish Woman.*
[4] Judith Reesa Baskin and Sheely Tenenbaum, *Gender and Jewish Studies: A Curriculum Guide* (New York: Biblio Press, 1994).
[5] *Ibid.*
[6] Paula Hyman and Deborah Dash Moore, eds., *Jewish Women in America: An Historical Encyclopedia* (New York: Routledge, 1997).
[7] See online http://www.mayan.org/mayan.asp.
[8] In her plenary address given at the Exploring Issues of Gender in Jewish Day School Education Conference held on February 13, 1996, author Nessa Rapoport spoke of the power of this ritual:

> I realized that after more than forty years of loving the seder with my heart, soul and might, I had not heard a single Jewish woman's name on seder night. I had never noticed that all the long beautiful night of the seder, all through the citations of Rabbi Eliezer and Rabbi Akiva, all through the paragraphs we added on the Shoah, on Soviet Jews, I could not look at this paradigmatic text and find this aspect of myself within it. If gender doesn't matter, such an absence makes no difference. But since it has mattered from the very beginning, it is powerful indeed to find Jewish women in a story about freedom and redemption.

See Jenna Kaplan and Shulamit Reinharz, eds., *Gender Issues in Jewish Day Schools*

(Waltham: Women's Studies Program & Maurice and Marilyn Cohen Center for Modern Jewish Studies, Institute for Community and Religion, Brandeis University, 1997).

[9]The poster series would later receive significant support from the Convenant Foundation and the Righteous Persons Foundation.

[10] See online http://www.bread-and-roses.com/index.html.

[11]It should, however, be noted that in its most recent set of posters, *International Women of Hope*, which highlights "the achievements of 12 internationally renowned women and their contributions in helping shape the lives of their respective countries," the Bread and Roses project chose a Jewish woman, Bella Abzug, to represent the United States.

[12]See Marcus, *American Jewish Women.*

[13]*I bid.*

[14]For information on these and other women in the JWA series, see online: http://www.jwa.org/exhibits/.

[15]Jacob Rader Marcus, *The American Jewish Woman: A Documentary History* (American Jewish Archives; New York: Ktav, 1981).

[16]*Ibid.*

[17] See Gerda Lerner, *The Majority Finds Its Past: Placing Women in History* (New York: Oxford University Press, 1979), 145 .

fig. 7 *Emma Lazarus*

fig. 8 *Rose Schneiderman*

fig. 9 *Bella Abzug*

Jewish Feminist Scholarship:
A Critical Perspective

Esther Fuchs

What is Jewish feminist scholarship, what kind of knowledge does it seek to produce, and what are the guiding questions of its practitioners? At first sight, these questions are formidable for anyone trying to tackle them; because so much can be categorized as Jewish feminist scholarship, a meaningful discussion of the subject seems almost impossible. Indeed, in the last two decades an outpouring of publications on this subject has been taking place in both the humanities and the social sciences, both in Israel and in the U.S. It is precisely this unprecedented outpouring that requires a reflective pause, an assessment of what has been achieved and what still lies ahead. In this paper I would like to suggest some directions for reflection.

The tremendous growth of the field requires that we begin to recognize it as just this, a new field of study. And because no field of study is devoid of a vision, an agenda, a basic understanding of the value of the pursuit of the particular knowledge it produces, Jewish feminist studies ought also to offer just such a map. This map remains provisional and open to re-drawing, but it should serve teachers and students alike. To the extent that Jewish feminist studies is part of a more general feminist enterprise in the academy, it cannot and should not easily forego the self-critical impetus that inspires much of feminist studies in general. Much as feminist studies is critical of traditional academic disciplines—of so-called objective scholarship—and the politics of knowledge as it relates to women, it is also critical of its own theories and methods, subjecting them to constant investigation and inquiry.[1] Feminist theory and praxis are based on a continued commitment to a political position in which knowledge is not a goal in itself, but rather is meant to bring about a change in perception and evaluation. As Liz Stanley has articulated the problem, "Succinctly, the point is to change the world, not only to study it."[2]

It is precisely this awareness of its position(s), and a historical consciousness of its own process of growth and development, that are missing in Jewish feminist studies. What, then, is the mission of Jewish feminist studies? What are the trends that dominate the field at this point? Are there any developments or transitions that can be discerned from an early or pioneering self-perception to a later one? My attempt is not so much to respond to these questions, but to argue for recognition of their importance.

What is most sorely missing in the majority of anthologies on Jewish feminist studies that have been published to date is a clarification of theoretical positions and a scholarly debate on the nature of the field. The prevalent tendency is to dismiss early work by Jewish feminist scholars and to replace it with the latest developments. Instead of engaging in cross-generational debate, instead of articulating and theorizing about the contributions of the early pioneers in Jewish history, Hebrew literature, and the Bible, "younger" scholars—whose age is not as important as the date of the most recent publication cited in their bibliography—dismiss rather than analyze their predecessors' work, simplistic as it may now seem to be. The old paradigm becomes inferior or "other"; the work in question becomes a stage for re-inventing knowledge as if from scratch, offering the "young" or "new" feminist a stage on which to perform her brilliant analysis; in the process she secures the desired institutional academic recognition or career advancement.[3] As Stanley, among others, points out, this very dismissal is an anti-feminist gesture, especially in the context of a field that is purportedly devoted to recovering the academic, literary, and cultural mothers who have been dismissed or suppressed by male-dominated scholarship.[4] While these so-called younger or new feminist scholars are careless about citing their predecessors, there is a general tendency to cite liberally the new fathers of the field and indeed to follow them both in theory and practice. The failure to recognize the mothers or even sisters in the field, a failure that is visible in the lack of theoretical debate among Jewish feminist scholars, leads inevitably to the retention of old scholarly paradigms from male-dominated academic practice as well as to disciplinary divisions. To a large extent, the field of Jewish feminist studies has been co-opted by male feminist scholars in rabbinic studies, modern Jewish literature, Kabbalah, history, and anthropology.

THE LACK OF DEBATE AND DIALOGUE

One of the few books published to date on the state and status of feminist inquiry in Jewish Studies is the excellent collection of essays titled *Feminist Perspectives on Jewish Studies.*[5] This valuable anthology assesses the impact of feminist criticism on the various sub-fields that make up Jewish Studies. Equally important is the survey of major feminist works and issues each essay offers. As the introduction notes, "The authors in this volume begin with the basic assumption that gender implies a hierarchy of values in which males have more power, their activities are seen as more important, and their traits are privileged."[6] The constrictions of objectivity masquerading as androcentrism and the interdisciplinary nature of feminist scholarship are clearly pointed out. This enables an inquiry into the public-private dichotomy to reassess the allegedly inferior contribution of women to Jewish culture and provide the reader with tools to reevaluate female interpretations and practices.

Most contributors to the volume seem to agree that resistance to feminist criticism is staunch and persistent. Feminist contributions to Jewish philosophy have been scant, and feminist contributions to Jewish history and sociology have not done much to bring about a paradigm shift in the field. On the other hand, gender seems to have become a basic category of analysis in biblical studies and, to a lesser extent, in Jewish literature. But what are the questions feminist scholars in all fields should be raising, what are the differences among and between the disciplines, what barriers can and should be transcended, and what are the most urgent problems requiring immediate attention? The unifying goal in each essay seems to be the creation of a paradigm shift, where gender becomes a fundamental category of analysis rather than merely a theme. However, the essays rarely venture beyond the disciplinary demarcations that delimit them. For instance, while the family is discussed in history, sociology, and anthropology, there is no effort to create interdisciplinary links to demonstrate how Jewish feminist inquiry can become an interdisciplinary enterprise. By using the "master's tools"—namely, the very construction of a discipline—the contributors remain separate and distinguished from each other, not modeling an interdisciplinary method of feminist inquiry.

Another missed opportunity is speculation on the links between Jewish feminist scholarship and its social base or the social movement that has spawned it: who are the women for whom these scholars speak?

Also needed is a self-reflective and self-conscious critique of the kind of feminism that inspires the volume as a whole: is it liberal feminist theory that seeks to create equality for women (that is, a better and larger share of the economic pie already available to privileged women), or does it seek to align feminism with other movements for social change? If so, what are those other movements? While the issue of exclusion and marginality emerges rather clearly from *Feminist Perspectives on Jewish Studies*, the problem of oppression and the politics of feminist scholarship are less well articulated.

The recognition that scholarship is both partisan and political is one of the basic insights of feminist inquiry as such:

> At the heart of feminist scholarship in all fields of study is an awareness of the problem of women's oppression and the ways in which academic inquiry has subtly subsidized it, a sense of the possibilities for liberation, and a commitment to make scholarship work on women's behalf.[7]

Yet this definition again begs the question: Who are the women we are fighting for? In like manner, *Feminist Perspectives on Jewish Studies* does not answer the question regarding whose oppression we are challenging in our committed scholarly work. Are we committed to the double exclusions of Middle Eastern Jewish women, of Jewish lesbians, of Ethiopian Jewish women in Israel? What is the role of class, race, and sexual orientation in constructing a new Jewish feminist scholarship? Is this scholarship inspired by a desire for social change, and does it have clear links to a social or political movement? Should Jewish feminist scholars work to prove the historical commitment of Jewish women to Jewish religion, or should they focus on the ways in which women, both Jewish and non-Jewish, have been victims of similar oppressions in different contexts? Do certain or all Jewish women collude in the oppression of other women, for example, of Palestinian women? In short, what are the political and social ramifications of a committed, non-objective, political scholarship of the kind described as the desideratum in this anthology's introduction?

The question about the kind of knowledge we seek to produce is raised as a theoretical precept in the introduction and in disparate essays, but the debate between integrationists and separatists is not spelled out. Do we wish to change the face of Jewish Studies as such, perhaps collapse the boundaries between the Bible and Mishnah and create a field of Jewish antiquity, or collapse the boundaries between Hebrew and English literature and create a new field of Jewish literature? If so, what would be the advantage to feminist inquiry of rethinking the very shape of the disciplines as currently constituted? For the purposes of feminist inquiry, why not collapse the boundaries of anthropology and sociology, both social science fields that study specific Jewish groups? Should we integrate literature and film studies into a new field of representational studies? What value might we find in collapsing the boundaries between theology and philosophy, boundaries that are not altogether necessary from a feminist perspective? In an essay on Jewish philosophy, Hava Tirosh-Rothschild raises a serious challenge to separatist feminist scholarship and the essentialism it implies: "The only difference is that what the traditional conceptions of women denigrate, feminist thought praises as ideal."[8] Yet, this separatism seems to be inadvertently at work in Tikva Frymer-Kensky's reading of biblical women and Susan Sered's article on Kurdish women. At this point I do not wish to take sides, but merely to show that serious points of difference and contention are not being made explicit and that this mode of presentation creates juxtaposition rather than conversation. This juxtaposition entrenches rather than challenges the disciplinary organization of Jewish Studies.

Perhaps more important than the lack of conversation between and among disciplinary contributors is the lack of recognition of feminist pioneers and predecessors. Though Frymer-Kensky admits that the recognition of patriarchy as a fundamental construction of biblical discourse is basic to biblical feminism, she nevertheless fails to mention the names of those scholars, some of them Jewish, who contributed to this recognition.[9] Judith Hauptman presents Jacob Neusner as the originator and pioneer of feminist thought in rabbinics, although he is clearly indebted to feminist critics in biblical studies and classics. Other contributors are likewise reluctant to mention pioneering or contemporary feminists in their field and disagreements with their work.

Scholars who wish to challenge the erasure of women from Jewish Studies disciplines must take pains not to erase other women. They must conscientiously look for the woman who inspired the man, the woman whose voice was appropriated by the male scholar before he became the new feminist authority speaking about and for women. It is crucial for Jewish feminist scholars to think through their mothers. Gender is not just a category whose social correlative is oppressed women; it is also constituted by women's history as a serial relationship established through time. Iris Young states: "As a series, woman is the name of a structural relation to material objects as they have been produced and organized by prior history."[10] I would add to this that Jewish feminist scholarship must begin with a theoretical expansion of previous scholarship and attempt to unfold and elaborate what has been started before. The recovery of women's voices ought to include the voices of feminist critics, including recent critics, and it ought to include those with whom we agree and disagree, those in our midst who have made a contribution and who have been suppressed or dismissed by male authorities, and those whose works no longer are the on the cutting edge of Jewish feminist scholarship.

The final point of difference I seek to articulate here regarding this extremely valuable contribution to feminist scholarship is its ethnocentric perspective. While three essays, "Toward a Feminist Sociology of American Jews," "The Problem of Gender in American-Jewish Literature," and "Jews, Gender, American Cinema," address the American scene explicitly, other articles, although they deal with immigration and assimilation, are only implicitly ethnocentric. Religion is a central concern in the chapters on the Bible, rabbinic studies, theology, and Jewish philosophy. The focus on religion reflects the fact that Jewish studies in the American academy is constituted to a large extent as a religious studies field. Scholarship on Jewish studies is likely to be indexed in religious studies journals and publications in the United States. In contrast, feminist studies in the Israeli academy does not necessarily revolve around the theme of religion or religious thought. There, political science, law, sociology, anthropology, and literature are the leading disciplines, with theology trailing behind rather than leading the way. Though major books and articles in history, sociology, literature, and political science have appeared, as well as interdisciplinary anthologies, there is a clear lack of dialogue with Israeli feminist scholarship. There is no debate regarding the issues that preoccupy each academic center. Yet it is precisely this kind of dialogue that promises to reconfigure the walls of disciplinarity and limits on the production of knowledge. A dialogue between primarily religious and primarily political definitions of Jewish femaleness will help clarify the arbitrary nature of both definitions, perhaps helping to produce a new configuration of Jewish feminism.

TALKING PAST AND AROUND EACH OTHER

Much has transpired since the publication of Elizabeth Koltun's *The Jewish Woman* (1976), but to a large extent the format of thematic juxtaposition and the privileging of religion apparent in this early anthology continue to dictate the general subject matter and structure of future anthologies.[11] While the anthology should be credited for calling attention to forgotten Jewish feminist activists like Bertha Pappenheim and Henrietta Szold, the book is visibly divided into religious rather than political categories (for example, "spiritual quest," "the life cycle and new rituals," "women in Jewish law"). While religion continues to dominate the 1983 anthology, *On Being a Jewish Feminist*, it also offers a much more trenchant critique of the Jewish response to feminism.[12] Unlike the earlier collection, this makes room for debate between an integrationist position, arguing for a "sociological" analysis of the Jewish woman's problem, and a separatist position, arguing for a "theological" analysis of the status of women in Judaism.[13] It may be concluded that while the first anthology is engaged with the women's share of the Jewish pie, the second is mainly interested in the shape of an altogether different pie.[14] Still, in both anthologies, articles appear in juxtaposition to one another, and the tension between religionists and secularists, for example, goes unexplored (this is more noticeable in the first anthology).

The elision of debate and the tendency to universalize the American framework as a universal Jewish one characterize the scholarly anthology, *Gender and Judaism: The Transformation of Tradition*.[15] Though she identifies the Israeli context as the one in need of more urgent attention, Tamar Rudavsky refers in her introduction to a Jewish women's movement whose characteristics are obviously American:

> Clearly, as the articles in the present volume amply demonstrate, the Jewish women's movement rides the fine line between maintaining the meaningful components of tradition, while at the same time working to transform the more oppressive elements of that tradition.[16]

But where or what is this movement? Who are its members and founders? If the members of the movement are white, middle class Ashkenazi women, should not their privilege as well as predicament be articulated? Though she refers to Alice Shalvi's comparative essay on Israeli and American Jewish feminisms, Rudavsky nevertheless reverts to the American framework as the natural social context for the conference papers in her collection. The fundamental problem of juxtaposition, that is, talking past and around each other, is visible in this anthology as well. Historical essays on Nahida Remy-Ruth Lazarus and Pauline Wengeroff appear side by side with essays on American Orthodox women, American reform rabbis, and modern Jewish women in European academic contexts. The admittedly important task of filling in gaps in knowledge and information about individual women in history and about movements and groups of Ashkenazi and American women is not complemented by a rigorous theoretical debate about the purpose or state of Jewish feminist inquiry. Nor is there a sense of the social context or contemporary social agents whose oppression is supposedly discussed here, either explicitly or implicitly. Though Rudavsky mentions a community and a social background, the book does not convey any clear sense of the group in question. This lack places the anthology squarely within a traditional Jewish academic context whose apparent purpose is to produce idealized and disembodied knowledge, rather than to change a socially oppressive situation. Given these issues, it is difficult to assess the purpose of this anthology.

Gender and Judaism consists primarily of essays on extraordinary women whose devotion to Judaism cannot be questioned; the few critical essays it does include refer mostly to Judaism as a religious context or establishment. Judith Baskin's *Jewish Women in Historical Perspective* can be also characterized as appreciative writing about women in Jewish history.[17] With the exception of Judith Romney Wegner, Judith Baskin, and Paula Hyman, these historical essays exemplify what I might call a reconstructive concern; that is, an attempt to describe the lives, contributions, and struggles of Jewish women in various historical periods. For the most part, a critical perspective on androcentric oppression is relatively understated in this anthology. While Hyman offers a critical assessment of immigrant American women's lives, juxtaposing them with the relative privilege of men, Ellen Umansky offers a rather optimistic assessment of the contributions of women to American religious and spiritual life.[18] This difference could have served as the occasion for a lively theoretical debate, mapping out the methodological trajectories of a critical versus an appreciative approach. Instead, the two articles are presented in juxtaposition, rather than in dialogical relationship.

The focus on women as agents is also salient in Judith Baskin's *Women of the Word: Jewish Women and Jewish Writing.*[19] As Baskin notes in her introduction, most of the twelve essays deal with distinct works by women authors writing in English, Hebrew, or Yiddish.[20] The search for a Jewish female experience animates Baskin's first anthology, while the search for a Jewish woman's voice in literature inspires the second. Despite the postmodern debate over the inherently problematic search for a self-present, or "natural," female experience or voice, both quests are warranted, at least as searches for a construct.[21] This construct is necessary as a sketched horizon, as a possible goal that must nevertheless be redefined and re-articulated.

The above anthologies clearly make the point that the search is necessary, and despite subsequent critiques, I still believe that hypothetical sketches of a "female Jewish experience" or "female Jewish voice" are necessary theoretical constructs, if only to serve as starting points for much-needed debate that will lead to greater clarification. The perceived lack in these anthologies is of conversation among and between the scholars represented rather than an awareness of postmodern interventions into the idea of female agency.[22]

As a subsequent anthology, *Active Voices: Women in Jewish Culture,* demonstrates, the analysis of Jewish female agency and creativity is by far the most salient scholarly activity in Jewish feminist scholarship.[23] In her introduction to *Active Voices,* Maurie Sacks argues that her purpose in focusing on women's voices and activities is to introduce a more balanced Judaism, one not dominated by religious issues or male concerns:

> We examine gendered behavior as it functions in a total Jewish socio-cultural environment, not just in the domain called "religion"....The present anthropological perspective informs a choice of chapters that address women as agents *within Jewish cultural systems.*[24]

Though Sacks explicitly argues for urgency in discussing cultural rather than specifically religious contexts, nine of the twelve essays in this anthology deal with religious systems and frameworks. More importantly, most of the female activities described take place in the margins of larger male-dominated cultural systems. Though some articles demonstrate that the female agents addressed offered an alternative interpretation of their roles in the margins of Jewish cultural life, the women never challenge their narrowly defined roles. The articles also do not explain how the women create an ethics of resistance or liberation.

The women discussed in this anthology do indeed remain "within Jewish cultural systems"—the word "within" being key to an assessment of their contribution. This location confirms that these women did not question or challenge the narrow parameters, the margins to which they were assigned by male culture. Sacks argues that "the female experience...pertains to an everyday Judaism in which women play powerful and focal roles."[25] "Powerful" and "focal" are indeed relational terms, and one must clearly identify the comparative grids to which these roles are being compared. Despite an emphasis on diversity and multiplicity, which is expected of anthropological inquiry, *Active Voices* seeks to identify the voice of the Ashkenazi, middle class, American or European woman.

It seems to me that I myself am not entirely free of the above charge. The volume I edited for the interdisciplinary journal *Shofar*, titled *Women in Jewish Life and Culture*, was based on conference presentations; it therefore reflected the diversity of the papers, each of which affirmed a different approach to a specific problem in a given discipline. My introduction, titled "Female and Jewish: Critique and Reconstruction," suggested that scholars within Jewish feminist studies are so busy reconstructing knowledge that they fail at times to keep an eye on the important question of critique. The reconstruction of a Jewish female past, or of a female-authored literature, is important as part of our attempt to recover erased subjects and agencies; at the same time, we must not forget to retain the critical edge that informed the earliest forays into Jewish studies. Beyond the specific argument of my introduction, my attempt was to create a context for debating the goals, the theory, and the methods of Jewish feminist inquiry and to establish a certain discourse that would make practitioners aware of their own responsibility in producing a new kind of knowledge. As I said, I am not sure my edited volume achieved what the other volumes failed to achieve. But I believe the time has come for Jewish feminists to pause and take stock of how far we have come in the past two decades and where we are going.[26]

MEN IN JEWISH FEMINISM

Even as the majority of disciplines in Jewish Studies continue to hide behind a façade of male objectivity and business as usual, even as they continue to resist feminist scholarship, some male scholars have gone the other way. The very same scholars who resisted my papers on Hebrew literature in the early 1980s are now cited by younger feminist literary critics as feminist authorities and celebrated as pro-feminist supporters and sympathizers.[27] Within a decade, feminist theory has become something men do alongside women, and the signature of the critic does not seem to matter, whether it is Dan Miron in Hebrew literature, Elliott Wolfson in Kabbalah, or Howard Adelman in history. Yet, if so much in feminist theory does indeed confirm the significance of the sex/gender of the writer, how can we pretend that these characteristics do not matter? Does it not matter if the feminist critic is male or female? Does not one of the principles of feminist scholarship confirm the importance of scholarship about, for, and by women? The question is not merely one of biology, essentialism, or even ideology, but, as Ann duCille points out in another context, it is one of simple professionalism.[28] Male feminist scholars are reluctant to cite women who preceded them. Jewish male feminists are also reluctant to refer to their own gender/sex and to problems inherent in their profiteering from a theory that is relatively well established in the non-Jewish academy. There is hardly an expression of discomfort or even self-consciousness by these males, nor has there been any attempt to address the problem of their co-opting feminist criticism or the domination by men of Jewish feminist scholarship. Indeed, the names cited by many feminist scholars are not those of pioneering women feminists, but those of the new fathers of Jewish feminism: Daniel Boyarin in rabbinics, Howard Eilberg-Schwartz in biblical studies, and Sander Gilman in literature. Yet, to the best of my knowledge, none of these men has attempted to articulate their position, to render it visible, to use it as a point of analytic departure. Over a decade ago, Elaine Showalter called attention to the invasion of feminist criticism by male practitioners who ignore the political implications of their unproblematic self-presentation as feminists, even as they occlude the contribution of pioneering feminist critics.[29]

In my opinion, the most serious problem presented by leading male authorities in Jewish feminism is the metaphorical appropriation of the position of women and the displacement of "woman" as the paradigmatic victim of oppression by the "Jew," a male subject. In *Freud, Race, and Gender*, Gilman claims a certain anteriority for the "Jew," both temporal and conceptual, positing that this image is the prototype of the image of woman in his work: "The language that Freud used about the scientific inability to know the core of what makes a Jewish male a male Jew was parallel to that which he used concerning the essence of the feminine."[30] While the Jew is the paradigmatic victim of racial hatred, the ultimate stereotype of abjection, woman, according to Gilman, is the image of beauty and epitome of desirability.[31] This binary construction gives primacy to the "Jew" over the "woman" as the foundational paradigm of the "other" in western mythology. If "woman" nevertheless did constitute an essential "other" in the European discourse of the turn of the century, it was the male Jew who suffered the consequences because, according to Gilman, "at the turn of the century, male Jews were feminized and signaled their feminization through their discourse, which reflected the nature of their bodies."[32] The Jew is the metaphorical woman of Europe. Because he is not a woman at all, there is something especially sordid in his representation as woman. Gilman does make use of the category of gender, but the object of his analysis is the male Jew. Gilman not only erases the Jewish woman as a category of analysis, doubly victimizing her, but he also presents misogyny as secondary to anti-Semitism, even though on the face of it he uses both race and gender as interarticulating categories of analysis.

The circumcised penis emerges as the primary sign of Jewish identity and the locus of anti-Semitic fantasies in Gilman's work, much as it emerges as the source of unresolved conflict for Jewish men in Howard Eilberg-Schwartz's *God's Phallus and Other Problems for Men and Monotheism*.[33] Here, too, the problem posed by the phallus is placed in the foreground, while the female body is all but erased: "Feminist theorists have yet to explore fully the question of how a male God is problematical for men's conceptions of self."[34] He chides feminists for failing to focus on male self-definitions, as if that is the task of feminist theory. In analyzing the implications of the invisible divine phallus for embodied masculinity, Eilberg-Schwartz argues for the urgency of prioritizing the male issue over the female. More importantly, he perceives himself as an authority, certainly enough of an authority to chide feminist theorists for neglecting the divine and human phallus/ penis.

For Eilberg-Schwartz, as for Gilman, femininity can have only metaphorical meaning. Thus, like Gilman, he attributes to ancient Jews a metaphoric femininity. According to him, the position of wife was taken by ancient Jews who sought to legitimize the marital metaphor as a fundamental articulation of the people's relationship to God: "The rabbis understood full well the fact that in the relationship with God, men must assume the position of wives."[35] The nation of Israel, once led by male priests and scribes, thus becomes feminized, and the question of women's oppression is occluded by making femininity a metaphor. If the entire nation of Israel is feminized and if the real drama is that unfolding between the disembodied male God and his male worshippers, there is really no need to discuss actual women as subjects or objects. To the extent that women appear in this analysis, they emerge as necessary divine images that ought to complement, but never replace, the divine father.

Feminization is the fundamental trope in Daniel Boyarin's *Unheroic Conduct*.[36] In Ashkenazi culture, male Jews constructed an ethos of feminized behavior: gentleness or *menschlichkeit* was the behavioral desideratum, while masculine aggression was a model that was by and large rejected as *goyish*. Boyarin endorses the feminist critique of Judaism as a system of oppression, but he justifies it only within the context of the traditional exclusion of women from Torah study. For the most part, as it does for Gilman and Eilberg-Schwartz, femininity has meaning to the extent that it characterizes Jewish culture and ethos. Femininity and even feminism become metaphors; the male Jew is embraced as a feminized man (Boyarin refers to him as a "sissy"). He argues for a celebration of the Talmud, despite its male-centered perspective, and an embrace of Judaism, despite its patriarchalism. The hierarchical asymmetry between women and men is a problem that can be corrected by a "radical reconstruction of the organization of gendered and sexual practices within our society (including necessarily the Jewish subculture)."[37] Boyarin believes that feminist goals are achieved by reclaiming "the eroticized Jewish male sissy"; his book is dedicated to the exploration of this prototype in Talmudic literature and culture.[38] His objective is to create the possibility of a traditionalist yet feminist Judaism.

In some ways, Borayin's thesis extends that laid out in much more simple form by Cynthia Ozick in her classic article, "Notes Toward Finding the Right Question," wherein she argues that the oppression of women is accidental, rather than essential, to Judaism.[39] Boyarin thus is an example of the scholar who presents his thesis as "a new thing in the world," rather than acknowledging the work of the feminist who preceded him.[40] Unlike other male feminists, Boyarin does, however, acknowledge the paradox in his identifying with what he claims as his role model, Bertha Pappenheim. Instead of rejecting the nineteenth century anti-Semitic conflation of Jews with women and feminism,

Boyarin validates this conflation and argues for its acceptance. This paradoxical move allows him to claim Pappenheim, an Orthodox feminist, as his idol and mentor.[41] As a Jewish male sissy, in other words, as a woman, Boyarin seems to justify his speaking for women; as a feminist, he justifies his defining the problems of Jewish feminism. Paradoxically, there is no attention to Jewish feminist debate, nor is there any attempt to situate himself as a male within such a debate or to acknowledge the influence of contemporary feminists. As a result, his male gender is erased as he claims female and feminist authority.

Jewish feminist scholars ought to welcome the cooperation of male feminists, but the distinction between cooperation and co-opting is often a fine one. Further, when men do not expressly articulate the problems inherent in their position in Jewish feminism, it is our obligation to remind them that along with all their sympathy and sincerity, men's feminist interventions necessarily bring with them implications of domination and appropriation.[42] To use Elizabeth Ermarth's words, to the extent that "feminism is a negotiation between women," men join the conversation as self-identified and self-acknowledged observers, supporters, or sympathizers.[43] They cannot and should not appropriate feminist discourse or women's voices.

THE NEED FOR CONVERSATION
The recognition that feminism is by definition a conversation among women, about women, and for women makes it all the more urgent for Jewish feminists who are aware of their exclusion from the larger body of feminist theory and scholarship to find a way of conversing among themselves. I define conversation as a discursive process of recognizing, investigating, and articulating the similarities and differences among the participants. That feminism requires debate and dialogue is one of the primary themes of the collection *Judaism Since Gender*, an excellent and daring anthology of provocative brief essays.[44] The introduction to the collection affirms that "the ongoing feminist analysis must continuously consider what we know and how we study."[45] The conversational nature of feminist theory is represented as one of the most urgent tasks of contemporary Jewish feminist theory. Part One, "Knowledges," consists of a series of conversations with Miriam Peskowitz. In her essay, "Engendering Jewish Religious History," she presents a provocative theoretical and methodological model. Peskowitz argues among other things for an understanding of knowledge as a

construction site, and for "engendering" as a contested discourse of study. Some essays in "Knowledges" do indeed confirm the need to challenge the male-centered or male-privileged construction of "Jew" or the field of Jewish literature.

There follows a kind of echoing, a reverberation of Peskowitz's argument (which is, after all, a fundamental feminist critique that began over twenty years ago). I use the word "reverberation" advisedly because there is neither the disagreement nor the elaboration or clarification that conversation is often expected to engender. Some essays discuss Orientalism, post-Zionism, racism, homophobia, and the enlightenment movement, issues that are essential to a re-articulation of Jewish Studies as an academic field rather than to the feminist enterprise per se.[46] Beth S. Wenger reaffirms Peskowitz's insight about rabbinic Judaism by insisting that Jewish modernity will also have to be reevaluated in terms of gender.[47] Other essays demonstrate the need for a new pedagogy and the importance of more established feminist patterns of inquiry, modeled on the "images of women" approach.[48] These essays—brief, suggestive and original—are exciting in that they point to the need for new approaches and reevaluations of an array of fields within Jewish studies. Nevertheless, and despite the fact that they are pointed and imaginative, I find it difficult to read this section as a conversation. The only piece that seems to engage Peskowitz is Rebecca Alpert's essay, "On Seams and Seamlessness," although it is written as a letter to Laura Levitt. Alpert takes issue with Peskowitz in regard to the writing of feminist history versus feminist midrash.

Part Two of the anthology, "Studies," presents exciting entries into traditional fields of Jewish Studies, such as rabbinics, medieval literature, and philosophy, and forays into depictions of Jews in Christian theology, literature, and Holocaust memoirs. Although innovative and thought-provoking, there is little debate here and certainly little conversation between and among feminist scholars about their respective projects and the possible relationships between them. The project of Jewish studies as such remains fractured; the project of Jewish feminist studies is even more so. While many essays forego the usual disciplinary boundaries, most remain within the circumscribed areas of Holocaust studies, medieval studies, and rabbinic studies without offering a general rethinking of the entire field of Jewish studies and its various sub-categories. While I agree that "a move toward canonized definition" is not as intellectually exciting as "conflict and multiplicity" or "glimpses

into fractiousness," what I miss in this exciting book is the promised
conflict and the lively debates that should emerge if a true scholarly
conversation is to ensue between and among Jewish feminist scholars.[49]
"A cacophony of unsettling and sometimes uncertain voices" and "the
joys of transgression" are better than silence, but can or should they
replace the much needed debate and clearly articulated disagreements
between modernist and post-modernist, or secular and religious, or
radical and liberal feminists?[50] Virginia Dominguez is correct to
emphasize that this anthology seeks not merely a change for Jewish
studies (namely, adding women to the topics covered within the area),
but an extensive transformation.[51] However, to achieve a radical
transformation we must understand the two or three major debates in
the field. I believe that this original book offers us "a way in," but we
still have a long way to go.

JEWS AND JUDAISM IN
THE WOMEN'S STUDIES CURRICULUM
While several anthologies have been published about the contributions
of feminism to Judaism and while feminism has been described as a
"breath of life" within contemporary Jewish American communities,[52]
less has been written on the contribution of Judaism to feminism. Most
Jewish feminists register a clear note of displeasure at what they construe
as anti-Semitism or anti-Judaism in the feminist movement at large and
in feminist scholarship in particular. The first anthologies that called
attention to the issue of anti-Semitism in the women's movement and
feminist scholarship were *Nice Jewish Girls, The Tribe of Dina,* and *Yours
in Struggle.*[53] A trenchant challenge to women's studies curricula was
articulated by Evelyn T. Beck in her article, "Jewish Invisibility in
Women's Studies," in which she points out "the consistent omission of
Jewish feminist work and Jewish women from the general women's
studies curriculum."[54] If Jewish themes do not fit snugly into the
women's studies curriculum, Beck suggests, this may be because the
analytic categories of sex and class as the primary basis for the oppression
of women are too rigid. She calls for a revision of analytic categories in
women's studies to enable a more flexible and inclusive framework. In
an equally incisive article, Susannah Heschel discusses the anti-Semitic
bias of German feminist theologians who identify Nazism with patriarchy
and patriarchy with Judaism.[55] Heschel analyses both feminist texts
and feminist responses to charges of anti-Semitism as symptoms of a

basic reluctance to take responsibility for Nazism and as a misplaced feminist tendency to arrogate to itself the exclusive role of victimized party. More recently, Amy Newman has documented misrepresentations of biblical stories of Israelite origins in feminist scholarship.[56] In her view, numerous distortions are based on the all too facile dichotomy between ancient goddesses and the Israelite male God, and some scholarly deficits can be traced to the use of secondary sources.

To some extent, the exclusion of Jewish feminism from women's studies can be understood as one manifestation of the omission of Jews and Judaism in general from multicultural curricula.[57] While the Jewish critique of the multicultural curriculum continues to evolve, Jewish feminist scholars ought to focus on the specific exclusion of Jewish women from women's studies curricula. One of the most urgent tasks of Jewish feminist scholarship must be the clarification and explanation for the collusion of misogyny and anti-Semitism. Rather than engage in apologetics for traditional Judaism, Jewish feminists ought to insist on the diversity of Jewish women and the plurality of Jewish feminist scholarship. This brings us back to the need for honest, lively, open-ended, and loving debate.

A critique of women's studies is productive as long as it does not end with a gesture of renunciation and closure. Anti-Semitism ought to be put in the same category as racism and sexism, so as to make it difficult if not impossible in the future to undertake any serious feminist analysis without rigorous attention to Jewish difference. The growing awareness within women's studies of its own ethnocentric limitations signals that the time is ripe for a cultural interpretation of the special victimization of the Jewish woman as a double outsider in non-Jewish culture.[58] Concepts, terms, and ideas devised by Jewish women, both traditional and secular, need to be elaborated in such a way as to explain their usefulness to feminist discourse and scholarship. The unique contributions of Jewish feminists like Betty Friedan, Gloria Steinem, Shulamit Firestone, Andrea Dworkin, and Adrienne Rich should become subjects of Jewish feminist scholarship in an effort to understand the role of Jewish identity in their revolutionary work. Instead of studying women exclusively within the historical or contemporary Jewish community, perhaps the focus ought to be broadened to the study of Jewish and Christian or Muslim women in history, or of Israeli and other Middle Eastern women, or of Jewish, Afro-American, Latina, and other ethnic communities. My reference to "community" need not infer that this kind of research should take place within the realm of sociology or history alone; comparative texts are essential as well. In such future comparative endeavors, scholars ought to attend to Jewish minorities, notably Middle Eastern women whose difference will shed light both on Ashkenazi women and on non-Jewish Middle Eastern women. Future scholarship in such comparative frameworks should lay bare the political tensions that have divided Jewish studies from other academic enterprises.

The differences within and the differences without should be theorized and articulated in such a way as to open and enable constructive debate. Even as our growing awareness of differences does not permit an easy generalization of what Jewish feminist scholarship may encompass, a reliance on easy pluralistic juxtaposition cannot replace serious scholarly dialogue among major trends in current Jewish feminist scholarship.[59] Thus, for example, the construct of the Jewish woman or the position of the Jewish woman between misogyny and anti-Semitism may serve as a point of departure for future theories in the field. It is just as significant to create a unified subject—fragile and contingent as it may be—as it is to recognize and respect our differences. Thus, while we agree to disagree, it is equally important to agree about what it is that matters to us all.[60] Introducing this missing conversation about our theoretical differences will create a space for us to construct and reconstruct the Jewish woman/feminist who is allegedly both the subject and the object of our study.

NOTES

[1] Jean Fox O'Barr, *Feminism in Action* (Chapel Hill and London: University of North Carolina Press, 1994); Nannerl O. Keohane et al, eds., *Feminist Theory: A Critique of Ideology* (London and Chicago: The University of Chicago Press, 1981).

[2] Liz Stanley, *"What is Feminist Praxis?"* in *Feminist Praxis: Research, Theory and Epistemology in Feminist Sociology* (ed. L. Stanley; New York and London: Routledge, 1990), 15.

[3] For an attempt to recognize new feminist scholarship, while at the same time revisiting and re-appreciating "old" terms and concepts, see Cheris Kramarae and Dale Spender, eds., *The Knowledge Explosion: Generations of Feminist Scholarship* (New York and London: Teachers College Press, 1992).

[4] Liz Stanley and Sue Wise, "Method, Methodology, and Epistemology," in *Feminist Praxis*, 20-60.

[5] Lynn Davidman and Shelly Tenenbaum, eds., *Feminist Perspectives on Jewish Studies* (New Haven: Yale University Press, 1994).

[6] *Ibid.*, 5.

[7] Ellen Carol DuBois, et al., eds., *Feminist Scholarship: Kindling in the Groves of Academe* (Urbana and Chicago: University of Illinois Press, 1985), 197.

[8] Hava Tirosh-Rothschild, "Jewish Philosophy," in *Feminist Perspectives on Jewish Studies*, 95.

[9] See Esther Fuchs, *Sexual Politics in the Biblical Narrative: Reading the Hebrew Bible As A Woman* (Sheffield: Sheffield Academic Press, 2000). Frymer-Kensky does not mention any of my essays on this subject dating from the early 1980s.

[10] Iris Marion Young, "Gender as Seriality: Thinking About Women as a Social Collective," in *The Second Signs Reader: Feminist Scholarship, 1983-1996* (eds. R. B. Joeres and B. Laslett; Chicago and London: The University of Chicago Press, 1996), 173.

[11] Elizabeth Koltun, *The Jewish Woman: New Perspectives* (New York: Schocken, 1976).

[12] S. Heschel, ed., *On Being a Jewish Feminist* (New York, Schocken, 1995).

[13] See Cynthia Ozick: "Notes Toward Finding the Right Question," 120-51, and Judith Plaskow, "The Right Question is Theological," in Heschel, *On Being a Jewish Feminist*, 217-222.

[14] See Ellen M. Umansky, "Females, Feminists, and Feminism: A Review of Recent Literature on Jewish Feminism and the Creation of a Feminist Judaism," *Feminist Studies* 14:2 (Summer 1988): 349-65.

[15] Tamar Rudavsky, *Gender and Judaism: The Transformation of Tradition* (New York and London: New York University Press, 1995).

[16] *Ibid.*, xiv.

[17] Judith R. Baskin, ed., *Jewish Women in Historical Perspective* (Detroit: Wayne State University Press, 1991).

[18] See Paula Hyman, "Gender and the Immigrant Jewish Experience," 222-42, and Ellen M. Umansky, "Spiritual Expressions," 265-87, in Baskin, *Jewish Women in Historical Perspective*.

[19] Judith R. Baskin, ed., *Women of the Word: Jewish Women and Jewish Writing* (Detroit: Wayne State University Press, 1994).

[20] Judith R. Baskin, "Women of the Word: An Introduction," in Baskin, *Women of the Word*, 17-34.

[21] See, for example, Linda J. Nicholson, ed., *Feminism/Postmodernism* (New York and London: Routledge, 1990); Judith Butler, *Gender Trouble: Feminism and the Subversion of Identity* (New York: Routledge, 1990); and Marysia Zalewski, *Feminism After Postmodernism: Theorising Through Practice* (New York and London, Routledge, 2000).

[22] The lack of dialogue and debate also characterize other important Jewish feminist anthologies; see, for example, Naomi Sokoloff, ed., *Gender and Text in Modern Hebrew and Yiddish Literature*, (New York: Jewish Theological Seminary of America, 1992), and Dalia Ofer and Leonore J. Weitzman, eds., *Women in the Holocaust* (New Haven: Yale University Press, 1998).

[23] Maurie Sachs, ed., *Active Voices: Women in Jewish Culture*, (Urbana and Chicago: University of Illinois Press, 1995).

[24]Maurie Sacks, "Introduction," 5-6. Emphasis is in the original.
[25]Maurie Sacks, "Introduction," 7.
[26]Esther Fuchs, "Critique and Reconstruction," in *Women in Jewish Life and Culture*, *Shofar* 17:2 (Winter, 1999): 1-7.
[27]See Esther Fuchs, "Introduction," in *Israeli Mythogynies: Women in Contemporary Hebrew Fiction* (E. Fuchs, ed; Albany: State University of New York Press, 1987).
[28]Ann duCille, "The Occult of True Black Womanhood: Critical Demeanor and Black Feminist Studies," in *The Second Signs Reader* (eds. R.E. B. Joeres and B. Laslett; Chicago: University of Chicago Press, 1996), 70-108.
[29]Elaine Showalter, "Critical Cross-Dressing; Male Feminists and the Woman of the Year," in *Men in Feminism* (eds. A. Jardine and P. Smith; New York and London: Methuen, 1987), 116-32.
[30]Sander L. Gilman, *Freud, Race, and Gender* (Princeton: Princeton University Press, 1993), 37. See also Gilman, *The Jew's Body* (New York and London: Routledge, 1991).
[31]Gilman, *Freud, Race, and Gender*, 47, notes: "What Freud constructed in his image of the feminine was the absolute counter image of the Jew: beautiful rather than ugly, and intensely narcissistic."
[32]*Ibid.*, 163.
[33]Howard Eilberg-Schwartz, *God's Phallus and Other Problems for Men and Monotheism* (Boston: Beacon Press, 1994).
[34]*Ibid.*, 5.
[35]*Ibid.*, 163.
[36]Daniel Boyarin, *Unheroic Conduct* (Berkeley: University of California Press, 1997), xxi.
[37]*Ibid.*, xvi.
[38]*Ibid.*, xxi.
[39]Cynthia Ozick, "Notes Toward Finding the Right Question," *On Being a Jewish Feminist*, 120-151.
[40]Boyarin, *Unheroic Conduct*, xxiii.
[41]Marion Kaplan, *The Jewish Feminist Movement in Germany: The Campaigns of the Jüdischer Frauenbund, 1904-1938* (Westport: Greenwood, 1979). Kaplan, who wrote about Pappenheim and wrested her from neglect in recent Jewish history, is mentioned in Boyarin's footnotes, but not explicitly as the first contemporary feminist scholar who put Pappenheim back on the map.
[42]Stephen Heath, "Male Feminism," in Jardine and Smith, *Men in Feminism*, 1-32.
[43]Elizabeth Ermarth, "On Having a Personal Voice," in *Changing the Subject: The Making of Feminist Literary Criticism* (eds. G. Greene and C. Kahn; New York and London: Routledge, 1993), 226-39.
[44]Miriam Peskowitz and Laura Levitt, eds., *Judaism Since Gender* (New York: Routledge, 1997).
[45]*Ibid.*, 6.

[46]See Laurence J. Silberstein, "Toward a Postzionist Discourse," 95-101; Ammiel Alcalay, "Finding a Language for Memories of the Future," 102-12; and Kalman P. Bland, "Medievals Are Not Us," 138-46, in Peskowitz and Levitt, *Judaism Since Gender.*

[47]Wenger, "Note from the Second Generation," in Peskowitz and Levitt, *Judaism Since Gender*, 113-19.

[48]See Amy-Jill Levine, "A Jewess, More and/or Less," 149-57, and Susan E. Shapiro, "A Matter of Discipline: Reading for Gender in Jewish Philosophy," 158-73, in Peskowitz and Levitt, *Judaism Since Gender.*

[49]Peskowitz and Levitt, *Judaism Since Gender*, 5.

[50]*Ibid.*, 2.

[51]Virginia Dominguez, "Foreword," in *Judaism Since Gender*, ix-xii.

[52]Sylvia Barack-Fishman, *A Breath of Life: Feminism in the American Jewish Community* (University Press of New England, 1995).

[53]Evelyn T. Beck, ed., *Nice Jewish Girls: A Lesbian Anthology* (1st ed.; Watertown: Persephone Pres, 1982); Melanie Kaye/Kantrowitz and Irena Klepfisz, eds., *The Tribe of Dina: A Jewish Women's Anthology* (Boston: Beacon Press, 1989); Elly Bulkin et al., eds., *Yours In Struggle: Three Feminist Perspectives on Anti-Semitism and Racism* (Ithaca: Firebrand, 1988).

[54]Evelyn T. Beck, "The Politics of Jewish Invisibility in Women's Studies," in *Transforming the Curriculum* (eds. J. E. Butler and J. C. Walter; Albany: State University of New York Press, 1991), 187-97.

[55]Susannah Heschel, "Configurations of Patriarchy, Judaism, and Nazism in German Feminist Thought," in Rudavsky, *Gender and Judaism*, 135-56.

[56]Amy Newman, "The Idea of Judaism in Feminism and Afrocentrism," in *Insider/ Outsider: American Jews and Multiculturalism* (ed. D. Biale et al.; Berkeley: University of California Press, 1998), 150-84.

[57]See Jonathan Boyarin and Daniel Boyarin, eds., *Jews and Other Differences: The New Jewish Cultural Studies* (Minneapolis: University of Minnesota Press, 1997); Marla Brettschneider, *The Narrow Bridge: Jewish Views on Multiculturalism* (New Brunswick: Rutgers University Press, 1996).

[58]See Mary Maynard and June Purvis, eds., *New Frontiers in Women's Studies: Knowledge, Identity and Nationalism* (London: Taylor and Francis, 1996).

[59]Debate and dialogue as part of the process of clarification and growth have been recognized as crucial for the ongoing production and progress of feminist scholarship. See Marianne Hirsch and Evelyn Fox Keller, eds., *Conflicts in Feminism* (New York: Routledge, 1990).

[60]For a debate on the value of certainty in Jewish feminist study, see Laura Levitt, "Slowing Down, Revving Up: Jewish Feminist Studies," and Hava Tirosh-Samuelson, "Against Dogmatic Skepticism," *Shma* (January 2000): 7-9.

Women as Prophets and Visionaries in Medieval and Early Modern Judaism

Morris M. Faierstein

To the memory of Jane Julian Crisci, z"l

It is a truism of Rabbinic Judaism that prophecy, in the classical sense, ended with Haggai, Zechariah, and Malachi.[1] However, contact with the Divine realm in a wide variety of forms, revelations from angels or other divine messengers, visitations from the prophet Elijah, mystical ascents to Heaven, and visions, while asleep or awake, continued throughout Jewish history.[2] Prophecy and prophetic revelation also played a particularly important role in the mystical school of Abraham Abulafia.[3] Though the majority of those who claimed these divine revelations and visions were distinguished scholars and mystics, there are also cases of ordinary men and women who were the recipients of heavenly revelations and visions. This study concentrates on the reports of Jewish women who in medieval and early modern times had divine revelations or visions. Many of these reports were connected with messianic movements. However, I focus on the question of divine revelation, considering the broader context of these revelations only when it is directly relevant to the theme of this study.

The reports of women who experienced divine revelations fall into several periods and communities. There is a report from the twelfth century, one from Sicily in the fifteenth century, several female visionaries in Spain immediately after the expulsion of the Jews in 1492, and a variety of reports in the late sixteenth to early seventeenth century in Safed and Damascus. Women were also represented in the messianic fervor surrounding the false messiah, Sabbatai Sevi, in the 1660s.

I

The first instance of a female visionary in the medieval period is found in a letter from the Cairo Genizah published by S. D. Goitein.[4] The heroine of the story was the daughter of Joseph the physician. The letter relates:

> On the 25th of Ellul 1120, the pious "daughter of Joseph the physician,"[5] who had led an ascetic life and had married during that year only under special pressure exerted by R. Daniel [son of the president of the Academy], appeared in public declaring that she had seen the prophet Elijah in a dream and had been told by him that the redemption of Israel was at hand.[6]

The caliph[7] who was in charge of the affairs of non-Muslims, hearing of the commotion that resulted from the messianic expectation aroused by this vision, ordered the leaders of the Jewish community to be imprisoned in the Mint at Baghdad. The caliph summoned a Jew who was active in government service and asked about the vision and who had seen it. When he heard that it was a woman, he ridiculed the whole story. That night, Elijah appeared to the caliph holding a pillar of fire in his hand. The caliph was struck with awe. The letter indicates that the Jews were released from prison.[8]

The daughter of Joseph the physician is described in this letter as a pious and ascetic woman. She had attempted to shun marriage, which was characteristic of women who aspired to sainthood in the Muslim world.[9] Thus, it could be argued that the appearance of Elijah to her was a sign of her spiritual attainment. What is novel in this case is that Elijah appeared to a woman in a situation where he would have been expected to appear to an important scholar or mystic.[10]

II

The Ottoman conquest of Constantinople in 1453 unleashed a wave of messianic yearnings and attempts by Jews around the Mediterranean basin to immigrate to the land of Israel.[11] In 1931, Jacob Mann published a document from the Cairo Genizah which speaks of a female prophetess.[12] He described it as a letter sent by a traveler from Catania in Sicily.[13] When the traveler arrived in Catania with his colleague, he heard of a woman who was prophesying in Centorbi, a village near the eastern coast of Sicily. They went to see her and found that she had been pregnant for more than nine months and had not yet given birth. They went to the synagogue for services, and the worshipers smelled a pleasant aroma when the woman stood outside.[14] After the services she went home and told her husband that she had been commanded by "the holy one"[15] that the whole congregation should come to the house and see what would happen. They saw her fall on her face, pleading and crying. She asked her husband to bring a tallit [prayer shawl or other covering] and cover her with it. A series of letters, the color of saffron, appeared on the tallit. She demanded to be covered with another tallit with no writing on the covering; as soon as she was, additional letters appeared. She then stretched out her left hand and a fluid in the shape of a person emerged from it. All those present tasted this fluid, which tasted of olive oil and had the smell of incense. The woman then prayed and raised her hands as if she were reciting the priestly blessing. Blood appeared on the tallit. She then said, "Give thanks to God and repent completely. Both you and all the places where you will take these shawls and all who will see these words and the shawls should repent, for so have I been commanded by the Holy One."[16]

On the Sabbath, the travelers were invited to her house after the morning prayers, where they had an experience similar to the first one. She told them that the end was near and those who would not repent would die by the sword or famine. Those who did repent would be saved. She told them that the oil that they had eaten would be given by God to Israel in the future. She told them to go to the synagogue for the prayers. In the synagogue they saw a fire enter and go to the opposite corner. Two of the men present fell to the floor. When they revived, they were asked what they had seen. They said, "We saw an angel with a sword in his hand and a large flame in his other hand."[17]

The writer interrupts his account of these prophesies to report the arrival of a non-Jew from Morea in southern Greece. This visitor was surprised that the Jews had not yet prepared for the arrival of the messengers from "the hidden king."[18] The visitor told them that the hidden king had sent letters to the kings of France and Germany, ordering them to aid his ambassadors in gathering the Jews and help them in their journey to Jerusalem. These letters also contained instructions for the rich Jews to aid their poor brethren in preparing for this journey. The visitor assured them that these ambassadors would soon arrive in Sicily. He also embellished his story with accounts of events he had witnessed in Spain and reports of events in other countries.

This document is not dated; a scholarly debate ensued as to its date. J. Mann, who published the document, dated it to the twelfth century on the basis of the paleographic evidence. Other scholars connected this story with messianic movements in the fifteenth and even the sixteenth century on the basis of the second part of the document.[19] A. Z. Aescoly suggested that it is difficult to date such stories purely on the basis of the internal evidence, since the dominant motif in the second part of the story, the advent of the ambassadors from a distant land who claimed to represent the ten lost tribes living beyond the mythic river Sambatyon, is a popular folk motif with a long history.[20]

Nadia Zeldes has recently reexamined this text.[21] She concludes that Aescoly's basic assumption, that this document was connected to the messianic events related to the fall of Constantinople, is correct. She also concludes that this document is not a letter, as previously assumed, but part of a larger document. In addition, she suggests a possible connection between this manuscript and a Sicilian document from 1456 that deals with several groups of Sicilian Jews who attempted to emigrate from Sicily to Jerusalem.

III

In Spain of the fifteenth and sixteenth centuries there was a wide variety of visionaries, Christian and Jewish, who claimed to have seen visions of divine figures.[22] In 1500, a year of messianic expectations among Jews,[23] there were three messianic or prophetic movements centered on converso women who claimed to have had heavenly revelations that their redemption from the exile of Spain was at hand.[24] The Jews would be led to the land of Israel, where they would again be able to practice Judaism. All of these movements were centered in the Extramadura region of Spain, in Cordoba, Herrera, and Chillon. Our knowledge of these movements is derived solely from the records of the Inquisition, specifically from interrogations of participants in these movements.[25]

In Cordoba, the city councilor Juan de Cordoba, his wife, four daughters, and family servants were conversos practicing Judaism in secret; they had also converted a Moorish servant girl to Judaism. According to the inquisitorial documents, they instructed the servant girl to sham coma-like trances. She then told the conversos that Elijah had taken her up to heaven during these "comas" and given her a message for them. The essence of the message was that if the conversos rejected Christianity and again embraced the teachings and laws of Judaism, God would deliver them from their captivity and Elijah would lead them to the land of Israel. Christian neighbors were told that these visions were of Jesus or Mary.

In addition to these visions, the home of Juan de Cordoba became a center for Jewish worship, where services were a mixture of Jewish and Christian rituals and practices.[26] This movement lasted for three years, from 1499-1502, when it was uncovered by the Inquisition. More than 300 people participated in this movement, and many made pilgrimages there from the whole region to see the prophetesses and participate in the religious services.[27]

The most widely discussed prophetess was Ines, the daughter of Juan Esteban of Hererra, a shoemaker and leather tanner. Like the others, her story is woven together from transcripts of interrogations by the Inquisition of conversos suspected of judaizing tendencies.[28] Ines was born about 1488 in Herrera; her mother died when she was still a young child. In the fall of 1499, she began to have dreams and visions of her dead mother and of a brilliant illumination that gave her messages for the conversos of her community. The illumination told her to inform the conversos that Elijah was coming soon. His coming would signal the beginning of the redemption of the conversos from their exile in Spain. In preparation for the advent of Elijah, they were told to believe in the Laws of Moses, fast on Monday and Thursday, observe the Sabbath to the extent they could, and give alms to the poor.[29]

Ines also had visions of ascensions to heaven. Juan de Segovia, one of the people interrogated by the Inquisition, described what he heard of Ines' visions:

How her mother who was already dead came to her and took her hand and told her not to be afraid because it was God's will that she ascend to heaven to see the secrets and to see marvelous things. And in like manner another young man who had died a few days before took her other hand, and the Angel who was drawing them upward thus said that they were taking her up to heaven where she would see the souls who were suffering in purgatory. And in like manner in another place she would see other souls in glory seated on chairs of gold. And likewise she told me that there seemed to be another higher place above her head where there was much murmuring, and that she asked the Angel: What are those sounds above? And the Angel said to her: Friend of God, those that make sounds up there are those who were burned on earth and now are in glory. And in like manner she saw three kinds of angels and other things that she told me but I don't remember.[30]

These visions made a great impression on many conversos in the area, who came to see Ines and to learn more about her prophecies. It is clear from the inquisitorial reports that she attracted a significant following. The Inquisition learned of Ines' visions; she was arrested, as were many other conversos in Herrera. We know from other documents that by August of 1500, Ines had been burned at the stake by the Inquisition, but the details of her trial have not survived.

A third prophetess was Maria Gomez of Chillon, a village not far from Herrera.[31] We know little about her, but she prophesied about the same time as the other prophetesses. Unlike the others, she was able to flee to Portugal and avoid arrest by the Inquisition, but her ultimate fate is unknown. She saw the other prophetesses and may have been influenced by them.[32] Her visions, heavenly ascents, and message of hope for the imminent redemption of the conversos were also similar. She too ascended to heaven, where she saw angels and the prophet Elijah. Like Ines, she also saw that Elijah would lead those conversos who believed in the Law of Moses, observed the Jewish fasts, gave charity, and observed the other Jewish practices enjoined by the other prophetesses. She saw a lavish banquet, reminiscent of rabbinic legends of the banquet prepared for the righteous in the messianic age and including the preparation of Leviathan, being readied for the conversos in the Promised Land.[33]

One of her prophetic visions is particularly interesting in that it shows the survival of rabbinic midrashic traditions among the conversos. This prophecy speaks of those who ascended to heaven while still alive, including Enoch, Serach the daughter of Asher the son of Jacob, and a number of others.[34] It should be noted that there was also a male prophet in Almadovar who had visions very similar to the three prophetesses that have been discussed. This prophet was active somewhat later, about 1540.[35]

An important question that has been raised about the converso prophetesses is the balance between Jewish and Christian influences on their visions.[36] As has been noted previously, during this period Spain also had many Christian visionaries. The Turkish conquest of Constantinople and the unification of Spain gave impetus to millenarian dreams among Spanish Christians. In addition, there was clear Christian influence on some of the rituals and ceremonies surrounding the prophetesses and their followers. John Edwards is typical of those who argue for the fundamentally Christian character of these visionary experiences. He writes:

However, despite this very definite Jewish flavor of the Cordoba and Herrera prophecies, it is nonetheless striking that the visions of the prophetesses in other respects correspond to the patterns of Christian visions in the same period and country which have been studied by the anthropologist William A. Christian.[37] Ines, for example, passed through purgatory on her way to the presence of God.[38]

There is a fundamental flaw in Edwards' argument. A comparison of the visions cited by W. A. Christian with those of the conversos shows that there is no correlation in the contents of the visions of the two groups. Central to all of the Christian visions is the appearance of the Virgin Mary. The converso visions are Jewish at their core. The Christian elements, to the extent they are present, are peripheral and reflect the religious syncretism that was part of the converso religious experience. In addition, the existence of Jewish female prophetesses and visionaries in other Jewish societies that contain elements of the converso visions further weakens this argument. The female visionary discussed above, from twelfth century Baghdad, also engaged in certain practices, such as shunning marriage and practicing asceticism, that reflected contemporary Islamic traditions about female sainthood.[39] However, this is not a reason to doubt the essentially Jewish nature of her experience.

There have always been cross-cultural influences between Jewish societies and their surrounding cultures. For example, Edwards sees the passage through purgatory on the way to heaven as a specific Christian influence on the converso prophetesses.[40] However, even here caution must be urged. Thus, two Jewish women in the sixteenth and seventeenth centuries had visions of being led through gehenna on their way to tours of heaven.[41] One was the wife of the famous kabbalist Rabbi Hayyim Vital in Safed;[42] the other was the daughter of Raphael Anav of Damascus. There is no reason to assume they were aware of or influenced by the experiences of the converso prophetesses. The only possible connection between them is the common store of Jewish legends about the messianic age and the afterlife. Furthermore, this motif of a journey to heaven or hell, or in some cases both, is very old and is found in early Jewish and Christian sources alike.[43]

Two additional factors must be considered in any discussion of the Jewishness of the converso prophetesses. First, our only sources about these visions are the records of the Inquisition, written in a Christian ecclesiastical environment. Thus, all extant information has been filtered through Christian concepts and terminology. It would be natural for the inquisitors to rephrase unfamiliar terms and concepts in language more consistent with their worldview. The substitution of purgatory for gehenna and other similar terminological shifts reflect the inquisitors' background and not necessarily Christian influence on the visions. As we have seen, there are clear Jewish parallels to the descriptions of the heavenly journeys by the converso prophetesses. These parallels strongly argue for the persistence of Jewish traditions among the conversos and the essentially Jewish nature of these visions.

Secondly, messianic longings and expectations were a part of all sectors of Jewish society in Spain during this period. Even members of the Jewish intellectual elite were actively involved in messianic speculation. The best known example is Rabbi Isaac Abravanel, one of the leading intellectual lights and communal leaders of Spanish Jewry during the period of the expulsion.[44] Thus, when our knowledge of the converso prophetesses is considered within the larger context of Jewish female visionaries in other societies and historical periods, there is no real reason to doubt that the core of their visionary experience was based on Jewish traditions.

IV

Rabbi Hayyim Vital (1542-1620) was one of the most important kabbalists in the revival centered on the town of Safed in the second half of the sixteenth century. Among his many works is a mystical diary, The Book of Visions, written for his own purposes and not intended to be published. Vital had messianic aspirations, believing himself worthy to be the Messiah at times and at other times a spiritual leader who would lead the Jewish people to repent of their sins and thus pave the way for the advent of the Messiah. Vital had a spiritual crisis around 1610-1612, brought on in part by his failure to succeed in either of his missions. He wrote a mystical diary in response to this crisis, wherein he reviewed his spiritual worthiness and the reasons for his apparent failure to fulfill the goals he had set for himself early in his life. In two parts of his diary, "Events in My Life" and "The Dreams of Others," he records a number of items relevant to the present discussion.[45]

In his Book of Visions, Vital discusses a number of women who had access to forms of positive contact with divine beings [maggidim][46] and visitations from angels and the prophet Elijah. A related phenomenon was possession by spirits, either positive or malevolent.[47] The most famous story of "possession" in this work is that of Raphael Anav's daughter.[48] The spirit that "possessed" Raphael Anav's daughter was not a malevolent spirit, but the pious scholar R. Jacob Piso, sent from heaven to bring a message to Vital. A week after his initial possession, R. Joshua al-Boom, a kabbalist in Damascus who was an expert in the magical aspects of Kabbalah, contacted an angel, one of the servants of the angel Zadkiel, so that Vital could ask a number of questions.[49] This angel told Vital the following regarding the spirit of R. Jacob Piso and his mission in entering the body of Raphael Anav's daughter:

> God only sent this spirit into the daughter of Raphael Anav to cause the people of Damascus to repent. The spirit was very pious and in his place in Paradise. Because of a small sin which he still had to repair he was sent to accept his punishment in a river where he was embodied in a fish which Raphael bought. When his daughter ate the head, he entered her and remained there for twelve days. On Sunday, the first day of Ab, the time for his ascent came and he ascended of his own will, not by means of any person's actions. On the previous Sabbath, he sent for you in the morning. You went there, but did not return again until Sunday, when the time for his ascent had already come. He had wanted to reveal divine secrets to you. His whole intent was that the world should repent. Several souls and angels descended with him on the Sabbath eve and they were all waiting to speak to you about this. However, you did not believe their words, and you lost all those secrets. God only sent them so that the people will hear about the awesome deeds of the Lord and through this they would repent.[50]

It is noteworthy and important for this discussion that the spirit did not enter Raphael Anav's daughter accidentally. It is clear from the angel's statement and from other evidence in the story that she was deliberately chosen as the medium for this spirit. Furthermore, her career as a clairvoyant did not end with this episode. Vital reports that she had further visitations from the spirit of R. Jacob Piso. In addition, she had visions of angels and even visits from Elijah, who had a message for Vital.

Vital even consulted Raphael Anav's daughter about the refusal of his teacher, R. Isaac Luria, to visit him in his dreams or in other visions. Luria transmitted an answer through her, which Vital did not understand. A few days later, she had another dream, wherein Luria asked for Vital's response. Luria was not happy that Vital did not understand his message. Several months later, Luria again appeared to her with another message for Vital. R. Jacob Abulafia, Vital's nemesis in Damascus, was the subject of another visit from the spirit of R. Jacob Piso.[51] In this case, the spirit voluntarily embodied himself in the girl, so that he could deliver the message to Abulafia; namely, that Raphael Anav's daughter was not a "helpless victim of an evil spirit," but a medium for divine messengers. [52] Consequently, her messages were taken seriously by Vital and even by his archenemy in Damascus, R. Jacob Abulafia.[53]

Raphael Anav's daughter was not the only woman credited by Vital with the ability to see divine beings. Vital reports:

> 5338 [CE 1578]: I was preaching publicly in Jerusalem one Saturday morning. Rachel, the sister of R. Judah Mashan,[54] was there and she told me that the whole time I was preaching she saw a pillar of fire over my head and Elijah, z"l, to my right supporting me. They both disappeared when I finished preaching.

She also saw a pillar of fire over my head[55] when I led the Musaf service on Yom Kippur in the synagogue of the Sicilian community in Damascus, in 5362 [1601]. The above mentioned woman was used to seeing visions, demons, spirits and angels, and most of what she said was correct from the time of her youth and through adulthood.[56]

Rachel was not the only female to see the pillar of fire over Vital's head. In 1568, Sa'adat, the wife of Jacob Nasar, saw a heavenly pillar of fire on Vital's head when he served as sandek[57] at a circumcision.[58] Many years later, in 1610, Simha, the wife of Cuencas, saw a pillar of light brighter than the sun over Vital as he left the synagogue.[59] Although this sign was seen by ordinary women rather than by great rabbis or scholars, it is significant that Vital had no problem attributing this phenomenon to women. He did not feel the need to attribute it to men, nor did he find it problematic or inconceivable that women would have these visions.

Another woman to whom Vital attributed heavenly visions was Francisa Sarah. Vital calls her, "a pious woman, who saw visions in a waking dream and heard a voice speaking to her, and most of her words were true."[60] Joseph Sambari, in his seventeenth century chronicle *Divrei Yosef*, says about her:

> In those days in Safed, in the upper Galilee, there was a woman who was wise and great in her deeds whose name was Francisa.

world. The sages of Safed tested her several times to see if there was substance in her words, and everything she said never failed to occur.[61]

Sambari goes on to describe several incidents when she predicted a number of events that occurred as she had predicted; he also records how the sages of Safed heeded her admonitions.[62] She was the only woman to whom a maggid was attributed; the only others reported to have had one were great kabbalists like R. Joseph Taitazak, R. Joseph Karo, and R. Moses Cordovero.

Vital's wife, Hannah, had a vision of a heavenly journey while she was in a coma. She described how she was first taken through gehenna, which was peaceful at the time because it was the Sabbath. Afterwards, she was taken to heaven, where she sought out the place that had been reserved for Vital. She described at length the glories of the place that had been prepared for him; of course, for him this was the most important part of her vision.[63] Vital describes having a similar experience when he too was extremely ill and in a coma.[64] Here we see Vital similarly had no problem crediting an experience to his wife that he also had and to which he attributed great significance. The similarities between the details of these visions and those of the converso prophetesses are striking, and, most significant, there is no possibility of direct influence between the two sets of visions. The only reasonable explanation is that both drew on a common store of Jewish legends and traditions about heaven and gehenna.

The third part of Vital's Book of Visions is devoted to dreams others had about him that reflect on his greatness and on his messianic mission. Of the seventy dreams that he reports, seventeen, or approximately one-fourth of the total, were dreams by women.[65] This, I would suggest, is a significant percentage, showing that Vital valued the dreams of women and considered them as significant as those of men. A careful reading of this part of the Book of Visions reinforces the conclusion that Vital made no distinction between the dreams of men and women; he valued both equally.

V

The Sabbatian movement of the 1660s was very different from the movements previously discussed. Rather than being composed of small groups of individuals who looked forward to and anticipated the imminent advent of the Messiah, Sabbatianism was a mass movement with an actual messianic claimant as its leader. Central to the Sabbatian movement was the breaking of previously accepted religious boundaries in all spheres of life. Among the Sabbatian phenomena was the eruption of mass prophecy among all sectors of believers in Sabbatai Sevi. This was seen as fulfilling the prophecy of Joel 3:1, "I will pour out my spirit upon all flesh, and your sons and your daughters shall prophesy, your old men shall dream dreams, your young men shall see visions."[66]

The female prophets who emerged during the height of the Sabbatian movement were likewise not a distinctive phenomenon but part of a mass movement. They are of interest in understanding the Sabbatian movement, but shed less light on the role of women as visionaries in medieval and early modern Judaism.[67] The mass prophesies ended abruptly with the apostasy of Sabbatai Sevi; the role of women in this prophetic episode ended as abruptly.[68]

CONCLUSION

Prophetic revelation and visions of divine beings continued throughout the medieval and early modern periods. Like prophecy in the biblical period, it was primarily a phenomenon experienced by men, but women were not entirely excluded.[69] The visions of the women who had prophetic revelations during these periods were consistent with mainstream, traditional Jewish beliefs. Even the converso prophetesses, whose connections with rabbinic traditions were more tenuous than most, still remained within traditional Jewish motifs and categories in their visions. While the need for a full analysis of prophetic revelation and divine visions in medieval and early modern Judaism remains, this study has considered one important aspect of this wide-ranging phenomenon.

NOTES

[1] *b. Sanh.*, 11a; *t. Sotah*, 13:2, and others.
[2] The pioneering study of this phenomenon is found in Abraham Joshua Heschel, *Prophetic Inspiration after the Prophets: Maimonides and Other Medieval Authorities* (ed. M. M. Faierstein; Hoboken: Ktav, 1996). The two articles in this volume cover the period from the close of the Talmudic canon until the thirteenth century.
[3] References to prophets and prophecy in the medieval period and the Abulafia school are found throughout the many works of Moshe Idel.
[4] S. D. Goitein, "A Report on Messianic Troubles in Baghdad in 1120-1121," in

Essential Papers on Messianic Movements and Personalities in Jewish History (ed. M. Saperstein; New York: New York University Press, 1992), 189-201.

[5] It is noteworthy that although she is the heroine of the story, we are not told her name. A similar example is the case of Raphael Anav's daughter, who occupies an important place in Hayyim Vital's mystical autobiography, *The Book of Visions*, in *Jewish Mystical Autobiographies: Book of Visions and Book of Secrets* (ed. M. Faierstein; New York: Paulist, 1999), discussed below, and hereafter referred to as *BV.*

[6] Goitein, "A Report on Messianic Troubles," 190.

[7] Goitein's term.

[8] *Ibid.*, 190f.

[9] *Ibid.*, 195. See also A. Schimmel, *Mystical Dimensions of Islam* (Chapel Hill: University of North Carolina Press, 1975), 426-435; M. Smith, *Rab'ia the Mystic and Her Fellow Saints in Islam* (Cambridge: Cambridge University Press, 1928).

[10] Elijah's appearance to save the Jewish community is a common motif in Jewish folklore. See A. Wiener, *The Prophet Elijah in the Development of Judaism* (London: Routledge & Kegan Paul, 1978), 139 and the sources cited there.

[11] Y. Baer, *A History of the Jews in Christian Spain* (vol. 2; Philadelphia: Jewish Publication Society of America, 1966), 292; Nadia Zeldes, "A Magical Event in Sicily: Notes and Clarifications on the Messianic Movement in Sicily," *Zion* 58: 356.

[12] J. Mann, *Texts and Studies in Jewish History and Literature* (vol. 1; Cincinnati: Hebrew Union College Press, 1931), 34-44. This text is also quoted and discussed in A.Z. Aescoly and Y. Even-Shemuel, *Ha-tenu'ot ha-meshihiot be-Israel: otsar ha-mekorot veha-te'udot le-toldot ha-meshihijuy be-Yisra'el* (Jerusalem: Mosad Bialik, 1956), 240-47, 286-89.

[13] Zeldes, "Magical Event in Sicily," concludes that it was part of a larger document and not a letter.

[14] Medieval synagogues did not have a woman's section; women typically stood outside and looked in through the windows during services.

[15] This could be either God or a heavenly messenger.

[16] Mann, *Texts*, 39; Aescoly and Even-Shemuel, *Tenuot*, 287.

[17] Mann, *Texts*, 41; Aescoly and Even-Shemuel, *Tenuot*, 287.

[18] This term has also been used to mean the Messiah or God himself.

[19] Full bibliographical details of this debate can be found in Aescoly and Even-Shemuel, *Tenuot*, 244-45 and 287.

[20] Among the better known examples are Eldad the Danite, who in the ninth century claimed he was an ambassador from the tribe of Dan. See, E.N. Adler, *Jewish Travellers* (New York, 1966), 4-21. The legendary Christian king Prester John was reputed to be either the ruler or neighbor of the ten lost tribes who lived on the other side of the legendary river Sambatyon. He is mentioned in a number of medieval Jewish chronicles. See ibid., index, s.v., *Prester John*. In the sixteenth century, David Reubeni appeared in Europe claiming to be the ambassador of the ten lost tribes, who would soon come with their army to liberate their brethren. Reubeni left behind an interesting diary of his adventures. See Aaron A. Aescoly et al., *Sipur David ha-Re'uveni: 'al-pi ketav-yad*

Oksford: be-tseruf ketavim ve-'eduyot mi-bene ha-dor, 'im mavo ve-he'arot (2nd ed.; Jerusalem: Mosad Bialik: 1993).

[21] Zeldes, *Zion*, 347-63.

[22] The Christian visionaries are discussed in William A. Christian, *Apparitions in Late Medieval and Renaissance Spain* (Princeton: Princeton University Press, 1981). A specific case study is Richard L. Kagan, *Lucrecia's Dreams: Politics and Prophecy in Sixteenth-Century Spain* (Berkeley: University of California Press, 1990). Women visionaries are also discussed in several of the essays in Mary E. Giles ed., *Women in the Inquisition: Spain and the New World* (Baltimore: The Johns Hopkins University Press, 1998).

[23] Aescoly and Even-Shemuel, *Tenuot*, 248.

[24] *Converso* is the preferred term for Jews who converted to Catholicism, but who still maintained some allegiance to Judaism and engaged in Jewish practices.

[25] The pioneering work on these movements is by Y. Baer; many of the primary documents were first published by Baer in *Die Juden im Christlichen Spanien* (2 vols.; Berlin: Akademie, 1929-1936). He initially summarized his research in his article, "The Messianic Movement in Spain during the Expulsion [Hebrew]," *Me'assef Zion* 5 (1934): 61-77. A more recent survey of these messianic movements is found in R. L. Melammed, *Heretics or Daughters of Israel: The Crypto-Jewish Women of Castile* (New York, Oxford: Oxford University Press, 1999), 45-72.

[26] J. Edwards, "Elijah and the Inquisition: Messianic Prophecy among Conversos in Spain c. 1500," *Nottingham Medieval Studies* 28 (1984): 80-81.

[27] This incident is discussed by H. Beinart, "A Prophesying Movement in Cordoba in 1499-1502 [Hebrew]," *Zion* 44 (1979): 190-200; Edwards, "Elijah and the Inquisition," also has a significant discussion of this story.

[28] The main studies of Ines of Herrera by H. Beinart are found in "The Movement around the Prophetess Ines in Puebla de Alcocer and Talarrubias [Hebrew]," *Tarbiz* 51 (1982): 634-58, and "The Prophetess Ines in Herrera, Her Place of Birth [Hebrew]," *I. Tishby Jubilee Volume* (Jerusalem, 1986), 459-506. His most recent summary of this incident can be found in H. Beinart, "Ines of Herrera del Duque: The Prophetess of Extramadura," in Giles, *Women in the Inquisition*, 42-52.

[29] Fasting was an important part of *converso* beliefs. See David M. Gitlitz, *Secrecy and Deceit: The Religion of the Crypto-Jews* (Philadelphia: Jewish Publication Society, 1996), 391-96.

[30] Beinart, "Ines of Herrera," 45.

[31] H. Beinart, "*Conversos* of Chillon and Siruela and the Prophecies of Maria Gomez and Ines, the Daughter of Juan Esteban [Hebrew]," *Zion* 48 (1983): 241-72.

[32] *Ibid.*, 243.

[33] On the tradition of the messianic banquet, see R. Patai, *The Messiah Texts* (Detroit: Wayne State University Press, 1979), 235-46.

[34] Beinart "Ines of Herrera," 46 and note 23, for the rabbinic sources of this tradition.

[35] Aescoly and Even-Shemuel, *Tenuot*, 306-7; Baer, *Juden in Christlichen Spanien*,

535-36.

[36] A recent discussion of this question is in Edwards, "Elijah and the Inquisition," 91-94.

[37] Christian, *Apparitions.*

[38] Edwards, "Elijah and the Inquisition," 93.

[39] See Goitein, "A Report on Messianic Troubles," 190f.

[40] Edwards, "Elijah and the Inquisition," 93.

[41] *Gehenna* is sometimes seen as the Jewish equivalent of Christian purgatory.

[42] Safed is in the Galilee region of Israel and was part of the Ottoman empire at that time.

[43] The basic studies of the early history of these journeys are contained in two books by Martha Himmelfarb, *Tours of Hell: An Apocalyptic Form in Jewish and Christian Literature* (Philadelphia: University of Pennsylvania Press, 1983), and *Ascent to Heaven in Jewish and Christian Apocalypses* (New York: Oxford University Press, 1993).

[44] On his messianic speculation see B. Netanyahu, *Don Isaac Abravanel: Statesman and Philosopher* (Philadelphia: Jewish Publication Society of America, 1972), 195-257.

[45] For more details on Vital and his diary, see the Introduction to *BV*. Citations are by part and section in this translation.

[46] A *maggid* is a divine messenger, usually an angel. The most famous *maggid* visited R. Joseph Karo, who believed his visitor was the personification of the Mishnah. On Karo's *maggid*, see R. J. Z. Werblowsky, *Joseph Karo—Lawyer and Mystic* (Philadelphia: Jewish Publication Society of America, 1972), and M. Beneyahu, *Yosef Behiri* (Jerusalem, 1991), 391-512. Another contemporary of Karo's who had a *maggid* was R. Joseph Taitazak. See G. Scholem, "The Maggid of R. Yosef Taitazak [Hebrew]," *Sefunot* 11 (1971-1978): 67-112.

[47] On the question of women and possession by spirits, see M. Faierstein, "Maggidim, Spirits and Women in Safed," in *Spirit Possession in Judaism: Cases and Contexts from the Middles Ages to the Present* (ed. M. Goldish; Detroit: Wayne State University Press, 2002).

[48] She is referred to in this manner because her name is not mentioned in any of Vital's discussions.

[49] al-Boom owned an ancient manuscript that taught him how to expel demons and spirits from persons who were possessed. He taught these practices to Vital. See M. Beneyahu, *Toldot ha-Ari* (Jerusalem, 1967), 291-95.

[50] *BV*, 1.23.

[51] Rabbi of the Spanish congregation in Damascus (1550?-1622?). He is mentioned often in *BV*. Abulafia also spent time in Safed and studied with many of the important figures there.

[52] The details of this incident are quite informative, but would take us too far from the central point of this discussion.

[53] *BV*, 1.24.

[54] A colleague of R. Hayyim Vital and student of R. Isaac Luria.

[55] There is a tradition that before his death, R. Moses Cordovero said whoever saw the pillar of fire that preceded his coffin would be his successor. R. Isaac Luria was the only one to see it. See D. Tamar, "The Greatness and Wisdom of Rabbi Hayyim Vital [Hebrew]," in *Rabbi Joseph B. Soloveichik Jubilee Volume* (vol. 2; Jerusalem/New York, 1984), 1300. The pillar of fire seen over Vital undoubtedly was meant to validate him as Luria's successor.

[56] *BV* 1.12

[57] The *sandek* holds the child during the circumcision. This is considered a great honor.

[58] *BV*, 1.26.

[59] *BV*, 1.27.

[60] *BV*, 1.18.

[61] J. Sambari, *Divrei Yosef* (ed. S. Shtober; Jerusalem: Machon Ben Zvi, 1994), 364.

[62] *Ibid.*, 364-66.

[63] *BV*, 1.17.

[64] *BV*, 1.19.

[65] Dreams by women are found in *BV*, 3.3, 3,7, 3.8, 3.10, 3.12, 3.15, 3.18, 3.19, 3.20, 3.28(27), 3.37(37), 3.45(44), 3.46, 3.47, 3.49, 3.50, and 3.66.

[66] On mass prophecy in Sabbateanism, see G. Scholem, *Sabbatai Sevi: The Mystical Messiah* (Princeton: Princeton University Press, 1973), 254, 417-23, 606; J. Sasportas, *Sefer Sisat Novel Sev*, (ed. I. Tishby; Jerusalem: Mosad Bialik, 1954), 60, 96, 147-48, 182.

[67] The Sabbatian prophetesses are the subject of a comprehensive article by A. Rapoport-Albert, "Al Ma'amad ha-Nashim be-Shabtaut," *Jerusalem Studies in Jewish Thought* 16 (2001): 143-327.

[68] Scholem, *Sabbatai Sevi*, 707.

[69] In the official rabbinic list of biblical prophets and prophetesses, there are forty-eight men and seven women. See *b. Meg.*, 14a.

Immigrant Jewish Women
Who Married Out

Keren R. McGinity

INDEPENDENT THINKERS

Immigrant Jewish women who intermarried in the early decades of the twentieth century were highly independent thinkers who refused religious conformity as a way of life. The Jewish women considered here immigrated to this country between 1886 and 1894 and subsequently married Gentiles. Their Eastern European places of origin were similar, likewise their Orthodox beginnings; as activists, they also shared some political views and experiences. The lives of Mary Antin Grabau, Rose Pastor Stokes, and Anna Strunsky Walling illustrate freedom of choice and expression in the New World. Not all of these immigrant women ceased to self-identify as Jewish or to exemplify Jewish values, as was presumed to be the case for those who married "out." They joined mainstream culture without entirely forgetting their heritage. In some cases, new religious identities were formed. All of their experiences expanded what it meant to be a "Jewish woman" in America. In addition, their stories shed light on the meaning of intermarriage by deconstructing some prior assumptions about why mixed marriages failed.

Antin, Pastor, and Strunsky are well-known historical figures because of their political activism and literary works. However, the personal details of life within their homes and marriages, and how their families responded to their marital choices, have received little attention to date. They are the focus here because they became celebrities of sorts as a result of their marriages to prominent non-Jewish men, their ambitions, and their professional accomplishments. The women in this chapter demonstrate that despite the lack of social acceptance, for some Jewish women intermarriage was a means of joining the dominant culture.[1] Although their marriages did not end as Cinderella fairy tales, each in its own way suggests something about the mechanics of intermarriage between Jewish women and non-Jewish men that defies conventional ideas about intermarriage and identity.

Immigrant Jewish women who intermarried shared certain characteristics with immigrant women who married co-religionists. Susan Glenn in her book, *Daughters of the Shtetl: Life and Labor in the Immigrant Generation,* contends that Jewish working women's involvement in two overlapping contexts, urban mass culture and political activism in the garment industry, eased constraints on female behavior. Such activity also fostered optimistic feelings among women about relationships with the opposite sex based more on a partnership model—not necessarily equal, but certainly more collaborative than Orthodox Jewish cultural patterns. Girls entered the workforce and became involved in union activities, thus expanding the traditional female sphere. Paradoxically, once they married, they settled into domestic life. Glenn writes, "One image emphasized women's ability to fight side by side with men to help earn a living and to struggle for workers' rights. The other stressed the respectability and romantic promise that women sought in the role of modern wife-companion." Moreover, "gender equality was never as important as working-class equality [for those involved in unions]." If women gained some modicum of social equality, it was the result of their radical activities rather than agitation specifically about women's needs.[2] This Jewish version of New Womanhood prompted those who intermarried, as well as those who in-married, to seek companionate marriages, but not necessarily equality with their husbands. In addition, if they did strive for gender equality in theory, it was generally unattainable in practice.

Like their immigrant sisters, Jewish women who married non-Jews chose their mates rather than accept arranged marriages. America presented many new opportunities for immigrant Jewish women, among them the ability to earn their own living and, with it, the potential to choose their own spouse. In contrast to their mothers, most of whom were parties to arranged marriages in the Old World, these immigrant women selected their own mates. According to Sydney Weinberg, author of *World of Our Mothers,* "Like the idea of a 'chief rabbi,' the marriage broker never really caught on in this country." Certainly, some immigrants still utilized the *shadkhen* [matchmakers] to help them secure an appropriate marriage partner, but they were increasingly in the minority. Although parental approval remained a factor, the ability to earn wages fostered unwillingness among immigrant Jewish women to marry someone chosen for them or whom they disliked. Shortly after they began to earn an income, young Jewish women married and began raising families.[3] While earning potential replaced the role of the matchmaker and the dowry, a middle-class ideal of respectability pervaded immigrant and American culture alike. Women were expected to stop working for wages after marriage. According to historian Elizabeth Ewen: "Both middle-class American culture and immigrant men in particular, considered it demeaning for women to work outside the home after marriage. It was assumed that husbands who allowed this were incapable of supporting their families on their own."[4] The male breadwinner ethic is also evident in intermarriages and often caused financial strife between spouses.

Antin, Pastor, and Strunsky succeeded in attaining contemporary marriage standards, notwithstanding criticisms for straying from the Jewish fold and mixed emotions from their in-laws. Marriage in America was defined by specific characteristics. As historian, Nancy Cott writes in *Public Vows: A History of Marriage and the Nation*:

> Political and legal authorities endorsed and aimed to perpetuate nationally a *particular* marriage model: lifelong, faithful monogamy, formed by the mutual consent of a man and a woman, bearing the impress of the Christian religion and the English common law in its expectations for the husband to be the family head and economic provider, his wife the dependent partner.[5]

When immigrant Jewish women selected for spouses men who were sufficiently well off not to require their wives' incomes, they fulfilled the American marital promise.

Getting married provided a way of participating in the American family ideal. As Riv-Ellen Prell writes in *Fighting to Become Americans,* "To create a new household and family was part of becoming attractive Americans with an outlook focused on pleasure and consumption"; in other words: "marriage was the route to Americanization."[6] Marriage as a purely social and economic arrangement had already begun to break down in the Old World, where young people began to request their parents' approval after falling in love. Western ideas about love and marriage infiltrated the *shtetlekh* [small Russian and Polish towns] and were reinforced among Jewish immigrant women in America; love, freely chosen, was what was important in the modern age, not *yichus* [prestige] brought to one's family.[7] As Cott argues, "Americans were very much committed to marriage founded on love....True love was envisioned as springing up of its own accord, neither obeying rational discipline nor answering family considerations or monetary concerns."[8] The immigrant character in one of Anzia Yezierska's stories exclaimed, "America is a lover's land."[9] Prell eloquently describes: "Romance and Americanization were baked together into a single wedding cake."[10] If an immigrant woman married for love rather than religion, as did all three of these women, she exemplified an American ideal and therefore the zenith of acculturation.

　　Religious differences, contrary to the claims of clergy and ethnic press authors, did not necessarily cause marital disharmony for immigrant Jewish women.[11] Political dissension and financial disagreements instigated the eventual erosion of all three of the marriages studied here. Whether, as the *Hebrew Standard* contended, the intermarriages of Antin, Pastor, and Strunsky actually influenced other immigrant Jewish women to consider marrying non-Jewish men is difficult to ascertain without direct testimony to this affect.[12] What is apparent is that these particular intermarriages sparked a continual outpouring of interest, coverage in the ethnic press, commentary by Jewish religious figures and organizations, and attention in mainstream media and popular culture. Understanding their intermarriage stories tells us as much about American history as it does about Jewish women's history.

MARY ANTIN

Mary Antin (1881-1949), author of the classic immigrant autobiography *The Promised Land*,[13] illustrates the ways in which intermarriage contributed to religious sampling without causing her to cease being Jewish as she defined it. Her early life was similar to many other Jewish immigrant women. Antin was born in the small Russian town of Polotzk, located within the Pale of Settlement, and immigrated to Boston aboard the steamship *Polynesia* on May 8, 1894.[14] It was here that her intermarriage took place, along with a quest for a new spiritual understanding of life's meaning. Antin met Amadeus W. Grabau, a German-American Lutheran geologist and paleontologist doing graduate work at Harvard, through the Natural History Club at Hale House.

　　She married him on October 5, 1901, in Boston (Antin was twenty, he thirty-one).[15] Edward E. Hale, Minister of the South Congregational Church, officiated.[16] Despite the social taboo against intermarriage, Antin's family never criticized her selection or that of her sister Ida, who also married a non-Jew.[17] Perhaps Antin's mother accepted her daughter's choice because she herself had been party to an arranged marriage. A woman who did not have a choice might wish that her daughter did. The fact that Grabau was an academic may also have earned him points in Antin's parents' minds. Although Antin's family did not object, her friends and benefactors certainly did. In a letter to English author Israel Zangwill announcing her marriage, Antin wrote:

I...hope that none of my old friends will think that I can spare them now. I want them all as much as ever, particularly since I have lost many to whom my marriage was displeasing on religious grounds. They might find these reasons unfounded if they could realize that I have not changed my faith.[18]

Antin questioned her Orthodox Judaism from a very young age. Although her queries began before she left Russia, they accelerated once she began the process of Americanization. Her parents did not deter the loosening of Jewish tradition. In fact, Antin's father had asked her mother to leave her wig, part of Jewish Orthodoxy, in Russia. And although they lit candles on the Sabbath, her parents kept their store open until Sunday, the Christian day of rest.[19] Once Antin began her American education, her pursuit of learning replaced traditional observance. As Jonathan Sarna describes it, "School became her surrogate house of worship."[20] Antin reveled in American ideals of freedom of choice. The prospect of American citizens choosing their own religion, or choosing whether to believe in God, was the ultimate freedom to Antin. She explained:

In Russia, I had practiced a prescribed religion, with little faith in what I professed, and a restless questioning of the universe. When I came to America I lightly dropped the religious forms that I had mocked before, and contented myself with a few novel phrases employed by my father in his attempt to explain the riddle of existence.[21]

Antin had already begun to explore nature's explanation for being and the process of evolution by the time she married a Lutheran man. The Natural History Club in Boston added new perspectives to her religious repertoire. According to Sam Bass Warner, "for her, the outings and lectures of natural history began a lifelong endeavor to unite her Judaic inheritance with the modern romantic tradition of Emerson and Thoreau."[22] And in Antin's words: "By asking questions, by listening when my wise friends talked, by reading, by pondering and dreaming,

I slowly gathered together the kaleidoscopic bits of the stupendous panorama which is painted in the literature of Darwinism."[23] This process was embellished by Antin's friendship with Josephine Lazarus, sister of the poet Emma. Lazarus believed in transcendentalism and insisted that, "in God's boundless universe all truth, all spirit are one, alike for the Jew and the Christian who live in the spirit and the truth."[24] This kind of thinking likely appealed to Antin because it helped to explain aspects of her own life, including her marriage to a non-Jew.

Antin was ambivalent about Judaism, but she did not abandon it for Quakerism, as Magdalena Zaborowska contends.[25] Both Antin's daughter and a friend, Rabbi Abraham Cronbach, have testified to the fact that she observed the major Jewish holidays at home after her marriage, while she also explored "many forms of religion and religious philosophy." Antin spent parts of her final years as a disciple of two different spiritual leaders, Meher Baba and Rudolf Steiner.[26] A relative contends that she "fully accepted being Jewish without accepting the dogma of the religious tenet."[27] While never formally converting to another religion, Antin clearly came to accept aspects of other religions as at least defensible, if not downright appealing. Writing in 1914, Antin showed definite signs of accepting some Christian precepts. "I know that 2,000 years after righteousness was urged on us we still have to be coaxed to behave ourselves," she wrote, alluding to the teachings of Jesus. "Christianity, as I understand it, is the Mosaic law expressed in another form."[28] It is also clear that the First World War figured in her thinking about the meaning of religion and brotherhood at home and abroad.

Within the larger historical context, Antin's diminished religiosity in terms of traditional Judaism was one example of a common trend. Although those immigrants who became less orthodox did not necessarily align themselves with another branch of Judaism, traditional critics used the lessening of observance as an opportunity to attack Reform Judaism. In an article entitled "Steps from Synagogue to Church," the author lambasted Reform Judaism as eventually becoming merely a variant of Christianity. The marriage of a Jewish woman from a famous family of Reform Jews to a Gentile in a church was cited to illustrate this point: "Were the young lady quite irreligious, and had she determined to marry a non-Jew, without any religious ceremonies, the matter would bear a different complection: it would represent another problem."[29] As others of her time may have done, Antin reflected on how changes in her religious practices would affect the spirituality and religious identification of her descendants:

> My grandchildren, for all I know, may have a graver task than I have set them....What positive affirmation of the persistence of Judaism in the blood my descendants may have to make, I may not be present to hear.[30]

While Antin's intermarriage may have added fuel to the fire of her religious meandering, the seed for this lifestyle was planted before she met her husband and continued to grow long after they parted ways. The historical evidence suggests that rather than keeping or discarding one identity or another, she continued to identify as Jewish and in other ways. In a 1925 letter to author Mary Austin, Antin described how she self-identified:

> I am not a Christian—not in any technical sense of adherence to orthodox Christian dogma; not in any popular sense. One friend defines me as "a Christian <u>and</u> a Jew," making a distinction from the popular rather distasteful conception of a "Hebrew Christian." I don't care what I am called, but I want to be sure I don't mislead anyone.[31]

This statement illustrates a coalescence of religious identities that defies simple categorization.

Antin's marriage and interests outside of Judaism did not prevent her identification with the Jewish people. In a powerful article written during World War II, Antin described how she rationalized the support she gave to a Catholic priest building a chapel to two Jewish men who similarly came seeking a contribution to start a Hebrew School: "It was known, of course, that I was married to a Gentile—a Protestant. Still it was assumed there were limits to my apostasy."[32] She had begun to read the New Testament: "I was not yet aware of the supreme role of Jesus of Nazareth in mediating the Hebrew tradition to the modern world. That was to come later; but already I was a queer enough fish from the orthodox Jewish standpoint."[33] Yet during a time of active anti-Semitism in the world, Antin identified as a Jew:

> For decades, I lived cut off from Jewish life and thought, heart-free and mind-free to weave other bonds. There was nothing intentional or self-conscious in this divorcement. It was simply that my path in life ran far from the currents of Jewish experience. Today I find myself pulled by old forgotten ties, through the violent projection of an immensely magnified Jewish

problem. It is one thing to go your separate way, leaving friends and comrades behind in peace and prosperity; it is another thing to fail to remember them when the world is casting them out. I can no more return to the Jewish fold than I can return to my mother's womb; neither can I in decency continue to enjoy my accidental personal immunity from the penalties of being a Jew in a time of virulent anti-Semitism. The least I can do, in my need to share the sufferings of my people, is declare that I am as one of them.

Finally, "In all those places where race lines are drawn, I shall claim the Jewish badge; but in my Father's house of many mansions I shall continue a free spirit."[34] Antin's use of the term "race" is fitting, as Jews did not make "the final transformation toward Caucasian whiteness" in common American understanding until after World War II.[35]

Antin believed that America held certain promises for women. Her autobiography asserted, "A long girlhood, a free choice in marriage, and a brimful womanhood are the precious rights of an American womanhood."[36] This contrasted with the traditional gendered view of Jewish women and marriage described in Antin's story "Malinke's Atonement." There she wrote, "What are daughters worth? They're only good to sit in the house, a burden on their parents neck, until they're married off."[37] In the Old World, women lived in a gender-defined world where learning and religion were reserved for men, and women were given the realm of domesticity to organize and master.[38] "It was not much to be a girl, you see."[39] She was saddened by what she considered to be her sister Frieda's premature marriage at the age of seventeen. Frieda's youthful union was common for immigrant women. Rose Cohen, another example, was introduced to a prospective husband at age sixteen.[40] However much she pitied her sister's fate, Antin did not attain what she had destined for herself after she was married. Having once set her goal on attending Radcliffe, Antin relinquished this idea when she married and with her husband moved to New York, where he assumed a professorship at Columbia University. She studied at Columbia's Teachers College and at Barnard College, but did not complete a degree.[41] Antin never did achieve the level of higher education that she had dreamed of throughout her Americanization, perhaps due to illness.[42]

Although Antin's marriage certificate listed her occupation as "At Home," she did not lead a domestic life.[43] Antin toured from 1913-

1918 on a national lecture circuit, speaking about the importance of immigration and the ability of immigrants to become good citizens; this was indeed work outside of the home.[44] In addition, she maintained the use of her maiden name in her published work. On the other hand, the fact that her profession was based primarily on the solitary act of writing articles, books, and related correspondence would imply that Antin did in fact succumb to the labor allocated to married women in America. Antin's "home" work was her writing. In the long run, she was left to raise her child single-handedly.

Her marriage deteriorated over time, accelerated by World War I. Conflicting nationalistic loyalties and wage competition, not religious differences, caused the eventual dissolution of her marriage. Grabau was of German ancestry, while Antin was fiercely patriotic about America. Therefore, when Grabau refused to acknowledge that Germany was in the wrong and Antin was supportive of the allies, it created significant friction between them. In later years, their daughter Josephine described her perception of Antin's and Grabau's differences by saying, "he was waving the German flag out of one window and she was waving the American one out the other."[45] A different rationale for discordance pertains to the discrepancy in their earning capacities. While Antin received lecture fees when she went on the national circuit as well as royalties from her writing, Grabau's salary at Columbia did not increase beyond $2,500 per annum even after he was promoted to full professor. In what perhaps was an example of the male breadwinner ethic, biographer Susan Koppelman confirms, "There is reason to believe that this disparity in financial success discomfited Professor Grabau."[46]

From this perspective, it is clear that a difference of religion was not a significant factor in their separation. Arthur Antin, Mary Antin's nephew, believes it played no part and rather that Grabau's pro-German feelings influenced the outcome of their relationship and contributed to his leaving the country.[47] In 1920, Grabau took a post as director of research for the China Geological Survey in Peking, where he remained until his death in 1946. Despite their mutual inclination toward divorce, their daughter "made such a fuss about it that they did not" obtain one.[48] Evidence suggests that Grabau sought a divorce and Antin refused; on what grounds is unclear. In a letter to her younger sister Rosemary, dated January 31, 1946, Antin wrote: "No, I am no longer agitated about A. There is nothing I can do, so I let go of the whole matter. The letters have stopped coming. I did send A. the lawyer's letter to show him officially that I could not execute this divorce."[49] She died three years later at age 68.[50] Antin was buried at the Mount Pleasant Cemetery in Hawthorne, New York. Although there are Jewish sections in the cemetery, section six, where her remains lie, is non-sectarian. Given Antin's spiritual journey, her final destination is not surprising. Nonetheless, visitors to her grave find small pebbles atop the tombstone, which indicate that Antin's Jewish relatives and friends did not forget her.

ROSE PASTOR

Rose Pastor (1879-1933) intermarried a few years after Antin and the resulting notoriety catapulted the public fascination with intermarriage from the stage to the pulpit, the ethnic press, the bookstore, and the film screen. While issues other than organized religion dominated her life, Pastor did not relinquish her identity as a Jewish woman. Born Rose Harriet Wieslander in Augustova, Poland, she immigrated to the United States (via a stay in London) in 1890 and later took her stepfather's last name of Pastor.[51] In 1901, she began to write letters and then eventually regular columns for the *Jewish Daily News (Yiddishes Tageblatt)*, a Yiddish newspaper. In 1903, Pastor moved from Cleveland to New York and joined the newspaper's staff.

Pastor wrote about intermarriage in her advice column, "Just Between Ourselves, Girls," under the pseudonym "Zelda."[52] An eighteen-year-old reader named "B.C." disclosed that she was in love with a Christian man two years her senior who wanted to marry her. Her father objected on grounds that a Jew should marry a Jew. The advice seeker wrote, "I think it very nice that a Jewess should marry a Christian. Don't you?...What would you advise me to do? Marry my Christian lover or listen to my father?" Zelda responded unambiguously that the girl should not marry him and her father was right. He "wants to save you from misery and shame; from social excommunication and from moral death; you know all this in the depth of your heart, in spite of what you are trying to fool yourself into believing."[53] Zelda admonished that should the girl take the ill-fated step, she would not be able to look her friends in the face, her father would curse her, and her mother's weeping would cause near blindness. These were strong words coming from someone who two years later married a Christian. Perhaps Pastor was trying to convince herself not to become romantically involved with a

Gentile, one in particular whose acquaintance she had made before issuing the advice against intermarriage.[54]

Pastor met James Graham Phelps Stokes, son of one of America's wealthiest Episcopalian families and a graduate of Yale's Sheffield Scientific School and the medical college at Columbia, when she was assigned to interview him for an article. Stokes worked at the University Settlement, founded in 1887, whose male college graduate residents, living among the poor, aimed to set good civic examples.[55] The interview was congenial, and the article ran in the *Jewish Daily News* on July 19, 1903. Stokes made clear that his Christianity was a private matter and that settlement work should be non-sectarian, to improve social and industrial conditions while avoiding class consciousness.[56] His words resonated with Pastor, who had to drop out of school at age 10 to make shoe bows, and their romance began.[57]

Pastor's mother did not articulate concern when they told her they planned to marry: "She showed neither surprise nor excitement, but looked glad, and said quietly, 'Well children, there's a lot of work to be done. I hope you will be very happy—and useful.'"[58] Pastor's mother's response was likely influenced by her own experience of not being allowed to wed a Gentile man. Pastor wrote in her autobiography: "So bound by tradition was my mother, she would not marry her Polish lover—out of faith and against her father's will."[59] Her mother had encouraged Pastor's trip with Stokes to Canada and perhaps welcomed the prospect of her impoverished daughter marrying a very wealthy man, regardless of his religious heritage. Pastor wrote, "He had 'seen' me home from the Settlement on many occasions and my mother liked him"; she considered him kind, thoughtful, and polite.[60]

Stokes described his fiancée to his parents as follows: "Despite her Jewish origin she is as Christlike a Christian as I ever knew—I don't know where to find another Christian who is truer to the teachings of her Master." His parents, who were on an extended tour of Europe and Africa, responded warmly in a cable to his letter that detailed his engagement: "We most sincerely congratulate you and wish you all joy and happiness. Give our love to Rose."[61] Not all of his extended family was equally supportive. Two of his aunts took him to Mexico, possibly to divert his attention from, in Pastor's words, the "Israelitish maiden."[62] Stokes's Uncle William Earl Dodge, an anti-Semitic xenophobe, complained to an assistant attorney general when Pastor's socialism

became too much for him.[63] Evidently, both her Jewish background
and her politics dismayed some of Stokes's relatives.

Their engagement evoked comments and headlines. Stokes's brother,
acting as the family's spokesperson and perhaps hoping to avoid scandal,
made their acceptance of Pastor public with the statement, "Miss Pastor
is an ideal woman, loving, true, tender hearted, gentle and intellectual.
She is a noble woman and has done noble work. The family is very
much pleased with the match. It is an ideal one in all respects."[64] Despite
the family's official position, rumors flew in the press. The front page of
the *New York Times* carried the headline, "J.G. Phelps Stokes to Wed
Young Jewess," on April 6, 1905. In this article, Stokes sought to rectify
two errors. The first pertained to his family's reported opposition to
their union. He said:

> That is entirely false. There is nothing but the utmost cordiality
> and delight. The second error is that there is a difference of
> religious belief between Miss Pastor and myself. She is a Jewess
> as the Apostles were Jews—a Christian by faith.[65]

Stokes sought to persuade people that his wife-to-be was different from
other Jews who maintained their distinctive lifestyles and customs, and
that theirs would not even be "intermarriage."

When confronted with an inquiry about her earlier advice column,
Pastor told the reporter, "I advised a Jewish girl…against marrying a
Christian, but that was not as some say because I am opposed to intermarriage. It was simply because it was obvious that the girl did not love
the man…and I was always opposed to loveless marriage."[66] This rings
of rationalization, but Pastor was hard pressed to explain her own action
given her earlier advice. Pastor perceived her match with Stokes as
intermarriage, even if he did not. While Stokes reassured his mother
that Pastor was "a very devout Christian…I have never met a nobler or
truer Christian," Pastor told friends that she was going to "make history"
by marrying the millionaire Stokes: "Riches and poverty, Jew and
Christian will be united. Here is an indication of a new era."[67]

Stokes's family shared Pastor's view that the marriage would join
dissimilar individuals. Although his mother responded unequivocally
to Stokes himself, she expressed surprise if not reservation to his brother.
"Is it not astonishing," Helen Louisa Stokes asked, "that a Phelps Stokes
would choose for his wife a poor girl of Russian Jewish parentage,
ancestry unknown?" Anson, Jr., reassured his mother that Pastor had a
sense of humor, good complexion, and sensible dress, and that her

"spiritual talent" was of a "very high order"; although she had "a Jewish look about the forehead and mouth," her nose did not.[68] This exchange demonstrates that Stokes's mother and brother noted Pastor's ethnic, religious, and socioeconomic differences along with the idea that she was at least not "too Jewish" looking.

Pastor and Stokes were married at St. Luke's church on July 18, 1905, her twenty-sixth birthday, and the reception was held at the Brick House, the Stokes's country home in Noroton, Connecticut. As at Antin's marriage, non-Jewish clergy performed the ceremony. Two hundred or so people attended. One of Pastor's journalist friends declined to attend because he opposed intermarriage.[69] The couple insisted that the word "obey" be omitted from the ceremony. At the time, Pastor did not explain why, but in her autobiography she later claimed the initiative for this deletion, contending that she had been little interested in the wedding preparations and had assured her husband-to-be that nothing was of much import; everything was fine. However, "on the inspiration of the moment I add, 'but I want the word "obey" eliminated from the service.'"[70] Though indiscernible in the photograph of the couple, Pastor supposedly wore a cross at her wedding.[71] But the *New York Times*, in describing the bride's attire in significant detail, noted that a pearl necklace was the only jewelry she wore.[72]

One can only speculate whether or not Pastor and Stokes discussed how they would keep and run their married household. While they were engaged, Pastor and Stokes traveled to Cleveland and attended a traditional Passover seder at a friend's house.[73] According to her biographers, Arthur and Pearl Zipser, the couple did not practice any "doctrinal religion,"[74] which implies that they observed neither Protestant nor Jewish religious laws. However, this generalization neglects to consider what threads of either their Christian or Jewish origin may have manifested themselves in the Stokes's marriage and practices. Paucity of evidence makes it difficult to know their exact manner of celebrating holidays; however, there are some hints. In a letter Stokes wrote to Pastor late one fall some years after their wedding, he told her that he ordered "something beautiful for the hall and trimmed the window box plants."[75] By the sound of it, their house was being decorated for the coming Christmas season, since a tree or wreath are often located in a front hall and plants are "trimmed" with holiday ornamentation. References to a "batch of cheery Christmas mail from Rose"[76] suggest season's greetings but deeper meaning is allusive. Without children to educate, we cannot know what religious tradition, if any, Pastor would have imparted from her Jewish background.

How couples negotiated married life depended on the intricacies of their relationship and gender. As Cott writes in *Public Vows,* "Turning men and women into husbands and wives, marriage has designated the ways both sexes act in the world and the reciprocal relation between them."[77] Housework was Pastor's domain.[78] It was Pastor who attempted to keep it simple by choosing paper napkins over linen ones and canned goods over cooking. Moreover, Pastor took Stokes's last name. During the incubation period of their pre-marriage relationship, Pastor had told Stokes, "you will be coming to my world, not I to yours....We will have a flat somewhere on the East Side, and live and work among the people."[79] Although this was true initially—the couple rented a six-room plus bath apartment on the Lower East Side—they soon moved into a new house on Caritas Island off Wallacks Point in Stamford, Connecticut (a wedding gift from his parents). In both locations they had hired help, suggesting that Pastor became accustomed to Stokes's way of life rather than the other way around.

At the outset of their relationship, Pastor's and Stokes's politics seemed more alike than not; both were committed to social betterment. For women active in the labor movement, such as Pastor, sharing political views with one's spouse superseded other concerns.[80] Pastor joined the Socialist Party and, using her childhood Yiddish, told a crowd at a rally that her husband's decision to join with her was "the happiest and grandest day of her life."[81] Over time their different modi operandi became apparent. Pastor noted this in her diary in 1913: "He [Stokes] is very dependent on my presence and dreads the thought of my going in to the strike without him, yet feels that he is not specially fitted for that <u>kind</u> of work in the movement."[82] Moreover, in her autobiography she described Stokes's seeking to avoid the crowds that pressed forward to shake their hands, while Pastor reveled in it:

> It was not until many years afterward that I realized why this was so with him. Then it was borne in on me that he loved the people in theory only; that there was no personal warmth in him for them. Often I thought I detected a look of contempt for some member or members of my class. He could not have dealt me a personal blow that would have hurt more. At times he would let fall a word...and I would chill with an undefined apprehension.[83]

The ghetto girl and the millionaire would not last.[84]

Distinct politics and gender inequity, not issues of religion, eroded the marriage in the long run. World War I increased the dissolution of common political ground. In a 1914 letter, Pastor described her horror about the war: "That stupendous slaughter house—the other side of the Atlantic—has had a most crushing effect upon me."[85] While both Pastor and Stokes resigned from the Socialist Party in 1917 because they supported the war and the party opposed it, only Pastor eventually sought to return to it.[86] She moved to the Left while Stokes moved to the Right. Pastor's outspoken politics made her the target of a government indictment and in 1918 she was convicted of attempting to cause insubordination, obstructing recruiting, and making false statements to impede the success of American forces and aid this country's enemies. The U.S. Circuit Court of Appeals ordered a new trial, and in 1921 the government dropped the case.[87] By this point the Stokes couple had become politically distant, she more radical and he significantly less so.

Earlier diary entries shed additional light on the demise of the Pastor-Stokes marriage. In one, Pastor described Stokes's displeasure at her interjection in a conversation he was having with someone else. She surmised, "now, and often before, my interest in the subject doesn't seem to count." Pastor chose to let this slide.[88] One year later, Stokes's conduct left a more permanent mark. After an exhausting speaking tour, Pastor stayed in bed late one morning, attempting to recover from bronchitis and a high temperature. She wrote:

> Today marked a deep change in me—mentally, spiritually—in my attitude toward G. He accused me of loafing...."Loafing!" I didn't reply. What's the good? But it put the iron in my soul, and this time I feel it's there to stay. The terrible loneliness of one's soul in such moments![89]

These experiences combined with their divergent politics, contributed to the breaking point that came in 1925 with their divorce. Maintaining class loyalty, Pastor stated that other than her marriage, "there is nothing remarkable to tell of my life. I was but one of an overwhelming number of working women when I came to this country and went into a cigar factory."[90] Her marriage helped make her famous because it was an interfaith union between a poor Jewish woman and a wealthy non-Jewish man.

Pastor's identity as a Jewish woman was subsumed in her beliefs and efforts on behalf of the working class. Just as education became

Studies in Jewish Civilization 14: Women and Judaism

Antin's form of worship, advocating a better way of life for the underprivileged became Pastor's. Although she would not be considered a practicing Jew by any means, her abundant social action demonstrated Jewish values. As historian Alice Kessler-Harris points out, the most prominent Jewish women who continued to be active politically after they married were those who intermarried.[91] Perhaps, their continued involvement served as an outlet for their modified self-identification as Jewish women. In Pastor's case at least, she worked as a Jew even if she did not observe as one.

ANNA STRUNSKY

As did Pastor and Antin, Anna Strunsky (1877-1964) married and eventually separated from her Protestant husband. Like Antin's and Pastor's marriages, differences in politics and financial perspectives— not religion—provoked the deterioration of Strunsky's marriage. While Strunsky identified as something other than Jewish in the years following her marriage, she continued to pursue issues of social justice. Strunsky was born within the Pale of Settlement in Bibinots, Russia, moved through Germany to England, and then immigrated to New York in the fall of 1886, settling on the Lower East Side.[92] Strunsky met her future husband through a mutual friend, famed author Jack London, with whom she had a prior relationship and would later co-author a book in 1903, *The Kempton-Wace Letters*.[93] William English Walling and Strunsky first noticed each other at a Thanksgiving picnic at which they talked long into the night. Five years later, in 1905, Walling wrote to Strunsky when he spotted a pamphlet she had written as chair of the Friends of Russian Freedom, calling for help and democratic reforms for the Russian people. Strunsky joined Walling in St. Petersburg in September, 1906, and their love blossomed amidst the volatile environment. Together they witnessed the shooting of a young student when he refused to rise and sing "God save the Czar!"[94] This experience ignited their romance.

News of Strunsky's and Walling's committed relationship, and the reactions of both sets of parents, were communicated long distance through multiple letters and cables. Strunsky wrote to her father that the shooting of the student "perhaps was the occasion which forced our love to our eyes and lips," inspiring "a new faith," and that they were "born again."[95] Strunsky's mother responded in Yiddish, "I thank God for taking you so far across a great distance to bring you happiness."[96]

Her mother's acceptance may have been influenced by her own experience; she had refused to consummate and escaped from an arranged marriage at the age of sixteen.[97] Her father's long letter expressed his utmost joy at her newfound love, with a small reference to Walling's finances. Her father considered Walling to be his son already and asked that she convey this to him, to kiss him, and to tell him that her father had "enough confidence in him to trust you over to him."[98] As if relinquishing a prized possession, Elias Strunsky handed over his daughter to Walling. "He got the greatest fortune" was a double entendre. Perhaps he thought financial security would be his precious daughter's future.

Not all parents were so open to the prospect of their Jewish daughters marrying non-Jews. Two *Forward* letters from 1926 expressed concerns about Jewish women's marriage prospects. In one, a family with four daughters living in the country was in a quandary because "here, it's impossible to marry off a girl, because there are no Jews, only Gentiles." Evidently marriage with a non-Jew was not considered a possibility. The parents wanted to send the girls to a big city, but not move themselves. The editor replied in this fashion: "We can only tell them that many Jewish families that are in the same position leave the small towns for the sake of their children. Others, on the other hand, remain where they are."[99] In a second letter, a mother confided that she once thought there was no difference between Jews and Christians, and that parents should not interfere if their child desired to wed a Christian. But now that her daughter had fallen in love with a Christian, she felt differently and tried to convince her daughter to end the relationship. The mother admitted: "True, it could happen that she could marry a Jewish man and after the wedding not be able to stand him. But with a Jew it's still different." The editor's response reinforced the mother's opinion and urged her daughter to understand that "the match is not a good one."[100] It is clear from these letters that some parents harbored the sentiment that even a bad Jew was preferable to a good non-Jew, a feeling Strunsky's father did not share.

The exchange with Walling's parents was more complicated, involving multiple letters and cables. He reassured them that he had known Strunsky for several years, she was considered a genius of a writer and speaker, and everyone loved her including all his friends. He concluded his description: "She is young (26) and very healthy and strong. Of course she is a Jewess and her name is Anna Strunsky, but I hope to improve that—at least in private life—but we haven't spoken much of such things." Apparently he sensed that her name, at least, would cause some concern. His father's initial response was a cable: "Surprised and anxious haste always dangerous your happiness ours." Walling cabled his assurance that he would do nothing in haste. Subsequent letters imply that his parents had reservations about his impulsiveness, not necessarily about Strunsky, yet he continued to assure them of her character and noble work. If they had other concerns, his parents' warning about "haste" was the only objection they put in print. Walling also revealed that Strunsky was not a "maid in waiting" and would not be a professional wife, but he was accustomed to hiring others to do the menial tasks in life anyway. He told his parents that their ambivalence made it "absolutely necessary" that he and Strunsky marry before returning to the US, and invited them to Europe to attend the marriage ceremony. Otherwise, he wrote, "I think you should send us the same free-hearted blessing her parents have."[101] The grounds for the Wallings's hesitation are not entirely clear, but his father's ill health at the time probably played some role. In any event, they did not travel to Russia. Letters from Walling and Strunsky allude to her foreign birth, but assure his parents that her father considered himself a full American and that she was American by upbringing, thus hinting that the Wallings's position may have been xenophobic. A letter from Strunsky to her father-in-law mentioned the "shock that unfortunate cablegram was," suggesting that it was more the abrupt timing of their announcement than the news itself.[102]

Walling's mother suggested that they return to San Francisco and marry in a manner that would please her parents. However according to the couple, intermarriage was best if it occurred on neutral European ground. Strunsky's response to her future mother-in-law, included here at length because it captures the predicaments of intermarriage, spelled out the complex reasons why she and Walling chose to marry far away and in a civil ceremony:

> My parents would of course love to have us married at home, but they are not opposed to our marrying abroad. They understand that a religious marriage is impossible. Neither English nor I belong to any creed and a religious ceremony would be farcical to us, at best, something less than sincere and beautiful. A greater reason still is that according to the law of Moses, I cannot marry English at all, and there is no rabbi in

the world who could listen to our troth without committing sacrilege! From the standpoint of the faith in which I was born I must be stoned to death for what I am about to do. My parents are very liberal yet I have heard them say they would rather see me dead than marry a Gentile. I should not record this at all for their attitude towards English is perfect. They believe in him so absolutely and have so perfect a picture of his nature, his strong, pure feeling, his idealism, that they count me blessed among the daughters of Zion, and they give me to him freely. It is transformation of their whole conception of nationalism, and I count it a miracle that our love should have brought it about. Their love for me helped, too, but if they had not felt deeply that English and I were tied by indissoluble laws of the spirit that we were one though every religion in the world cried otherwise, they would have withheld their consent.

You see, therefore, how it is we cannot marry at home. The Jewish religion would unite us only if English became a Jew, and another form of religious marriage is equally impossible for me. It would mean conversion on my part to have even a Unitarian minister officiate, and it would literally kill my mother....So we look upon our being in Europe as the kindest possible arrangement of Fate. It is a fortunate escape for us.[103]

In this same letter she also told Walling's mother that her attitude was not "too soft or servile" and that this suited him fine. She contended that their love was the "strong good love of equals." To her credit, Rosalind Walling wrote back to both children, sympathizing with Strunsky's parents, admiring their devotion to their religion, and admitting that previously she did not know "it was not allowed to use the Jewish rites in marriage with a Gentile." She commented, "I have seen that there is more opposition in Jewish families than in Christians to mixed marriages but I didn't know the laws were so severe."[104] The many letters Strunsky wrote to her in-laws, addressed "Dearest Mother and Father," indicate that her relationship with them grew strong with time. As with the Pastor-Stokes match, the Strunsky-Walling engagement prompted headlines—about a talented authoress and a rich Yankee, both Socialists, becoming betrothed in Russia. Strunsky's intermarriage illustrated the modern American ideal of romantic love. In a news clipping, Strunsky reportedly "defended passionately the ideal of marriage based on romantic ideal."[105] After she wed, she wrote to her family that, "Our love is as free as the soul. We hold each other and will hold each other forever, by no force in the world except the force of love."[106] Strunsky epitomized the Jewish immigrant woman's ascendancy to Americanism through her commitment to marry a man of her choice whom she loved.

While Strunsky explained to her mother-in-law that she had no intention of converting to another religion, her words also betray a woman who distanced herself from the faith she inherited at birth. In a July 1, 1906, letter to her family addressed "Dearest people," Strunsky described the civil ceremony that took place on June 28 and commented: "We consider it of no more importance than getting a passport."[107] The marriage ceremony, something sacred in Jewish tradition, held no import for her. In response to a letter from her father-in-law that might have expressed concern about how the two would meld their different backgrounds, Strunsky wrote, "Neither English nor I have an axe to grind, no small panacea to propose; we have no dogma that we are aware of. I think, therefore, we shall not miss our mark."[108] Her married life, however, came to involve more Christian tradition than she might have initially imagined.

Although there is little historical evidence detailing Strunsky's and Walling's domestic life, a few pieces are rather telling. They eventually left Russia and, after visiting family in Chicago and San Francisco, settled in New York. In 1916, the couple bought a house in Greenwich, Connecticut.[109] On December 21, 1918, Strunsky wrote a letter to her mother-in-law describing the glee she felt about their Christmas tree:

> The greatest news is that I bought a beautiful, large Christmas
> tree for the children, had it set up in the parlor, and last night
> I trimmed it, so that we can have it for Hayden's birthday
> tomorrow. It is lighted by electricity, and it is the loveliest tree
> I have ever seen!

She described the children's delight when they came downstairs in the morning and spotted the tree. Her concluding sentence is most revealing: "Dearest, I have never before had a Christmas tree, but I hope to trim a Christmas tree every remaining year of my life—it is such a delight-giving experience."[110] This indicates that for the first twelve years of marriage, during which she bore several children, Strunsky and Walling did not have a Christmas tree. The change over time illustrates further dilution in her allegiance to her heritage and an acceptance of her husband's. Some Jews who did not intermarry had Christmas trees, in an effort either to Americanize or not to deprive their Jewish children of what their Gentile friends enjoyed. However, Christmas and Easter holiday cards sent by their young daughter Georgia imply that Strunsky and Walling raised their children to observe at least two Christian holidays.[111] Found among Strunsky's personal papers is a wide assortment of Christian religious literature, as well as ten publications by the Society of Friends. A membership card for The Wider Quaker Fellowship, bearing the name "Mrs. W. English Walling," is among her personal items. Yet Strunsky also chose to keep the advertisement booklet from a Jewish funeral home containing the laws for mourners and dates for Jewish holidays from 1960-1965. Like Antin, Strunsky's religious identity changed by adding aspects from other traditions; this is not to say that she entirely ceased to be Jewish.

Gender and economic imbalances soon presented problems in the Strunsky-Walling marriage. The summer they wed, Strunsky wrote in her diary about Walling's tone of voice when speaking to her about a minor matter: "Authority only means disrespect and irritation against perceived weakness in another's personality. It was not loving—it is not to be found in the spirit of a comrade."[112] Economic disparity soon became a point of contention when she wanted to come to the aid of her relatives and he did not. That September she wrote in her diary:

> Well, I tell myself, I must work, I must earn—when I earn I shall do what I can. I have no right to what is not my own...I begin to feel estranged from him, distanced by a brutal fact, that he has and I have not, that there is a barrier....If I cannot earn my bread and he can than I feel inferior to him.[113]

A month later, Strunsky made an entry detailing the bitter loneliness she felt: "I am lonely. I feel very much outside of his life....Why must I live in loneliness and doubt?...How lonely and isolated I feel!"[114] The intermittent loneliness Strunsky documented when Walling seemed absorbed only in his work or distant from her made Strunsky more aware of her own need to work, which was hindered by the demands of motherhood placed squarely on her shoulders.

While newly married, Strunsky remarked that she, too, "had a 'Cause' as men have."[115] However, an entry ten years later illustrates that Walling operated as he pleased, while Strunsky kept the home and children together. In 1916, Walling made a cutting remark, questioning whether anyone could get any "service" out of Strunsky. She remonstrated, "What about my serving the babies day and night!"; there was much more she could have added about serving others. He left himself open so that he could decide whether to travel to Boston, telling her he never tied himself up if he could avoid it. "'That's splendid,'" she told him with sarcasm. "I always tie myself up. I love freedom, but I have so many duties always."[116] Strunsky outlined her views on marriage in a five-page undated essay. She advocated a "Revolution in the home, and the function of woman as home-keeper, home-drudge, or house-manager. That eats away our intellectual life, our poetry, our comradeship. The home must be kept by both men and women."[117] Within her own home, Strunsky had an unequal share of the upkeep. Her domestic responsibilities made their marriage more gender traditional than she had envisioned. True equality between spouses was not attained.

Initially, Strunsky intended to continue using her maiden name professionally after she married; however, she eventually gave in to convention on this point. The summer they married, Strunsky wrote to her brother about having to sign a paper concerning Walling's property and made the comment, "I signed Anna Strunsky Walling, my legal name—but all of my other letters and writings I sign Anna Strunsky." Strunsky's thumbing her nose at convention caught the attention of the press. A December, 1906, *Chicago Daily News* headline read: "Scorns the Name of Wife/Mrs. Walling Wants to Be Known as Anna Strunsky, Though Married." She explained her position well: "This taking of a husband's name by a woman when she marries is one of the symbols of the merging of her individuality into his. It is a convention against which I protest."[118] Less than two years after they wed, Walling got his wish to "improve" her last name. Strunsky's continued use of her maiden named must have caused her in-laws some consternation. She assuaged in 1908: "Father, dear heart, I shall never grieve you again by using my maiden name, for I want my daughter's name for whatever I write and do."[119] Strunsky's decision to modify the use of her name, counter to her original plan, illustrates one way that gender influenced marriage. In what her biographer James Boylan calls another "symbolic retreat from the notion of equality in marriage," Strunsky purchased a wedding ring nearly three years after she and Walling wed to avoid misunderstanding about them among people unfamiliar with their status.[120]

Strunsky and Walling went different political directions, as did Antin and Grabau, Pastor and Stokes. While she supported peace efforts during World War I, he associated the American peace movement with German subversion and strongly disapproved of her involvement. In addition to political disagreement and issues of gender inequality, financial concerns added considerable stress to their crumbling marriage. Several years before their actual divorce, Strunsky wrote to her mother-in-law: "So to my mind whatever difficulty exists arises mainly from the fact that English, who is a genius, was not a bread winner and was never intended to be one."[121] Although she spoke and wrote of economic equality, Strunsky's own life did not exemplify this. There is no historical evidence indicating that their different religious backgrounds played a role in their 1932 divorce.

TIKKUN OLAM

Antin, Pastor, and Strunsky practiced *tikkun olam* [repairing the world]. As writers, political activists, and labor leaders, all three women, each in her own way, exemplified the Jewish values of caring for others and seeking social justice. While these can be considered secular humanitarian ideals, it is conceivable that their experiences as minorities and their Jewish backgrounds contributed to their concerns and career pursuits. They may not have appeared "Jewish" in the eyes of the organized Jewish communities or the larger society. However, their actions on behalf of the less fortunate and their sincere determination to make the world a better place for all people, despite marrying "out," can be considered a transformation of what it meant to be a Jewish woman in America in the early twentieth century.

While the lives of the women discussed in this chapter were similar in the ways and extent to which each woman navigated her life after marriage almost entirely outside the Jewish fold, this was not necessarily the case for all Jewish women who intermarried during the early decades of the twentieth century, immigrant or otherwise. Some women sought acceptance within the Jewish community. When Nellie Gutenberg married Clarence Dowd, they both signed a pledge orchestrated by Rabbi Leo M. Franklin of Congregation Beth El in Detroit. It read: "We the undersigned hereby solemnly promise that should children be born of our union we will to the best of our ability rear them in the Jewish faith."[122] Presumably, this rabbi stipulated that he would officiate at their marriage ceremony provided that they swear to raise the children as Jews, suggesting that matrilineal descent was not considered sufficient in this case. Other extant pledges appear to be signed by a Jewish man and a non-Jewish woman. Hence, such promises were sought regardless of the gender of the Jewish party. It must have been quite difficult to find a rabbi who would officiate, with or without a pledge.

Moreover, intermarriage could accentuate rather than diminish a woman's Jewish identity. In an anonymous 1929 article titled "My Jewish Wife," the Gentile author, who described himself of Nordic origin and nature, states he felt compelled to write of his marital experience. His wife, who emigrated from Russia, "has never been able to escape the fact that she is a Jewess" and was "deeply race conscious." They married in haste after a three-week courtship and had been married five years when he wrote: "My wife, suddenly inducted into the Nordic world, has been made all the more deeply conscious of her race." His greatest criticism against his wife was that she was overly sensitive about anti-Semitism, which he admitted was plentiful. In addition to trying to mold him to conform to her ideal of a college professor, he reported that she ceaselessly tried to prove herself an asset to him. He considered unnecessary her insistence that he tell people she was Jewish to avoid inadvertent discrimination and embarrassment.[123] Clearly, like Antin, Pastor, and Strunsky, the woman in this case did not relinquish her Jewish identity. Instead, she exemplified the contradictory nature of marital assimilation.

While there were other immigrant Jewish women who intermarried 1900-1929, only those whose life stories were preserved for other reasons provide details. The histories of Mary Antin Grabau, Rose Pastor Stokes, and Anna Strunsky Walling are exceptional because of their marital choices and their impact on mass media and popular culture. Electing to marry non-Jewish men had consequences for their identities as Jewish women by increasing their exposure to Christian practices and thinking. Antin and Strunsky investigated other religions and, more likely than not, modified their identities as Jewish women to include other ways of thinking that were not Jewish. Although they each maintained some contacts with their Jewish families and friends, these three women did not stay within the immigrant Jewish fold, but rather crossed over to their husbands' circles. However, none of these women ever explicitly renounced her Jewish identity. In fact, Antin and Pastor claimed "the Jewish badge." While scholars and community leaders asserted that those who intermarried ceased to be Jews, the experiences of women who actually intermarried offer a more varied interpretation of the meaning of intermarriage and Jewishness. One could indeed intermarry and remain a Jew, provided the definition of "Jew" be enlarged.

Great care must be taken in evaluating the ways in which the women migrated away from their immigrant backgrounds or retained their religious-ethnic affiliations. While intermarriage contributed to their different lifestyles, it was not the sole reason for secularization, religious experimentation, or the decline in Orthodoxy. When Antin, Pastor, and Strunsky elected to marry men of their own choosing and for reasons other than purely economic or to bring prestige to one's family, they did so along with many of their immigrant sisters who married Jewish men. The modern conception of romantic love rather than arranged marriages pervaded American immigrant culture. These three women followed the majority of Americans in conforming to the marital model of free choice.[124] For some immigrant Jewish women, marriage represented freedom and along with this freedom came secularization. Becoming American could supersede attachments to tradition, particularly for immigrant Jewish women who intermarried. The intermarriages considered here were very different from their mothers' arranged marriages, and, with the exception of Strunsky, their families were significantly smaller than those of the Jewish immigrant, who in the first decade of the century had five children on average.[125] They all also married at ages older than did most immigrant women.

The tradition of patriarchy, which (in Ewen's words) demanded that "female children be subordinate and inferior and that immigrant daughters were allowed little leeway in their desire for independence, schooling, and sexual freedom,"[126] does not seem to describe these women's lives. Nevertheless, while each woman strove to achieve equality to some degree in her marriage, all shouldered the traditional female responsibilities of running a household and, in Antin's and Strunsky's cases, of also being responsible for childcare. The taking of their husbands' names also reflected the prevailing gender custom. A partnership of equals was sought but not achieved, at least within the confines of their marriages. However, the reasons behind the dissolution of these unions, revolving as they did around divergent politics, illustrate the ways in which these immigrant Jewish women carved out independent lives for themselves. Strunsky's insistence that she, too, had "a Cause" conveys this very well.

While the First World War played a significant role in the women's lives, neither the great depression nor the ratification of the Nineteenth Amendment, granting women suffrage, seems to have influenced their marriages in any direct way. All of the women studied here were sufficiently well off to have hired help at various times during their marriages, though finances diminished considerably once they separated from their husbands. Although their actions seem to indicate otherwise, they did not claim to be feminists; Antin defiantly told President Theodore Roosevelt: "The truth is that I am very cool about the suffrage— by no means against it, but not warmly interested in securing it. I simply haven't got religion on the subject, and you cannot count on me until I have."[127] Even someone who had been involved in the birth control movement could self-identify as other than a feminist. Pastor wrote shortly before her death, "I have never been a feminist as such."[128] Nevertheless, passage of the Nineteenth Amendment may have influenced the political perspectives of Antin, Pastor, and Strunsky, giving them the confidence that their sense of nationalism could stand independently from their husband's, as did their votes. In any case, the evidence demonstrates that religious differences were not responsible for their marital disunions. Intermarriage did not bring about unhappiness and divorce; political variance from their husbands and gendered economics did.

ACKNOWLEDGMENTS

I would like to express my sincere appreciation to Mari Jo Buhle for her ceaseless encouragement and bountiful constructive criticism. Many thanks, also, to Howard Chudacoff and Lynn Davidman for their numerous and insightful editorial suggestions. Any errors herein are mine. A summer research experience at the Jewish Women's Archive inspired my desire to study Jewish women. A junior research grant from the Hadassah International Research Institute on Jewish Women at Brandeis University and fellowship support from Brown University provided the fuel, thereby adding to my confidence about pursuing a study of intermarriage across the twentieth century. The preparation and publication of this chapter was made possible, in part, by a grant from the Memorial Foundation for Jewish Culture. In my dissertation, titled "Still Jewish: A History of Women and Intermarriage in America," I discuss communal reactions as well as popular culture representations, which are omitted here due to space constraints.

NOTES

[1] Julius Drachsler, *Democracy and Assimilation: The Blending of Immigrant Heritages in America* (New York: MacMillan, 1920), 122, 123, 128, 130, 143, 250, and Table F, calculated that 1.17 percent of New York City Jews (immigrants, second, and third generation) intermarried in the years 1908 through 1912. Although it is probable

that some marriages went undetected due to name changes, the number of immigrant Jewesses who intermarried prior to 1930 was still likely small. See also Fred Massarik, et al., *National Jewish Population Study: Intermarriage, Facts for Planning* (New York: Council of Jewish Federations and Welfare Funds, 1971), 10.

[2]Susan Glenn, *Daughters of the Shtetl: Life and Labor in the Immigrant Generation* (Ithaca: Cornell University Press, 1990), 210, 238, 39.

[3]Sydney Stahl Weinberg, *The World of Our Mothers: The Lives of Jewish Immigrant Women* (Chapel Hill: The University of North Carolina Press, 1988), 205.

[4]Elizabeth Ewen, *Immigrant Women in the Land of Dollars: Life and Culture on the Lower East Side, 1890-1925* (New York: Monthly Review Press, 1985), 230.

[5]Nancy Cott, *Public Vows: A History of Marriage and the Nation* (Cambridge: Harvard University Press, 2000), 3.

[6]Riv-Ellen Prell, *Fighting to Become Americans: Jews, Gender, and the Anxiety of Assimilation* (Boston: Beacon Press, 1999), 71.

[7]Glenn, *Daughters of the Shtetl*, 157.

[8]See Weinberg, *World of Our Mothers*, 128; Glenn, *Daughters of the Shtetl*, 157; Cott, *Public Vows*, 150-151; Ewen, *Immigrant Women*, 228, 250.

[9]Anzia Yezierska, "The Miracle," in *Hungry Hearts* (New York: Signet Classic, 1996; 1920), 93.

[10]Prell, *Fighting to Become Americans*, 68.

[11]"Inter-Marriage: A Sermon Suggested by Elias Tobenkin's 'God of Might'," 11 April 1925, Ferdinand M. Isserman Papers, Series B. Sermons and Addresses, Subseries 1, General, box 11, folder 3, American Jewish Archives, Cincinnati; "Just Between Ourselves Girls," *The Hebrew Standard*, 14 April 1905.

[12]"Just Between Ourselves Girls"; "Intermarriage," *The Hebrew Standard*, 21 April 1905.

[13]Mary Antin, *The Promised Land* (Boston and New York: Houghton Mifflin, 1912).

[14]*Contemporary Authors: A Bio-Bibliographic Guide to Current Writers in Fiction, General Nonfiction, Poetry, Journalism, Drama, Motion Pictures, Television, and Other Fields*, Hal May, ed. (Detroit: Gale Research, 1986), 118:22. Passenger Lists of Vessels Arriving at Boston, MA, 1891-1943 (Waltham, MA: National Archives) T843, microfilm roll 10, vol. 16-17, Jan. 1-June 30, 1894.

[15]Susan Koppelman, "Mary Antin," in *Dictionary of Literary Biography Yearbook: 1984* (Detroit: Gale Research), 227.

[16]City of Boston, Registry Division, Certified Copy of Record of Marriage No. 4500, Recorded 8 October 1901.

[17]Arthur Antin (Mary Antin's nephew) to the author, 16 April 2001.

[18]Mary Antin to Israel Zangwill, 8 October 1901, *Selected Letters of Mary Antin*, Evelyn Salz, ed. (Syracuse: Syracuse University Press, 2000), 37. Thanks to Evelyn Salz for collecting Antin's letters from far and wide.

[19]Antin, *Promised Land*, 247.

[20]Jonathan Sarna, *The Jews of Boston: Essays on the Occasion of the Centenary (1895-1995) of the Combined Jewish Philanthropies of Greater Boston* (eds. Jonathan Sarna

and Ellen Smith; Boston: Combined Jewish Philanthropies of Greater Boston, 1995), 14.

[21]Antin, *Promised Land*, 331.

[22]Sam Bass Warner, Jr., *Province of Reason* (Cambridge: Harvard University Press, 1984), 26.

[23]Antin, *Promised Land*, 330.

[24]Oscar Handlin, "Foreword," in Antin, *Promised Land*, x.

[25]Magdalena Zaborowska, *How We Found America: Reading Gender Through East European Immigrant Narratives* (Chapel Hill: University of North Carolina Press, 1995), 54.

[26]Koppelman, "Mary Antin," 230.

[27]Arthur Antin to the author, 16 April 2001.

[28]Mary Antin, "God and His World," in *Ford Hall Folks, A Magazine of Neighborliness* 3:3 (1 November 1914): 1-2, Mary Antin Papers, American Jewish Historical Society, Waltham, MA (hereafter cited as Antin AJHS).

[29]"Steps from Synagogue to Church: The Way of the Wealthy Jewish Family, Which Passes From Reform Judaism to Apostasy," *The Day*, 13 October 1923: front page.

[30]Antin, *Promised Land*, 248-49. Mary's daughter and granddaughter both married non-Jews. Interestingly, her great-granddaughter Jeanne married a Jewish man, Michael Neuwirth, and is raising her daughter Eliana as a Jew. Thus "the persistence of Judaism" resurfaced despite three consecutive generations of intermarriage. Jeanne Ross-Neuwirth, conversation with author, 21 February 1997, and baby naming celebration, 19 August 2000.

[31]Werner Sollors, "Letter from Mary Antin to Mary Austin, March 11, 1925," in *RSA Journal* 7:111.

[32]Mary Antin, "House of the One Father," in *Common Ground* (Spring 1941): 36.

[33]Antin, "House of the One Father," 37-38.

[34]Antin, "House of the One Father," 41.

[35]Matthew Frye Jacobson, *Whiteness of a Different Color: European Immigrants and the Alchemy of Race* (Cambridge: Harvard University Press, 1998), 176.

[36]Antin, *Promised Land*, 277.

[37]Mary Antin, "Malinke's Atonement," in *Atlantic Monthly* 108:3 (1911): 303.

[38]Ewen, *Immigrant Women*, 39.

[39]Antin, *The Promised Land* 33.

[40]Rose Cohen, *Out of the Shadow: A Russian Jewish Girlhood on the Lower East Side* (1918; Ithaca: Cornell University Press, 1995), 201.

[41]Pamela S. Nadell, "Introduction," in Mary Antin, *From Plotzk to Boston, 1899* (New York: Wiener, 1986), xiii.

[42]Koppelman, "Mary Antin," 227.

[43]City of Boston, Registry Division, Certified Copy of Record of Marriage No. 4500, Recorded 8 October 1901.

[44]Warner, *Providence of Reason*, 29.

[45]Elizabeth Anne Ross, telephone interview by author, 14 October 1996.

[46]Koppelman, "Mary Antin," 231.

[47]Arthur Antin to author, 16 April 2001.

[48]Elizabeth Anne Ross, telephone interview by author, 29 October 1996.

[49]Mary Antin to Rosemary Antin, 31 January 1946, Antin AJHS.

[50]"Miss Mary Antin, Wrote Noted Book: Russian Jewish Immigrant Who Won Acclaim Here With Her 'Promised Land' Dies at 67," *Special to the New York Times*, 18 May 1949, 27. Elizabeth Anne Ross, telephone interview by author, 14 October 1996. Antin was born in June 1881 and died the month before her sixty-ninth birthday. The age indicated in the *New York Times* reflected the misconception that she was two years younger, based on an earlier falsification by her father. See Keren R. McGinity, "The Real Mary Antin: Woman on a Mission in the Promised Land," *American Jewish History* 86:3 (September 1998): 291.

[51]Rose Pastor Stokes Papers, Yale University, Group 573, Box 1, Folder 5 (hereafter cited as RPS Yale).

[52]Arthur Zipser and Pearl Zipser, *Fire and Grace: The Life of Rose Pastor Stokes* (Athens: University of Georgia Press, 1989), 1.

[53]"Just Between Ourselves, Girls," *The Jewish Daily News*, English Department, 12 August 1903.

[54]I am indebted to Lynn Davidman for this insight.

[55]James Boylan, *Revolutionary Lives: Anna Strunsky and William English Walling* (Amherst: University of Massachusetts Press, 1998), 55.

[56]Rose Harriet Pastor, "The Views of a Settlement Worker: A Talk With J.G. Phelps Stokes," *The Jewish Daily News,* 19 July 1903.

[57]Zipser and Zipser, *Fire and Grace*, 13.

[58]*I Belong to the Working Class: The Unfinished Autobiography of Rose Pastor Stokes,* Herbert Shapiro and David L. Sterling, eds. (Athens: University of Georgia Press, 1992), 99-100.

[59]Shapiro and Sterling, *I Belong to the Working Class*, 4.

[60]Shapiro and Sterling, *I Belong to the Working Class*, 96.

[61]James Graham Phelps Stokes to his mother Helen Louisa and father Anson, March 1905. Cable from mother to son. Columbia University Archives, Special Collection, Butler Library. Cited in Zipser and Zipser, 34.

[62]Shapiro and Sterling, *I Belong to the Working Class*, 100.

[63]Zipser and Zipser, *Fire and Grace*, 176, 181.

[64]*Philadelphia Evening Telegram*, n.d., 1905, clipping in Box 75, Columbia University. Cited in Zipser and Zipser 37.

[65]"J.G. Phelps Stokes to Wed Young Jewess," *New York Times* 6 April 1905.

[66]*New York Sun,* 7 April 1905; *Philadelphia Press*, 8 April 1905. Cited in Zipser and Zipser, 36.

[67]James Graham Phelps Stokes to mother, 12 April 1905. Zipser and Zipser, *Fire and Grace*, 36, 43.

[68]Helen Louisa Stokes to Anson Phelps Stokes, Jr., 15 April 1905; Anson Phelps Stokes, Jr., to Helen Louisa Stokes, 20 April 1905; Anson Phelps Stokes, Jr. Papers,

Yale. Cited in Stanley Ray Tamarkin, "Rose Pastor Stokes: Portrait of a Radical Woman, 1905-1919" (Ph.D. diss., Yale University, 1983), 23, 25.

[69]Zipser and Zipser, *Fire and Grace*, 44.

[70]Shapiro and Sterling, *I Belong to the Working Class*, 104-5.

[71]Prell, *Fighting to Become Americans*, 70; Zipser and Zipser, *Fire and Grace*, 44.

[72]"East Side's Poetess is Now Mrs. Stokes: Wedding of Miss Pastor and Rich Settlement Worker," *New York Times*, 19 July 1905, 7.

[73]James Graham Phelps Stokes to Helen Louisa Stokes, April 21, 1905, JGPS Papers, Yale University. Cited in Tamarkin, "Rose Pastor Stokes," 149.

[74]Zipser and Zipser, *Fire and Grace*, 41.

[75]*Ibid.*, 118.

[76]*Ibid.*, 230.

[77]Cott, *Public Vows*, 3.

[78]Zipser and Zipser, *Fire and Grace*, 46, 49.

[79]Shapiro and Sterling, *I Belong to the Working Class*, 97.

[80]Weinberg, 212.

[81]Tamarkin, "Rose Pastor Stokes," 202.

[82]Pastor Stokes diary, January 9, 1913. RPS Yale, Group 573 Box 12, Folder 1.

[83]Shapiro and Sterling, *I Belong to the Working Class*, 131-32.

[84]Prell has identified the ghetto girl stereotype as a Jewish woman who withheld wages from her family because of her love of fashion and who dreamed of wealth and success. Contained within the stereotype is the fear that Jewish women would abandon the community because it did not have the Prince Charmings to fulfill their fantasies. Prell, *Fighting to Become Americans*, 24-25, 36, 40.

[85]Rose Pastor Stokes to Butler Davenport, September 4, 1914. Call/accession number A/S874. Schlesinger Library, Radcliffe Institute, Harvard University.

[86]Zipser and Zipser, *Fire and Grace*, 170-173.

[87]*Ibid.*, 189; 197.

[88]Pastor Stokes diary, March 20 or 30, 1914, RPS Yale, Additions 1984, Group 573, Box 13, Folder 1.

[89]Pastor Stokes diary, March 27, 1915, RPS Yale, Additions 1984, Group 573, Box 13, Folder 1.

[90]Shapiro and Sterling, *I Belong to the Working Class*, ix-xvii.

[91]Alice Kessler Harris, "Organizing the Unorganizable: Three Jewish Women and Their Union," in *Labor History* 17:1 (Winter 1976): 8 and fn. 9.

[92]Boylan, *Revolutionary Lives*, 6-8. Boylan gives the year 1877 as Anna's birth year (3 and 270), but the publication information and other sources list 1879. I use 1877 to be consistent with her primary biographer.

[93]*Ibid.*, 16.

[94]Boylan, *Revolutionary Lives*, 94-95.

[95]Anna Strunsky to Elias Strunsky, undated fragment, Box 5, Huntington Library, San Marino, California. Cited in Boylan, *Revolutionary Lives*, 95.

96 Mother to Anna Strunsky, 15 February 1906, box 4, Huntington Library, San Marino, California. Cited in Boylan, *Revolutionary Lives,*103.

97 *Ibid.*, 6.

98 Elias Strunsky to Anna Strunsky, 15 February 1906, Anna Strunsky Walling Papers, Yale University, Box 11, Folder 153, Reel 10 (hereafter cited as ASW Yale).

99 1926 Letter, *A Bintel Brief: Sixty Years of Letters From the Lower East Side to the Jewish Daily Forward,* Isaac Metzker, ed. (intro. I. Metzker; foreword and notes H. Golden; Garden City: Doubleday, 1971), 147-48.

100 1926 Letter, *Ibid.*, 149-50.

101 William English Walling to his parents, 29 January 1906; Cable from Willoughby Walling to William English Walling, 17 February 1906; William English Walling to parents, 17 February 1906. Another 1906 letter, undated. ASW Yale, box 19, folder 266. There is the possibility that English reduced Anna's age by two years; if indeed she was born in 1877 (not 1879), she would have been 28 when he wrote the letter to his parents. If English's letter is to be trusted, other sources cannot.

102 Anna Strunsky to Willoughby Walling, 23 March 1906, ASW Yale, box 13, folder 194, reel 13.

103 Anna Strunsky to Rosalind Walling, April 1906, ASW Yale, box 13, folder 194, reel 13.

104 Rosalind Walling to Anna Strunsky and William English Walling, April 1906, ASW Yale, box 13, folders 189-199, reel 13.

105 "They Were in Love: Friend Pays Tribute to Jack London," *New York World Telegraph,* n.d., ASW Yale, box 37, folder 435.

106 Anna Strunsky Walling to her family, 1 July 1906, ASW Yale, box 11, folder 153, reel 10.

107 Anna Strunsky Walling to her family, 1 July 1906, ASW Yale, box 11, folder 153, reel 10.

108 Anna Strunsky Walling to her in-laws, 29 July 1906, ASW Yale, box 13, folder 194, reel 13.

109 Boylan, *Revolutionary Lives*, 225.

110 Anna Strunsky Walling to Rosalind Walling, 21 December 1918, ASW Yale, box 14, folders 200-209, reel 14.

111 Christmas (1948) and Easter (n.d.) cards from Georgia Walling to Anna Strunsky Walling, ASW Yale, box 13, folders 189-199, reel 13.

112 Strunsky Walling diary, July 11, 1906, ASW Yale, diary #4-1, 1906, box 23, folder 302.

113 Strunsky Walling diary, 3 September 1906, ASW Yale, diary #4-1, 1906, box 23, folder 302.

114 Strunsky Walling diary, 21 October 1906, ASW Yale, diary #4-1, 1906, box 23, folder 302.

115 Strunsky Walling diary, 25 or 28 October 1906, ASW Yale, diary #4-1, 1906, box 23, folder 302.

[116]Strunsky Walling diary, 12 September 1916, ASW Yale, diary #5, box 23, folder 303.

[117]Untitled, undated essay signed "Anna Strunsky Walling," ASW Yale, box 34, folder 414, loose pages.

[118]"Scorns the Name of Wife/Mrs. Walling Wants to Be Known as Anna Strunsky, Though Married," *Chicago Daily News*, 1 December 1906.

[119]Anna Strunsky Walling to Rosalind and Willoughby Walling, 26 February 1908. ASW Yale, box 13, folder 195 (reel #13). Cited in Boylan, *Revolutionary Lives*, 125.

[120] Anna Strunsky Walling to Rosalind Walling, 23 April 1909, ASW Yale, box 13, folder 195. Cited in Boylan, *Revolutionary Lives*, 160.

[121]Boylan, *Revolutionary Lives*, 228-29; 263-64.

[122]Intermarriage pledge signed 22 December 1918 by couple married by Rabbi Leo M. Franklin, Detroit: American Jewish Archives, Cincinnati.

[123]Anonymous, "My Jewish Wife," in *The Menorah Journal* 16:5 (May 1929): 456-61.

[124]Cott, *Public Vows*, 8, 151.

[125]Weinberg, *World of Our Mothers*, 220.

[126]Ewen, 189.

[127]Mary Antin Grabau to Theodore Roosevelt, 2 August 1913, Harvard University Government Documents, microfilm A88, series 1, reel 179.

[128]June Sochen, *Herstory: A Woman's View of American History* (New York: Alfred Publishing, 1974), 295.

Finding Women in the Story of American and Omaha Reform Judaism

Karla Goldman

"Go forth from your native land and from your father's house to the land that I will show you. I will make of you a great nation, and I will bless you." These words are recorded in the Torah portion *Lech Lecha* as God's command to Avram, instructing him to leave his home and journey to Canaan.[1] The same words could also be used to describe what happened to Jewish immigrants who left everything they knew and risked everything they had in order to commence a dangerous voyage that they hoped would bring them to a new home in an unknown land. Even without God's assurance of their ultimate success, millions of European Jews made the journey to the United States. Here, in this new world, they found an atmosphere of acceptance and tolerance unprecedented in Jewish Diaspora experience. And we have become a great nation in terms of accomplishment, affluence and influence. Like Avram, we have faced many challenges, but we are indeed the recipient of myriad privileges and blessings.

Much as in the Bible, the narrative through which we learn and understand this journey with all its challenges, failures, and successes has come down to us chiefly as one told and acted out by male protagonists. This has been the case regarding our understanding of American Jewish life in general and even more so with respect to the specific development of American Reform Judaism. This is hardly surprising. The founders and early leaders of American Reform Judaism concentrated their efforts on formalizing synagogue rituals and behavior, in the process introducing a level of decorum and aesthetics that would convince observers and participants of the respectability of American Jews. Authority in these institutions was restricted to religious and lay leaders, who maintained the historical tradition of male leadership. No women rabbis were ordained by Hebrew Union College or any other rabbinical seminary until 1972.[2]

Given these conditions, it would seem appropriate to tell the story of American Reform Judaism and its complex, often passionate, attempts to make sense of an ancient religion in a new land through the story of its notable men: rabbis like Cincinnati's Isaac M. Wise and Omaha's William Rosenau and Leo Franklin, and committed lay leaders like Isaac Oberfelder and Frederick Cohn, both presidents of Omaha's Temple Israel. After all, these were the founders and symbolic representatives of American Reform Judaism.[3] Just as we learn about Judaism by learning about Abraham, identified by tradition as the founder of the Jewish people, it is logical to suppose that that the best way to understand more recent Jewish history is to learn the stories of its leaders.

Yet, we know that the struggle of any people to find its way in a new land could never be solely the work of men. The Torah portion referred to above alerts us to this truth. Avram was not alone in the venture to Canaan. Sarai, Lot, and all the souls they had brought into their house in Haran were also asked to make this journey; they were asked to take these risks without the personal assurance of blessing and covenant that God vouched to Avram. No less significantly, the prosperous advance of Avram's household was not purely the result of Avram's efforts, but, as the text acknowledges, was gained largely on account of Sarai's sacrifice. And of course, ultimately, the descendents promised to Abraham would be as much the product of Sarah's and Hagar's faith as of his own.

We are blessed as a people with a body of literature that has for thousands of years remained powerfully evocative of the struggle to understand our place in the world. But for all its timelessness, the biblical text, in which we still invest so much, obfuscates the spiritual struggles and sacrifices of the women mentioned or unmentioned in its pages, preventing some among us from feeling that we can fully share its legacy. After all, might we not have as much to learn from the story of Sarai, who ventured into the unknown on the basis of assurances from her eccentric husband, as we do from Avram's willingness to trust in God's commands? In response to this challenge, creators of contemporary midrash have gone back to the biblical world of our matriarchs, elaborating upon Sarah's hopes or the stories of the other matriarchs, as exemplified in the popular novel, *The Red Tent*.[4]

Sitting in the sanctuary of the historic Temple Israel in Omaha, Nebraska, we may be moved to consider a past much closer to our own time and experience, one that we do not have to re-imagine so much as reexamine. Let us consider how it was that American Jews took on the challenge of carrying on the inheritance of their mothers' and fathers' houses. I would like to suggest that we cannot understand this story or our own place in it if we do not recognize the central place that women have taken in preserving, transmitting, and redefining our ancient religion as we have moved through a new land.

American Jews very quickly came to understand that their synagogues had to provide different places for women than those that had become accepted in Europe. In traditional European synagogues women sat sequestered in balconies, separated by barriers of latticework, curtains, and grills. Unmarried women rarely attended regular worship services, and married women generally appeared only on Saturday mornings.[5] In America, changes in Jewish women's religious identity found architectural expression as early as 1763. In the Newport, Rhode Island, synagogue dedicated in that year, women sat in an open balcony, free from the opaque barriers of European sanctuaries. As perhaps indicated by this open balcony, synagogue presence was becoming more important for American women.[6] This was also evident in 1792, when male leaders of New York's Shearith Israel congregation tried to ban all young unmarried women from the front row of their women's gallery. This effort to control female behavior demonstrated that a number of unmarried New York women had decided that in the new world they too, drawing upon the example of their church-going neighbors, would find a place in the synagogue.[7]

In 1851, at Rabbi Isaac Mayer Wise's new congregation, Anshe Emeth, in Albany, New York, and in 1854, at New York City's Temple Emanu-El, men and women sat together in family pews. This innovation, unique to the United States, was prominent among the practical changes eventually adopted by an emerging American Reform movement.[8] In the wave of synagogue building that followed the Civil War years, Jewish congregations across the country dedicated grand synagogues that declared their proud presence upon the landscapes of numerous American cities. Men with uncovered heads sat next to women in these impressive edifices, which offered an updated version of Jewish worship and became emblems of Jewish prosperity and respectability.[9] Thus, in 1884, when Omaha's Temple Israel built its first synagogue building at 23rd and Harney Streets, it offered a choir, an organ, and, for the first time in Omaha, a synagogue sanctuary where, in keeping with a by-now established pattern for Americanized Jewish congregations, men and women sat together at worship.[10]

In most of these late-nineteenth century synagogues, women far outnumbered men in regular synagogue attendance, a pattern unprecedented and without parallel in Jewish experience.[11] By their mere presence, first in the balcony and later in the family pews of their Reform temples, American Jewish women changed the structure and nature of Jewish public worship. If the nineteenth century introduction of family pews did not succeed in changing women's religious status or affording them access to religious leadership, it did confirm the evolving notion that going to synagogue should be a central part of their image of themselves as Jewish women. Although this adoption of mixed seating was not accepted by millions of more traditionally inclined East European Jews who arrived in America at the turn of the century (including those in Omaha), the model of women's inclusion as a way to show meaningful acculturation had been firmly established in American Judaism.[12]

Initially, traditional synagogue organizational structures and a concerted Reform emphasis on male-led worship service meant that Jewish women—unlike contemporary Protestant women of the time—were kept out of much of the community's work and were slow to develop meaningful sisterhood-like groups. Nonetheless, in many communities and at the behest of male communal leaders, Jewish women would often organize to support synagogue building projects.[13] In Omaha, a Ladies' Benevolent Society was created in association with the Temple in 1885 and promptly held a charity fair that yielded a profit of $2,200, half of which went to the congregation, presumably to pay its outstanding building debt. This was not an insignificant sum given that the total cost of the Temple building opened a year earlier was $4,500.[14]

In the 1890s, the increasing needs of millions of new Jewish immigrants, the emergence of Ray Frank as a prominent Jewish woman orator and the model of public activism offered by the leaders of the National Council of Jewish Women (NCJW, founded in 1893) propelled acculturated Jewish women into a myriad of new roles and organizations.[15] This sudden influx of women workers greatly expanded the life of the community and helped to redefine the life and role of the synagogue.[16] For example, in 1896, the creation of a local NCJW section in Omaha led to the founding of a school for Russian immigrants.

Moreover, involvement in local NCJW work of planning schools, classes, and public meetings connected Omaha women to a broader world of Jewish women's rights activists, even as it highlighted Jewish women as public figures in a way that was probably unprecedented in Omaha.

This emerging activism also found expression in the more than two thousand dollars the Temple's Ladies' Society contributed to the congregation in 1898. A sisterhood was founded in 1903.[17] This sisterhood has special significance; it was founded by Rabbi Abram Simon before he left with his wife, Carrie Simon, to take a new pulpit in Washington, DC. Ten years later Carrie Simon would be the moving force behind, and the first president of, the National Federation of Temple Sisterhoods (NFTS), founded in 1913.[18] The creation of NFTS added force and substance to the work of old and new sisterhoods, creating a voice for women in Reform Judaism and offering a model of organization and activism that helped transform local congregations.[19]

The introduction of sisterhoods greatly expanded the scope and reach of congregations across the country, as women volunteers turned their attention to the social, educational, organizational, and religious life of the community. Through the 1890s and into the twentieth century, Temple Israel's women's organizations occupied themselves with raising money to decorate and repair the existing Temple and to contribute toward the construction of a new building. Investing their energies in organized effort, these acculturated Jewish women filled the new structure, located at 1908 Park Ave, as well as other temples across the country, with a rich spectrum of Jewish communal life. Sisterhood workers filled numerous posts for which current synagogues require extensive paid staffs.[20]

The struggle for and success of the 1920 Women's Suffrage Amendment to the United States Constitution helped to open up the question of women's political roles within Jewish congregations. Women's active presence in so many spheres of communal life made it difficult for communities to deny the legitimacy of women's claims to representation in governance and among synagogue trustees. At Temple Israel, the congregation's president requested in 1916 that the Sisterhood send a representative to the Congregation's board of trustees meetings. A 1939 amendment to the congregation's constitution mandated that the Sisterhood president serve as a member of the synagogue board; later this provision was expanded to require the presence of two Sisterhood representatives on the board.[21]

Later still, the important roles taken by women in so many realms of synagogue life made it impossible for liberal Jewish denominations to maintain resistance to opening the sphere of religious leadership to women who were willing to bear the burden of entering the previously exclusively male world of the rabbinate. In the almost thirty years since Sally Priesand's ordination as the first American woman rabbi, as women have assumed the symbolic and spiritual leadership of numerous Jewish religious communities across the United States, change has seemed to come at a much faster pace. The presence of women rabbis has changed the Jewish landscape in many arenas. "Gender-sensitive" liturgies; reexamination of notions about God, religious leadership, and patriarchal traditions; the shifting boundaries of family and gender identities that once seemed fixed—all of these have added layers of both creativity and complexity to today's Jewish world.

We could certainly compile a history of Temple Israel by focusing on the lives of its illustrious leaders, men like Rabbi Frederick Cohn and Rabbi Sidney H. Brooks who each nurtured and shaped this community for many years, or like Rabbis William Rosenau, Leo Franklin, Abram Simon, and Aruth Lelyveld, who all went on to have a notable impact on the national Jewish community. But if we speak solely of these rightfully honored men, we have only part of the story. We miss the long history of women who chose to come to American synagogues, who sat through long services and sermons, and who so often did the heavy lifting for their congregations. They did not reap the kind of public reward that came so often to male leaders, but we may be allowed to hope that they found their own kind of blessing in shaping their communities and in making community possible. Without these women, Judaism in America and American synagogues would look and be much different today.

As Jews, we stand on our past. We take our ancient and modern texts, our traditions, our rituals, our understanding of Jewish historical and religious experience, and we try to build meaning. In days like these, when so much of our world feels arbitrary and unsettled, many of us are looking long and hard for something solid to hold onto. Ironically, perhaps, the massive loss of life caused by terrorist violence has sensitized us to the richness of every individual's story.

When we begin to seek women's presence in the stories that we tell ourselves about who we are as Jews and Americans, we realize that bringing women into Jewish history does not require reinventing what happened—it only requires deepening the questions we ask and the stories we tell. When we understand that changed expectations for women's religious roles are part of a long tradition, when we recognize that tensions between Jewish and American expectations for women's religious roles have long shaped our communities, when we see how even women who did not think much about the broader significance of their own religious choices actually helped to shape the course of American Judaism—then we can begin to take our own questions and our own stories a little more seriously. We have already received many blessings, but our journey is not over. We are still struggling to make sense of an old faith in a new land.

NOTES

[1] In addition to making a Symposium presentation, Dr. Goldman delivered an extended Friday night sermon at Temple Israel, the Reform congregation in Omaha, Nebraska. This article is based on her sermon on that occasion; *Lech Lecha*, covering Gen 15:1-16:16, was read during the weekend of this Symposium.

[2] Pamela Nadell, *Women Who Would Be Rabbis: A History of Women's Ordination*, (Boston: Beacon, 1998).

[3] Michael A. Meyer, *Response to Modernity: A History of the Reform Movement in Judaism* (New York: Oxford University Press, 1995). For a useful and lengthy bibliography on many aspects of the American Reform movement, see online: http://www.faqs.org/faqs/judaism/reading-lists/reform/.

[4] Anita Diamont, *The Red Tent* (New York: St. Martin's Press, 1997).

[5] Michael Kaufman, *The Woman in Jewish Law and Tradition* (Northvale: Aronson, 1993).

[6] Karla Goldman, *Beyond the Synagogue Gallery: Finding a Place for Women in American Judaism* (Cambridge: Harvard University Press, 2000), 41-44.

[7] See Goldman, *Beyond the Synagogue Gallery*, 51.

[8] Meyer, *Response to Modernity*.

[9] Goldman, *Beyond the Synagogue Gallery,* 93-95, 129-33.

[10] Suzanne Richards Somberg and Silvia Greene Roffman, *Consider the Years, 1871-1971, Congregation of Temple Israel, Omaha, Nebraska* (Omaha: Congregation of Temple Israel, 1971), 16, 19.

[11] See Goldman, *Beyond the Synagogue Gallery.*

[12] *Ibid.,* 203-5.

[13] *Ibid.,* 137-50.

[14] Somberg and Roffman, *Consider the Years,* 16-17.

[15]See Faith Rogow, *Gone to Another Meeting: The National Council of Jewish Women, 1893-1993* (Tuscaloosa: University of Alabama Press, 1993), 9-35. See also NCJW, Inc., online: http://www.ncjw.org/about/ourstory.htm
[16]See Goldman, *Beyond the Synagogue Gallery*, 172-92.
[17]Somberg and Roffman, *Consider the Years*, 68.
[18]Mark I. Greenberg, "Simon, Carrie Obendorfer," in *Jewish Women in America: An Historical Encyclopedia* (eds. P. Hyman and D. D. Moore; vol. 2; New York: Routledge, 1997), 1260-61.
[19]See online: http://rj.org/wrj/.
[20]Somberg and Roffman, *Consider the Years*, 32; see Goldman, *Beyond the Synagogue Gallery*, 188-92, 205-8.
[21]Goldman, *Beyond the Synagogue Gallery*, 211; Somberg and Roffman, *Consider the Years*, 68.